Green Fading into Blue

ALAN ROSS

Green Fading into Blue

Writings on Cricket and Other Sports

André Deutsch

First published in Great Britain in 1999 by
André Deutsch Limited
76 Dean Street
London W1V 5HA

www.vci.co.uk

A catalogue record for this book is available from the British Library

ISBN 0 233 99451 3

Typeset by Derek Doyle & Associates
Mold, Flintshire
Printed in the UK by MPG Books Ltd,
Bodmin, Cornwall

To David Sylvester
and
In memory of Sussex Cricketers

You came, and looked and loved the view
Long-known and loved by me
Green Sussex fading into blue
With one gray glimpse of sea

Alfred Tennyson

Contents

Introduction

The pieces collected here, mostly, but not all, on cricket, derive in the main from a period, 1950–70, when the going was good and English cricketers, brought up on an even more demanding county schedule than now, were simply the best. No one felt then any need to tinker with the programme. We have today too many one-day competitions that no one remembers and too many overseas tours merging into one another and reducing the temperature. An exaggerated emphasis on fitness at the expense of technique has also led to considerable damage. I cannot imagine the stalwarts of my youth hurling themselves about in such undignified fashion to save the odd single. Instead, I see with my mind's eye the legendary elders of the time looking on with amused tolerance, Alec Bedser at mid-on or John Langridge at slip, Leonard Hutton at mid-off or Jim Laker in the gully. Of course, they had to run sometimes.

Writing about sport, whether cricket or football, is a question of perspective, of evaluating situations and finding equivalents. It is one thing for this to be resolved in paint or a photograph, which isolates an image without comment, quite another for it to be achieved in words, with their extra dimension and responsibility. I was lucky in the two decades in which I wrote about cricket and football for the *Observer* to have been able to practise on some of the greatest, Hutton and Stanley Matthews, Peter May and Colin Cowdrey and Edward Dexter, on Alf Ramsey and the three Ws, on Ray Lindwall and Keith Miller. At the same time, my heart was always as involved parochially as internationally, in the rough industrial environment of White Hart Lane and the sea-scented air of Hove. The challenge for a writer is to convey the music of the game, a sweetly-timed cover drive by David Gower or a long, defence-splitting pass by Glenn Hoddle, without neglecting its nuts and bolts. In the whole picture the defiance of a Trevor Bailey is often as important as the heroics of an Ian Botham, that wholly adventurous super-star, half charlatan, half avenging angel, who hit sixes with glorious abandon, took wickets with the most harmless-seeming of deliveries, and who proved, ultimately, endearingly vulnerable.

After Leonard Hutton's retirement it was never quite the same, although there was still the grand manner of May and Cowdrey and Dexter, the intransigence of Boycott. After the brief fireworks of Frank Tyson, there was still the pace and lovely action of Trueman, the accuracy of Statham, the probing cut and thrust of John Snow. Laker and Wardle, curmudgeonly connoisseurs of alternative spin, had their bright moment. For a decade or so there was the Pickwickian bounce of Godfrey Evans behind the stumps, Alec Bedser's swinging fast medium smacking into his gloves only inches from the batsman's ear.

For a while England kept winning but with less conviction. Peter May and Colin Cowdrey, great batsmen and opposite temperaments, each won important series, and later on there were exciting flourishes under Brearley, Gower, Ray Illingworth and Mike Gatting. But the power was running out and for a while only the Herculean efforts of Graham Gooch, villainously moustached and Victorian, his bat like a railway sleeper, kept England afloat.

Among opponents in these years I think first of the classical beauty of Greg Chappell's batting, the athletic magnificence of the West Indian fast bowlers Holding and Marshall, the savagery of Vivian Richards. There was too much short-pitched fast bowling tolerated for too long, but against that one could balance the high-spirited exuberance of Kapil Dev, the romantic all-round skills of Imran Khan. I wish more of them surfaced in these pages, their subjects reminders of a lifelong passion.

In the first section of this book I have included accounts of some of the most crucial and exciting Test matches involving England during my two decades of reporting. Most of those mentioned above were at some time involved. I was fortunate that in the six overseas tours I covered we lost not a single series and won in both Australia and the Caribbean. The final section concentrates on the individual, not the match, cricketers, footballers, boxers, Real Tennis professionals, women hockey players, snooker stars, on and off duty.

Before I began to spend my winters abroad with MCC I travelled the length and breadth of England covering football and savouring the industrial north and midlands. They were the glory days of Tottenham Hotspur and I can still, forty years later, reel off without difficulty the names of all those who graced the grass of White Hart Lane under the silky captaincy of Danny Blanchflower and the managements of Arthur Rowe and Bill Nicholson. There are some reminders of those days here. Gates of 50,000 or more were then commonplace, cloth-capped spectators convivially jammed together on the terraces. Now a measly 20,000 are demurely seated. Denis Compton I saw once or twice hugging the touchline for Arsenal before putting over immaculate crosses. Thereafter he was a martyr to pain, the postwar summers when he and Edrich gorged themselves at Lord's followed by fewer and fewer of those inventive or fighting innings that were his hallmark. I see him batting against Hugh Tayfield at the Wanderer's, Johannesburg, tied to his crease like a dog in his kennel by mercilessly accurate off spin. You could sense the mind straining to escape but the legs were moored. Denis lived in a fashion far beyond the reach of most professionals, both cricketers and footballers then financially at the bottom of the sporting heap. He was the most charming of creatures, though we quarrelled regularly about South Africa.

Sussex, whom I wrote about as often as I was allowed, have always been a 'family' team, with exotics like Ranji and Duleep, Pataudi and Melville and Imran Khan, occasionally thrown in. Even now, the father and son, brothers and nephew tradition, begun in the last century by 'old' George Cox, continues with Lenhams and the Newells. Before them were the Tates and the Gilligans, Langridges and Parkses, the Oakes and Busses, hardly a match going by without a brother or son in the side. A raffish club always, in keeping with Regency Brighton, often in the dumps, but sometimes a shooting star. I suffered and rejoiced with them as over nothing else from the earliest of days. There is little alas about them here, though some innings by Hugh Bartlett and Jim Parks gave me as much pleasure as anything I can remember.

In the mid-1960s I developed an addiction to racing. Brought up in Bengal I inherited from my father a love of racehorses, cigars and whisky. Having been a frequent attender at my local Sussex courses,

Plumpton, Fontwell and Brighton, I one day nervously bid for a hurdler, hoping I might eventually see it placed. It was very cheap and immediately broke down. I tried again with a yearling to be trained at Lewes for the flat by my friend Gordon Smyth, a regular at Hove and a useful cricketer. It died of a twisted gut before it even sniffed a racecourse.

Since training fees were only £11 a week at the time, I decided to have one final go, and if it didn't work, give it up and return to betting. I bought for £600 a skinny three-year-old grey called Acrovat and asked Alan Oughton to train it at Findon. His first runs were not promising but when he was just about due for the chop he suddenly bestirred himself and, ridden by Josh Gifford, won three races in a row.

The next few years were a kind of dream. Acrovat paid for himself by alternately running abysmally and then winning at long odds. He won six races altogether. He was followed by Blameless Stall, who won five hurdle races, by Zaras Pearl who won four, by Harvest who won four quality steeplechases. Round the Twist, in his turn, won five. Encouraged by this I acquired two modestly priced year-ling fillies, Cigarette Case and Parvati. Trained by Gordon, they won seven races between them and were placed a dozen times each, at Newbury, Ascot and Lingfield. They were sold eventually for several times what they cost, to go to stud. I hated to see them go and watching them trudge round the sales ring at Newmarket eyeing me balefully I felt like a traitor. It has long been too expensive a game, except for Arabs, millionaires and syndicates.

The second section here consists of poems. I wrote my first cricket poem, 'Cricket at Brighton', in the 1950s and my most recent one, 'Late Gower', in the early 1990s. My poem 'Stanley Matthews' dates from 1948 and 'Gary Lineker' from 1991. Poetry about sport has not much of a history, being in general of the rather hearty Newbolt variety, but over the years I have tried at various times, in a more modern idiom, to recapture racehorses, cricketers, golfers, and footballers in action, to suggest both a living likeness and a sense of period. Although Yeats, Sassoon, Larkin and Francis Thompson have written poems on racing and cricket that linger in the mind, the most haunting poem I know is by the American poet Marianne Moore about the great Iberian Real Tennis and pelota player, Pierre Etchebaster. 'There is no suitable simile,' she concludes. 'It is as though / the equidistant three tiny arcs of seeds in a banana / had been conjoined by Palestrina; / it is like the eyes / or say the face, of Palestrina by El Greco / O Escudero, Soledad / Rosario Escudero, Etchebaster!'

There are no perfect similes of course, but one can try to preserve a style, restore an action, rehearse an elegance.

I had the illusion that, when I no longer had to go to an office, I would be able to potter about at Hove or Lord's in the summer, at White Hart Lane or Twickenham in the winter. It hasn't turned out like that. I still go to an office and my visits to Lord's and the cricket places of Sussex are few and far between. My interest, however, is no less, in the fortunes of England in Test matches, on the rugby field or at Wembley, and of Sussex wherever. Television may not bring you the atmosphere or the intimacy but it provides a significant increase in detail.

Some of the happiest days of my life have been spent watching and writing about cricket. In my youth I learned much from Robertson-Glasgow, Ian Peebles, Cardus and Swanton, each of whom became friends. Diverse personalities, they stamped the game with their own distinctive styles. More nearly my contemporary, John Woodcock was a happy companion to most of the events in this book, Robin Marlar, Tony Winlaw and Henry Blofeld to a good few. The Press Box, despite the odd sourpuss, was in my day a very jolly place. Whatever the tensions on the field, often passionately reflected, there was nothing that an evening drink or two couldn't disperse.

PART I
Great Matches

2nd Test, Australia v England, Sydney, 1954

Eng
land, having put the Australians in at Brisbane in the First Test, lost by an innings and 154 runs, Australia making 601 for 8 declared, England 190 and 257. This match had to be won if the series was to be saved; or so it seemed.

ENGLAND

L. Hutton, c. Davidson, b. Johnston	30	c. Benaud, b. Johnston	28
T. E. Bailey, b. Lindwall	0	c. Langley, b. Archer	6
P. B. H. May, c. Johnston, b. Archer	5	b. Lindwall	104
T. W. Graveney, c. Favell, b. Johnston	21	c. Langley, b. Johnston	0
M. C. Cowdrey, c. Langley, b. Davidson	23	c. Archer, b. Benaud	54
W. J. Edrich, c. Benaud, b. Archer	10	b. Archer	29
F. Tyson, b. Lindwall	0	b. Lindwall	9
T. G. Evans, c. Langley, b. Archer	3	c. Lindwall, b. Archer	4
J. H. Wardle, c. Burke, b. Johnston	35	l.b.w., b. Lindwall	8
R. Appleyard, c. Hole, b. Davidson	8	not out	19
J. B. Statham, not out	14	c. Langley, b. Johnston	25
Extras (l.b. 5)	5	Extras (l.b. 6, n.b. 4)	10
Total	154	Total	296

FALL OF WICKETS. *First innings*: 1–14, 2–19, 3–58, 4–63, 5–84, 6–85, 7–88, 8–99, 9–111. *Second innings*: 1–18, 2–55, 3–55, 4–171, 5–222, 6–232, 7–239, 8–249, 9–250.

AUSTRALIA

A. Morris, c. Hutton, b. Bailey	12	l.b.w., b. Statham	10
L. Favell, c. Graveney, b. Bailey	26	c. Edrich, b. Tyson	16
J. Burke, c. Graveney, b. Bailey	44	b. Tyson	14
R. N. Harvey, c. Cowdrey, b. Tyson	12	not out	92
G. Hole, b. Tyson	12	b. Tyson	0
R. Benaud, l.b.w., b. Statham	20	c. Tyson, b. Appleyard	12
R. Archer, c. Hutton, b. Tyson	49	b. Tyson	6
A. Davidson, b. Statham	20	c. Evans, b. Statham	5
R. R. Lindwall, c. Evans, b. Tyson	19	b. Tyson	8
G. Langley, b. Bailey	5	b. Statham	0
W. Johnston, not out	0	c. Evans, b. Tyson	11
Extras (b. 5, l.b. 2, n.b. 2)	9	Extras (l.b. 7, n.b. 3)	10
Total	228	Total	184

FALL OF WICKETS. *First innings*: 1–18, 2–65, 3–100, 4–104, 5–122, 6–141, 7–193, 8–213, 9–224. *Second innings*: 1–27, 2–34, 3–77, 4–77, 5–102, 6–122, 7–127, 8–136, 9–145.

Bowling Analysis

AUSTRALIA

First Innings	O.	M.	R.	W.	*Second Innings*	O.	M.	R.	W.
Lindwall	17	3	47	2	Lindwall	31	10	69	3
Archer	12	7	12	3	Archer	22	9	53	3
Davidson	12	3	34	2	Johnston	19.3	2	70	3
Johnston	13.3	1	56	3	Davidson	13	2	52	0
					Benaud	19	3	42	1

ENGLAND

First Innings	O.	M.	R.	W.	*Second Innings*	O.	M.	R.	W.
Statham	18	1	83	2	Statham	19	6	45	3
Bailey	17.4	3	59	4	Tyson	18.4	1	85	6
Tyson	13	2	45	4	Bailey	6	0	21	0
Appleyard	7	1	32	0	Appleyard	6	1	12	1
					Wardle	4	2	11	0

ENGLAND WON BY 38 RUNS

First Day: There was a violent thunderstorm during the night, and, though the drizzle that succeeded it stopped about breakfast-time, the weather was not conducive to gaiety. Nor was the light good. Driving to the ground, one might have been on one's way to Old Trafford. By eleven o'clock, modest crowds were streaming through the avenue of heavy palms that links the city tramlines to the cricket ground; the gates, however, were not open, and they were obliged to wind themselves on to the end of a queue well-equipped with raincoats, parasols and umbrellas. Twenty minutes before play was due to begin the sun came out, the audience permitted to enter. The rumour was that Bedser, regardless of the conditions, would not play: it turned out to be correct, and there were few who did not think it folly. It looked just the day for him, the atmosphere heavy, the wicket a genuine green-top. Hutton, however, lost the toss, and Morris, most bravely in view of Brisbane, put England in to bat. Had Hutton won this, the nastiest of tosses to win, Bedser's absence would probably have obliged him to choose to bat in any case. Yet despite the wicket's apparent greenness, Morris was taking some considerable risk. His action showed how little he thought of England's two spin bowlers. Hassett, sitting next to me at lunch, subsequently committed himself to stating that it was not a risk he would have dared to take.

Hutton and Bailey, therefore, came out with stoical countenances, Lindwall going through his habitual unloosenings, the umbrella-field folding round the striker. Hutton took guard, warily eyeing the arc of five slips and two close fine legs, chewing slowly. Thus does a keeper, entering the cage, sense the tiger.

Hutton, in the first over, turned Lindwall for two off his leg stump with loose wrists and delicate application of the guiding hand, a stroke to calm nerves. A few balls later he leaned a full toss past gully for four. Archer bowled tight at the other end, just short of a length, which is the right foil to Lindwall, who barters runs for wickets generously in his opening overs. Without either third man or deep fine leg, any stroke that beats the close arc is worth four runs. Morris provided Lindwall with his usual 'Carmody' field, and Lindwall, keeping the ball right up, moved it a lot both ways. Lindwall works up gradually to full pace, preferring to let the shine do the work for him in the early stages, and his first three overs were not fast. Hutton nowadays prefers to steer away, rather than hit, the

11

widish half-volley, with body not truly over the ball, and Lindwall generally attacked this area. Bailey played Archer with dead bat and back foot outside the off stump for three successive maidens. Johnston then came on for Lindwall. The first half-hour was weathered, with fourteen runs scored, all off Hutton's bat. Lindwall, however, had retired only to change ends, and now, in his first over from the Noble Stand end, a breeze blowing in from cover, he sent Bailey's middle stump somersaulting. The ball dipped in late, and Bailey, late down on it, was yorked. May is always an agreeable sight at number three, for while not being incapable of airy waves outside the off stump, he gives an immediate impression of impending assault. Moreover, he encourages, with his full backlift, the idea that the fall of the first wicket was of little account. He was not long in, though, for, after several firm strokes, he drove at an in-swinging half-volley from Archer with insufficient control, and the ball shot off the inside edge straight at Johnston's midriff fine of short square leg. Graveney, next man in, for some minutes made no sense at all, straddling his legs as if playing leap-frog and withdrawing his bat at the last second. Lindwall found various edges subsequently, Graveney pushing and missing at both him and Archer, and taking the ball on the thigh when it came down the line of the leg stump. Hutton, smoothly efficient early on, was rendered strokeless by a combination of misery and accurate attack. So it continued till the interval, at which England were 34 for 2 after ninety minutes of increasing discomfort. Archer had bowled seven overs for four runs and one wicket. This was the first of four successive gloomy pre-lunch sessions for England.

Graveney looked better for his lunch, playing Lindwall firmly off the front foot and once driving Johnston with elegant swing past cover. He is, however, a player of yacht-like character, beautiful in calm seas, yet at the mercy of every change of weather. There are no obvious faults in construction but the barometer has only to fall away a point or two from fair for way to be completely lost and the boat broached to, if not turned for harbour. Lindwall bowled two magnificent overs to Hutton, varying swing and pace, adjusting them each ball as he attacked one stump and then another. Hutton was never allowed to let one go by with certainty, nor did he receive a ball of length short enough for it to have straightened out. The trajectory was full and gradual, the ball holding up at the end of its flight for the breeze to drift it across. Hutton played thoughtfully and without impatience, but there were no pickings at either end. A whole hour more passed before Hutton turned Lindwall through the short legs to send up the fifty, which had taken 150 minutes. Lindwall wound up with two bouncers of great savagery that curved Graveney back like a sapling, and then demanded his sweater. Davidson bowled in place of him, which meant that two left-handers were in operation, Johnston wheeling away at varying speeds from the other end. Davidson was lively and quick off the pitch, but the ball usually went straight through after pitching. Johnston alternated between floating the ball away towards the slips, and digging it in, rather quicker, just short of a length on leg stump, two fielders crouching off the batsman's hip. Together, with the score 58, they took the vital wicket: Hutton flicked at an in-swinger pitching on his legs and Davidson at leg slip flung himself yards to his right, catching the ball right-handed (the wrong hand for him) grass-high. The stroke was technically perfect, the ball kept well down and steered fine of the wicket-keeper. Hutton stood bemused, uncertain of what had happened, much as an actor might, who having delivered a line with cutting irony, finds it answered with words not in the script. Slowly, very slowly, he walked from the wicket. Before he can have got his pads off Graveney joined him, pushing out at a ball from Johnston that, pitching a foot outside the off stump, was proceeding towards third slip. Graveney helped it on its way and Favell, a puppyish fielder, frisky in the chase, took a low tumbling catch.

Cowdrey and Edrich were therefore obliged to start again from scratch, rather as if beginning the innings, but with the knowledge that none were to follow. Neither looked unduly disconcerted. Cowdrey glided Johnston still finer than Hutton had done, the pupil instructing the master as it were, and received four runs. Edrich pulled a no-ball from Archer to the square-leg boundary, and his bat continued to make healthy noises. Cowdrey, calm and relaxed, was disposed to treat the bowling with no more than the deference expected of youth. Twenty were added: then Archer, who had taken Edrich's wicket at Brisbane, got one to lift abruptly on the off stump and Edrich, already in position, could not avoid giving Benaud a gentle catch at gully. Tyson arrived, and Lindwall could hardly get his sweater off quick enough. His eagerness was pardonable, for he quickly knocked back Tyson's leg stump. Evans, who for some weeks has played any ball on the off as if handing point his bat to hold, moved back to, and inside, a half-volley from Archer, and was caught by Langley. Three wickets had fallen for four runs and Archer, in ten overs and one ball, had taken three for eight. England at tea were 94 for 7, Cowdrey 18. Benaud dropped Cowdrey in the gully to the tinkle of teaspoons, but it was of small account, for Cowdrey, trying to force Davidson, was caught at the wicket five runs later. He had played admirably, but the ship was too badly holed and he was obliged to try and salvage what he could.

Appleyard put the hundred up, displaying a model forward stroke before Hole snatched a low fast snick at first slip. Wardle, who had been cavorting about as though wearing someone else's glasses, stabbing his bat a yard inside or outside the ball, now suddenly saw Johnston plain and with great good spirits hit him for 17 in one over. Four came from a strapping cover drive made on the hop, two upper-cuts sent second and third slip on futile chases to the boundary, and three hefty swings, made with bat and legs as far apart as the human frame can stand, just cleared the field for 2, 2 and 1. Benaud, running back, got his hands to one of these, but, to the delight of the Hill, failed to hold it. Statham, soberly professional at the other end, cut and drove when opportunity offered, but was largely content to observe Wardle with the good nature of one who had long outgrown such crudities. The 150 went up, and Morris began to bear the air of a stage manager who sees two comedians inserting unrehearsed jokes in an act already running late, and only reluctantly engaged at all. Eventually Burke caught Wardle at long-on very quietly, but not before 43 runs had been added in twenty minutes for the last wicket. No sooner was the ball pocketed than a great bundle of clouds, gathering for some while, sent the players off at the double, as fast as they had run all day.

With only half an hour left, Australia seemed safe till the morning. But the rain departed as rapidly as it had appeared, and finally Hutton had time to give Statham and Bailey two overs each. Morris and Favell scored 18 with discourteous hurry, until, with two balls to go, Bailey made one lift on the leg stump and Hutton at leg slip picked the ball politely off Morris's glove. It seemed almost too unobtrusive to have really happened.

Second Day: Favell and Burke set off at such a gallop under the loose grey clouds of noon that it looked as though England's 154 would be overtaken before lunch. Tyson was good for only two wild overs, and Statham was glanced and cut by both batsmen. Favell was quick to detect the length of the ball, and he lay back and thrashed anything at all short. Burke had a pale air of permanence about him, and he offered few edges. Fifty went up in forty-four minutes, and the field was unflatteringly spread for two fast bowlers reckoned to be as quick as any in the world. Hutton switched Statham, and brought Bailey on at the opposite end from the evening before. Bailey, by adroit and systematic attack on the region of the off stump, first halted, then drove back Australia. He kept a precise and determined length at no more than medium pace, pitching the ball on roughly the same spot, but using his bowling crease so variously that the angle and margin of swing altered constantly. There was little short enough to hit away off the back foot, little quite full enough to drive. As the ball pitched, it ran away towards the slips, so that the forward stroke had to be made outside the line of flight. Now and again Bailey, bowling a faster one straight, had Burke shuffling behind it in a hurry; and sometimes, after Favell had pushed forward to several in a row, one came back sharply at him, causing him to jab it down awkwardly in front of short leg. Both felt for, and missed, the ball that was delivered, with surprising bounce off the seam, as obliquely as possible.

Rightly enough, Bailey in the end dismissed them both, caught off identical strokes by Graveney at second slip. Favell departed at 65, leaning forward and getting an outside edge, and Burke at 100, immediately after lunch. Graveney held Favell ankle-high and Burke more easily at shoulder level. Harvey was an hour over six runs, two of his scoring shots sending the ball skimming past the heads of May and Cowdrey in the gully. He seemed, however, to have settled down for the day when Tyson, whom Hutton had brought on for Statham, made one kick sharply. Harvey, already into his stroke, could not withdraw in time, and Cowdrey took as simple a catch in the gully as Benaud had done to remove Edrich from a similar ball. The lunch score of 100 for 2 had become 104 for 4. Tyson, bowling with admirable control and much fuller length from a shortened run, now made the ball both lift and break sharply back from the off. Hole, like many modern Australian batsmen, curves his back and bends his knees at the wicket, but he drove Bailey with so splendid a stroke to the cover boundary, having cut imperiously between slip and gully from the start, that patriotism and pleasure were made to struggle for supremacy. He had made only 12, several late cuts bringing no more than one run each, when Tyson slanted his leg stump. He is not happy against real pace. His back lift, circular rather than straight, is high, and he was no more than brushing pad with bat when the ball was through him. Benaud, morally bowled numerous times before scoring, was badly dropped when playing Tyson with the break into Graveney's hands at short leg. Bailey, in a spell of seventy minutes between lunch and tea, had both Benaud and Archer scraping forward and missing so monotonously that the stomachs of the three slips must have been turning over continuously with ungratified apprehension. Had Archer's bat possessed whiskers, it would assuredly have forfeited them several times over.

Nevertheless, they were together at tea, albeit poised as precariously as curates on a dowager's Regency chairs. Statham, returning for Tyson, had Benaud l.b.w. with a ball that both came back and kept low; but Graveney's missed catch had cost 20 runs. Appleyard had his first bowl of the series and, after several introductory balls of quality, was struck for four and six successively by Archer, who, wretched so long, seized on him with the relish of one who suddenly sees a familiar face in a hostile, crowded room. The second of these unexpected blows took Australia past England's score.

Archer was moving out of the precincts of banditry into the quiet suburbs of middle-order respectability, when the new ball became due. Davidson, his partner since tea, had helped him to add fifty in the same number of minutes, though both were frequently defeated. Nevertheless, in the intervals they made bold and imaginative strokes, Davidson driving splendidly to extra cover, where Hutton was slow to put a fieldsman. Australia's lead was fattening disagreeably when Davidson hit across a ball from Statham and lost his leg stump. Archer, one short of his fifty, was then beautifully caught by Hutton at third slip, Tyson having not long before taken the new ball. Lindwall drove and cut his way into double figures, the ninth Australian to do so, before he swung at a tired bouncer from Tyson and obliged Evans to catch him off his glove. Things had moved at so rapid a pace that, were Johnston or Langley to get out quickly, England would be faced with seven or eight minutes' batting.

Hutton, therefore, commanded Tyson to bowl down the leg side, which he did, to Johnston's keen disappointment, even beyond the range of the latter's one-handed sweep. With exactly ten minutes left, Bailey rattled Langley's middle and off stumps in the manner of one who could take a wicket whichever ball he wished. Australia, all out for 228, were 74 ahead. But, due primarily to Bailey, who had taken the first three wickets, England were not out of it. They had attacked, and, if they were to have any hopes of winning the match, they had to continue to do so.

Third Day: The pattern was little different from that of England's first innings, though the recovery came earlier and was longer sustained. Bailey once again looked devoid of shots, lasting this time for forty minutes, but without ever seeming likely to do other than delay the inevitable. Hutton had no alternative to Bailey to open the innings with him; a week ago he and Bailey had put on ninety for the first wicket against Victoria. Yet, watching Bailey now against Lindwall and Archer, his unsuitability was painfully made evident. An opening over of half-volleys from Archer was patted gently back, with only two fielders in front of the wicket. An opening batsman must be able sometimes to drive the over-pitched ball, and Bailey, for all his solid virtues lower down the order, holds his bat in such a manner as to preclude the free swing of the left elbow. He made of his bat the usual barricade, but, with Hutton ruminative, that was too unambitious in the circumstances. In Archer's fourth over, the first three having been maidens, Bailey failed to get behind a ball that moved away late off the seam, providing Langley with the simplest of catches. He endured for forty minutes, during which, apart from hitting a full toss from Lindwall for four, he made the scoring of runs appear well-nigh impossible.

May at once forced Archer several times hard to mid-wicket, thereby encouraging Hutton to a more spritely gait, which is what often happens. Hutton glanced Johnston for four, drove him firmly past cover and then turned Archer a shade uppishly through the short-legs for four more. Fifty came up, the lead was cut to twenty-four, and English hopes rose with the sun, that was now free of cloud for about the first time since the match began.

At 58 the left-arm combination of Johnston and Davidson was at work, Lindwall having bowled very fast, but with little swing, for three-quarters of an hour. Johnston had not long changed ends when Hutton, checking a stroke made well away from the body at a wide half-volley, succeeded only in steering it towards Benaud's head in the gully. Hutton does not always drive with his left foot at the pitch, preferring sometimes to hit it later and squarer, with arms extended. He was not over this ball, which was thrown disconcertingly into the wind. Had he continued the stroke, he would probably have cleared Benaud and got four runs to third man.

Graveney, having narrowly avoided edging his first ball, similar to the one that took Hutton's wicket, groped forward, left leg down the line of the leg stump, at the third, also pitched on or outside the off stump and leaving him. This ball, bowled over the wicket and moving diagonally from leg to off across the batsman's body, is one that Johnston has bowled thousands of times. Graveney was well inside it and Langley took the catch almost apologetically. Over cold lobster at lunch the talk was not surprisingly of how long the match could now last – talk that was soon made to appear absurd by Cowdrey and May playing Lindwall and Johnston in bright sun but cool breeze with an ease of manner that betokened innocent digestions. May scored continually in the area between square leg and mid-on; his bat swings naturally across his body, and anything not well pitched-up outside the off stump he was able to force into that space. When Archer came on, he hooked him hard for four. Bowlers tend to pitch short to May, for he lays into the over-pitched ball with uninhibited savagery. Davidson took over from Lindwall, and Cowdrey drove him sweetly several times through the covers, as well as once to the sightscreen. Bat and pad come down as one when Cowdrey drives, and so truly is his not inconsiderable weight distributed that he seems never to need to do more than lean quietly forward. His natural instinct being to play off the front foot, he is less quick than May to move back on his wicket and force the shorter ball through gaps on the on-side. He is, therefore, for the moment, the easier player to pin down.

At 118 Benaud came on to bowl the first of seventeen overs, interrupted only by tea. Cowdrey and May had raised the score by sixty before he began, but he quickly found a length, and Cowdrey especially found himself restricted to forward strokes that had not the power to beat a deepish ring of off-side fielders. Johnston bowled also to a field set half-way to the boundary on both sides of the

18

wicket, and, though every so often both batsmen moved their feet and hit the ball hard, the safer shot was the checked forward push. Harvey, Favell and Burke, however, are not fielders to encourage the repeated stealing of runs. Lindwall after tea had another long, foxy and accurate spell, bowling with constant changes of pace, sudden venom and ancient guile. By five o'clock, nevertheless, a hundred had been added, all of them along the grass, since Graveney's dismissal. Cowdrey for a short while looked to have tired, made restless also by the fact that there was under half an hour left for play. He reached fifty, however, not long after May, who seemed sensibly to be encouraging him to further assault, rather than to withdrawal. But, with the score 171, the time ten-past five, Cowdrey, going down the pitch to a googly from Benaud, failed just to get there. Continuing his stroke, he lifted the ball, which went high and straight to Archer at long-off, the only occupied place behind the bowler. Wretchedly disappointing as the fall of Cowdrey's wicket in this manner was, to others as patently as to him, he and May had set, through their wise blend of patience and aggression, a new value on any runs that were to come. For three hours, in their contrasted styles, they had batted with unforced authority, the one upright, flowing and lithe, the other powerful with the gentleness of strength. May split the air with the noise of his strokes, Cowdrey the field with the ease of his timing. There was little to choose between them in the correctness of their technique, the natural assertion of their breeding.

It was to be expected now that Edrich and May would settle for survival. But not a bit of it: Edrich began by hooking Johnston for four, off-drove him for another, and then, swinging violently at a no-ball, unsighted Langley who let it speed through to the rails. In the next over Benaud dropped one short, and Edrich, with forearm only, pulled him for the swiftest four of the day. May, finding Edrich's mood as infectious as it was surprising, hit Johnston wide first of mid-on, then of mid-off. When the field dropped back he pushed him for singles. Thirty-three runs were scored in twenty minutes before a perspiring Morris was able to lead his team to shelter. This was champagne, when one had prepared for indigestion tablets.

The pitch, having sown its wild oats on the first two days, appeared during the afternoon to have acquired a taste for domestic calm. However, the new ball would be due when play began in the morning, which meant that May, who was two short of his first century against Australia, and Edrich would need to see the shine off. England at 204 for 4, 130 runs ahead, had still a long climb to make.

Fourth Day: May reached his hundred off Lindwall's second ball, turning it for two past Johnston at backward short leg. This innings of crisp drives, powerful on-side placings and, most important of all, a certainty suggesting that he knew himself the equal, if not the superior, of Australian bowling, marks the end of May's first Test period. Henceforth, however, he will need to throw off his present unhappy characteristic of being a second innings batsman. He should by nature be the architect of a match, not its restorer.

During this first over of Lindwall's, bowled with the old ball, drizzle began to block out the sky over Botany Bay, thickening quickly, and sending everyone scampering in as soon as it was finished.

Twenty minutes later the headlands of the Bay were once more visible over the cabbage-tree palms behind the pavilion, and play continued. Morris, because of the wet outfield, delayed taking the new ball, using Johnston and Davidson in the meantime. Edrich played Johnston agreeably through the covers for four, and was then all but caught and bowled by Davidson, who bowled steadily for half an hour.

At twenty-past twelve, the real moment of crisis, Lindwall took the new ball. He bowled two out-swingers fairly wide: the third ball, swinging in, pitched on the middle stump and May, watchful for the out-swinger, was late on it and yorked. It was Lindwall's first wicket of the innings, costing him fifty runs. May had appeared perfectly comfortable, though Johnston and Davidson, attacking his off stump at a good length, never allowed him to get going. The loss of this wicket, caused by Lindwall's control over the new ball and his understanding of the psychology of the batsman faced by it, put an end to the possibility of a commanding English score. Australia were again on top.

Tyson made several reassuring forward strokes to Lindwall; then, moving forward to make another, he found the ball shorter, and momentarily perplexed, hesitated. The ball lifted steeply and, before he could do more than turn his head away, hit him on the back of the skull, shooting down to fine leg as knowingly as if it had come off the centre of the bat. He went down at once, throwing his arms back helplessly. It was a sickening blow. Lindwall's bouncers are not of the childish, 'telegraphed' variety common to most fast bowlers. They pitch only just short and get up almost straight. Tyson is not at the best of times quick on his feet, and he was on the wrong foot anyway to duck. He was eventually led off by two ambulance men, patently uncertain whether in heaven or hell, but with a very bad headache whichever it was.

Evans was dropped at slip by Hole first ball, holding his bat out as in an Edwardian photograph, well away from his body. On the stroke of lunch, what seemed the ultimate disaster occurred. Edrich, concentrating resolutely on keeping his wicket, moved forward and then drew his bat away from a slower, shorter ball from Archer, going well wide of the off stump. He was in position far too soon, however, and his bat dropping as he let go his right hand, turned the ball on to his stumps. The score was 232 for 6, England 158 ahead.

During lunch the opinion was that Tyson, who had been taken to hospital for an X-ray, was unlikely to bat or bowl again in the match.

Evans wasted no time in placing Archer politely into Lindwall's hands at third slip. He was barely half-way to the pavilion when Tyson, pale, but not otherwise visibly shaky, strode out past him. He was nobly received, and played quietly and efficiently, driving Johnston for four to extra cover and Archer straight, before Lindwall bowled him for the second time in the match. Wardle hit Lindwall to the square leg boundary and was then l.b.w. Five wickets had fallen to the new ball and only forty-six runs been scored; which meant that, with the last pair together, England were 176 runs ahead. With the pitch as placid as it had been all day, this seemed at least a hundred short of a reasonable proposition.

That looked to be the opinion of Statham and Appleyard, who, with the modesty of bowlers pure and simple, played unobtrusively for some overs of considerable swing from Archer and Lindwall. Appleyard again revealed a forward stroke of some merit, and a bat of such pallidness that one feared it would get sunburned. However, it had its longest outing yet, its owner even cutting Davidson for four with a stroke of governessy severity. Statham, by habit, is a batsman of adventure and hazard, but he seemed for once quite interested in the technique, as opposed to the more esoteric sensations, of batting. He placed his body behind Lindwall's good ones, declining to lift his head or sweep round towards the square leg umpire. He smote a half-volley all along the ground to the sightscreen, and cut Lindwall hard down past gully for another four. Pleased with these strokes he repeated them off Davidson for a similar number of runs. Lindwall demanded his sweater, Davidson was encouraged into his. Statham continued to slant the ball through the slips by skilfully angling his bat. He was the first to lose patience, though, swinging wildly at Johnston when it was beginning to look as though he had found an individual kind of orthodoxy rather attractive, and snicking the ball to Langley. Appleyard was left caressing his bat like a bridegroom. Forty-six runs had been put on, which brought the contribution of the last English pair to 89 for the match. The first-wicket partnership in both innings had been more than doubled. More important, it showed that it was worth while for the last few batsmen to take a little trouble. Runs scored for the last wicket, a fact that English bowlers have been slow to learn, count just as much as any others. Langley in the two English innings held five catches and let through no byes. He is a wicket-keeper whose considerable virtues lodge behind a rubicund, homely and undemonstrative exterior.

At twenty minutes past three Australia began their fourth innings, needing 223 runs to win. It was not generally thought, on this wicket, to be a task likely to extend them. Statham's first over, however, bowled into the wind, was of such liveliness that most preconceptions were quietly shed. His second ball swung in sharply, and Favell, covering his middle and off stumps, was hit firmly on the pads. A confident appeal was disallowed, the ball perhaps rising enough to have frisked over the bails. The fourth ball lifted, and Favell, with a semi-circular scoop, steered it wide of Edrich a foot above his head. Edrich, though he got both hands there, could not hold it and the ball went through his fingers for two. Favell was within an inch of being bowled two balls later. The last ball of the over skidded off the inside of his bat for four to fine leg, Favell anxiously seeking its whereabouts. Altogether an over which, since it was without reward, seemed likely to dishearten any bowler. Tyson, downwind, worked up a fine speed, but Morris pushed the ball confidently into vacant regions round square leg and, when Tyson bowled him a full toss, sliced it between first and second slip to chip the paint from the pickets. A black spaniel, seeing no fielder, squeezed on to the field, retrieved the ball, and cantered elusively about as if reluctant to allow Morris another go at it. In Statham's next over, the last before tea, Morris seemed to take leave of his senses. He went to hook a good-length ball, missed, and was appealed against for l.b.w. Next, he slashed vainly at out-swingers three times in succession. Finally, despairing of contact, he swung well above a ball only fractionally short on the leg stump. It kept low, hitting him on the pads. This time he was out. Harpo Marx could barely have dreamed up such antics.

At 37 Favell, possibly curious, after his earlier good fortune, about Edrich's abilities, guided an away-swinger from Tyson straight at his head. Edrich, standing deep, held a much faster travel-ling ball with both hands clasped together in a boxer's acknowledgement. Favell's habit, playing a good-length ball on the off stump, is to move back along the line of the leg, his bat at the moment of contact showing itself more to the sky than to the bowler – a common fault among players who place their feet for the cut.

Harvey played at, and was only a thickness of oil off, his first two balls from Tyson, both of which lifted over the off stump. Subsequently, he made certain of getting well behind the ball, not scoring much, but slowly establishing a right of tenure. After half an hour of high-spirited attack, Statham and Tyson were rested, Appleyard and Bailey coming on to concentrate on Harvey's leg stump. Anxious for another wicket Hutton called up Wardle, who bowled two maidens to the intransigent Burke, before bringing back Tyson and Statham for a final assault. Harvey, however, was now proceeding without trace of uncertainty, and, having seen the fast bowlers off, found time to take two fours off Wardle in the last over of the day. Thirty-five runs only were added in eighty minutes after Favell's departure, Harvey making 26. Australia, 72 for 2, needed 150 more. England could hope for nothing from the pitch.

Fifth Day: The first overs bowled by Statham and Tyson confirmed the worst fears of the night before. The pitch was corn-coloured, the light excellent, and Harvey and Burke played each ball in the middle of the bat with time to spare. The Hill was not much over a third full, the stands rather less so: a few sunbathers lay stripped to the waist on either side of the scoreboard. A light breeze ruffled the flags and

Australia, one imagined, would be high and dry by tea-time.

Burke has so little backlift, and, generally, preserves an air of such immovable detachment, that it was some time before one became aware that a yorker of exceptional speed from Tyson had uprooted his off stump. Two balls later Hole's middle stump rattled against its fellows; the ball was of similar pace, perhaps a couple of inches shorter. Tyson, using a run now little longer than Tate's, dropped his shoulders and hung his arms loosely in his habitual follow-through. But the stumps were awry, and the slips leaping like salmon as Hole disconsolately made his way past them: 77–4–0.

Benaud joined Harvey and, playing solidly off the front foot, looked disagreeably less out of composure than might have been expected. Tyson kept up a tremendous pace, forcing Harvey back on his stumps, so that, although he was putting the middle of the bat to the ball, he was detained at one end. Benaud took runs here and there from Statham, earning each one. With the score 100 Hutton rested Statham and brought on Appleyard to bowl into the wind. Benaud pushed forward at his first ball, which hung a little before turning in between bat and pad to shave the leg stump. He seemed to prefer the pace of the others, which he thumped hard to mid-off. Appleyard is not, nevertheless, a safe bowler to drive indiscriminately, for he varies his pace and makes the ball hold up at the last second, before dipping into the batsman. Just such a ball Benaud, fancying a half-volley, attempted to sweep to mid-wicket six runs later. He swung early, therefore across, and sent the ball swerving high to square leg. Tyson stood under it, gazing upward and weaving anxiously from side to side. Palpably it drifted and equally obviously Tyson misjudged it. At the last moment he lunged forward on bended knee, extending his hands as for the sacrament. The ball found them, miraculously.

At lunch Australia were 118 for 5: forty-six runs had been scored in ninety minutes, 105 more were wanted. At five minutes to two, with the total 122, Tyson bowled a ball very fast and slightly short outside the off stump. Archer leaned away as if to cut, but his bat was still ascending when the ball broke back and shattered his wicket.

Harvey was being kept as much as possible from the bowling, both Tyson and Statham forcing him to play back off his ribs with three men a pitch's length away on the leg side.

At 127 Statham, bowling into the wind, hit the shoulder of Davidson's bat, and Evans, who had not been taking the ball cleanly, made several yards to snatch the ball with both hands outstretched from in front of second slip. He rolled over and over but kept his gloves aloft. Davidson himself might have caught such a catch; not conceivably anyone else. The ball flew from the bat-maker's name as if it had come in contact with a spring.

Lindwall took eight off the rest of that over, mostly through the covers. A single by Harvey then brought him face to face with Tyson. The first ball came sharply back from a length and Lindwall did exceptionally well to stop it. The crowd had visibly stiffened, musing, as perhaps was Lindwall, on the possibility of something very fast, straight and short. The second ball pitched about six inches in front of Lindwall's off stump, which it hit long before Lindwall had gauged its length; 136–8–8, Tyson 5 for 54.

The scoreboard at this point showed a certain confusion, due to an unprecedented number of people being required at the Members' Gate. In consequence the name of Dr F. Rosati found itself temporarily inserted into the batting order in the only vacant space, which, however much it might have dismayed its possessor, seemed exceedingly sharp practice.

At half-past two, the score 145, Statham hit Langley's off stump with an in-swinger, breaking the base off. Johnston therefore emerged preceded by an umpire carrying a replacement – an embarrassing accompaniment for the batsman, obliged to walk fifty yards in a file of two. Australia were 77 runs behind.

Johnston stabbed at his first two balls: the first nearly removed his off bail, the second got him the benefit of the doubt after an appeal for l.b.w.

Harvey now threw off the protective colouring he normally wears at the wicket and decided on all-out attack. It was later suggested that he might well have done this before; in fact, he was given no chance. Prescience lagged behind events.

He soon made up for it. His timing magically returned to him, and he hit the ball away off the back foot almost regardless of its length on both sides of the wicket. He scuttled for threes and twos when he wanted them, and declined long singles. Hutton did his best to prevent this sudden monopoly of the strike, but the accuracy and speed of his fielders let him down again and again. Johnston, rarely asked to play more than two balls an over, was not above despatching them one-handed to the long-leg boundary. Twice he treated Tyson thus.

After eighty minutes' onslaught against the wind, Statham came off. Bailey bowled, and was immediately hit straight over his head by Harvey. Not long before, Harvey had hooked Tyson hard to fine leg where Bailey, standing a few yards in, had gone forward only to find the ball clear him and bang the palings first bounce. Harvey's score moved from 64, when Johnston entered, into the eighties. The joke was turning a little sour. Australia required forty-six, which was little more than these two had already put on.

Tyson, almost at the end of his tether, was bowling with considerably lowered arm. Johnston stopped the straight balls with deceptive protestations of amazement; Harvey, beyond the reach of bowlers, had left fallibility trailing him.

The last ball of an over from Bailey, struck high on the rise by Harvey, slowly climbed the bank at mid-wicket, beckoned on by numerous small hands as it slackened pace.

Johnston therefore was faced with the prospect of a whole over. Hutton must have thought hard before offering it to Tyson, whose weariness was making him bowl helplessly down the leg side. He did so, however, though probably it would have been Tyson's last. Johnston picked one off his boot to get four to fine leg. He followed another past his hip, not able to reach it. To yet another wide of the leg stump he extended his bat, this time caught up with it, and Evans, standing back, safely took the ball.

Harvey, 92 not out, had reinstated himself amongst those who provide the legendary innings of cricket. For this was surely one such.

So England, on an afternoon of ignored time and weather, had won by 38 runs. Tyson became only the third fast bowler ever to take ten wickets in a Test match for England against Australia, Larwood having done so in 1932–33, and Farnes in 1934.

That night in Prince's we celebrated marvellously. Christmas was only two days off and we had, after all, received the best present anyone could have wished for. An American from Philadelphia, who had made a special trip to see the match, entertained the team: he had once played for the Gentlemen of England some decades ago in obscure circumstances, and his enthusiasm seemed only equalled by his generosity in the cause of English cricket. He had watched England draw the Second Test at Lord's in 1953, when Bailey and Watson batted throughout a day of unbearable tension, and he had gone to West Indies in the following winter, when England were two down, and stayed to see the rubber squared.

It had been a memorable day, one fit to compete with any hauled out of the past by those who had witnessed the battles of 1902, or who had watched with innocent eye the achievements of Trumper and Hill, of Spofforth and Albert Trott, of Braund and Richardson. The bowling of Tyson and the batting of Harvey on 22 December 1954 was the contribution of a new generation to the classical repertory of cricketing drama. In one match Tyson had reimposed the menace of speed on Australian batsmen. At Brisbane it seemed that, as much by luck as by good judgement, Australia had inflicted psychological blows on England's speed attack from which immediate recovery could not possibly be hoped. Hutton, too, had no feasible alternative to his fast bowlers: he was committed to them virtually in sickness as in health. Tyson's run, cut by over half, still showed the same shuffle and change of feet: but from three raking strides he managed to get his left shoulder quite as high as before and the increase in control was astonishing.

It had to be remembered that it was once again Bailey who started the fight-back on the second day, when Australia were scoring at a rate enough to put any bowler out of composure. He performed the duties that Bedser had so often done since the war on good wickets. He moved the ball consistently and sufficiently from a good length to reduce batsmen, hitherto scoring freely, to the defensive push that, like a virus, brings in its train a whole host of other symptoms.

Hutton, that evening at Prince's, was pointedly asked by an Australian journalist, 'Did you miss Bedser at all?' and, with the diplomatic twinkle that has become instinctive to him in public, he replied: 'We always miss Alec.'

It was not the least part of Hutton's triumph in this match that the decision to leave out Bedser, criticized almost without exception by correspondents of both countries, was honourably justified. Both Wardle and Appleyard, one of whom played in Bedser's place, made vital runs: and though Wardle bowled scarcely at all, the balance of the attack was improved as much by the fact that there were only three pace bowlers present, as through the performances of the two slower ones.

In a way this match was also a vindication of Hutton's predominantly defensive field-placing. Morris persisted with the close 'umbrella' field – five slips, two leg slips – that does not permit of third man or long leg. England scored some thirty or forty extra runs in this way, though possibly one extra wicket was taken by these two men being up close. Hutton, almost as soon as he could decently do so, dropped his third slip back to the boundary; long leg never came up at all. On several occasions Tyson, Bailey and Statham bowled only to one slip. I can't recollect a chance being missed on this account, and at least forty runs were saved. Against this, Hutton provides his slow bowlers with a field so spreadeagled from the start that what little self-confidence he allows them anyway must soon evaporate.

Yet he captained England during these days with patience, skill and admirable control. He kept his bowlers as fresh as circumstances allowed, and, though he asked much of Bailey, Tyson and Statham in turn, he never failed to get a response. He attacked whenever possible, and he made the most of periods of enforced defence. He may not, off the field, draw his players out or encourage their confidences: still less may he build them up as individuals. But he led them in this Second Test match, in frequently trying conditions, with a most exemplary calm.

That night at Prince's, with the corks popping over plates of oysters, the band thudding behind the shuffle of dancers, was the most exciting of the tour. Later, coming out into Castlereagh Street, with the stars sparkling as though they were part of the Christmas decorations, one felt an elation altogether out of proportion. But, after all, we had been present at a rebirth, one situated so appositely in the year, that the sense of wonder communicated itself as in happiest childhood. Christmas may rightly belong to children: but it is still capable of surprising grown-ups.

The Third Test, played over the New Year at Melbourne, was just as exciting. England, on the first day, were reduced to 41 for 4, but largely due to a magnificent 102 by Cowdrey, reached 191. Australia, recovering from 134 for 7, were all out 231, Statham taking 5 for 60. May made 91 in England's second innings of 279, leaving Australia to make 240 to win. Tyson, bowling at great pace, took 7 for 27, and Australia were all out 111.

At Adelaide, after both sides were about level in the first innings, Australia were again bowled out for 111, Tyson, Statham and Appleyard taking three wickets each. England, set to make 94 to win, lost Hutton, Edrich, and Cowdrey to inspired bowling by Miller for 18, but Compton pulled them through and the match was won by five wickets.

The Fifth Test, ruined by rain, would almost certainly have gone to England. Batting first, England declared at 371 for 7, Graveney 111, Compton 84. Australia had made 221 and 118 for 6, Wardle taking eight wickets in the match.

2nd Test, West Indies v England, Port of Spain, 1960

The First Test, played in Bridgetown, Barbados, was a high-scoring draw, England making 482 and 71 for 0, West Indies 563. Barrington, Dexter, Sobers and Worrell all made centuries, Sobers 226, Worrell 197 not out.

While M.C.C. were disporting themselves among the oil refineries at Pointe à Pierre, West Indies were having an open practice at Port of Spain.

Two places were in doubt: those of McMorris, who had been run out for nought at Bridgetown, and Scarlett, the off-spinner, whom Singh's success had put in jeopardy. McMorris failed in each innings of the trial, so that virtually put paid to him. Nurse of Barbados was summoned at a few hours' notice, but in the event the selectors plumped for Solomon, one of the successes of the India-Pakistan tour, to open with Hunte. Singh, as we expected, replaced Scarlett. This was a justified gamble on the lines of the Ramadhin-Valentine gamble in 1950, for Singh was virtually without first-class experience.

This meant that two Jamaicans were rejected. McMorris and Scarlett, both complaining of the hostile atmosphere of the crowd, even during net practice, flew home before the Test.

In this instance, the changes seemed common sense. But throughout the time we were in the Caribbean we heard criticism of the 'horses for courses' or 'proportional representation' policy of West Indian selection committees. The home player, it was repeated, stood at an overwhelming advantage when a Test was due to be played in his island. Many were those who regretted the chauvinism that showed itself equally in attitudes to the concept of Federation as to picking the best Test team.

Yet an atmosphere of mutual trust and confidence among the players is not always helped by the Press. On the second day of the Port of Spain Test the following paragraph appeared in *The Nation* (formerly *P. N. M. Weekly*):

> I want to say clearly beforehand that the idea of Alexander captaining a side on which Frank Worrell is playing is to me quite revolting. Whatever the result of this series I shall mobilize everything I can so that Frank should captain the team to Australia. In 1957 during the tour in England I endured the long days of misery which need not have been. To send to Australia as captain in 1960 a man who has never been there before would be a betrayal. Show me one single individual who will come out and say 'I believe Alexander will be a better captain than Worrell for such and such reasons'. No one will dare ... If Frank is not appointed it will be over wide and public protest ... That Worrell was not captain in 1957 in England was a scandal known to everybody. I shall go into detail as to the mischief this kind of thing causes. I have kept silence for 25 years. I shall do so no longer.

The article was signed C. L. R. James, the name of a locally known literary critic, cricket enthusiast and political editor.

Now whatever the rights and wrongs relating to John Goddard's reluctant acceptance of captaining the unfortunate 1957 touring side, Mr James must know that Worrell was offered the captaincy of the side that went to India and Pakistan. At that time Worrell was studying in England and for perfectly sound reasons he felt it impossible to interrupt his work. In face of Worrell's refusal Alexander was appointed and, generally speaking, did a good job. He never made any secret of the fact that he was the second choice.

It was not therefore surprising – especially in view of the fact that he is a resident of Jamaica while Worrell is a bird of passage with annual commitments in England – that Alexander was reappointed. The fact that he had been to Cambridge and was lighter in colour than some does not affect his genuine qualifications for the job. At

Bridgetown he showed himself a much improved wicketkeeper and batsman, and a shrewd, determined captain on the field.

Who but a malicious xenophobe could write, during a Test match, 'that the idea of Alexander captaining a side on which Frank Worrell is playing is to me quite revolting'? *Revolting* is the parlance of the irresponsible agitator. Worrell's great gifts as a player, his intelligence and charm, and no doubt his capacity for leadership, cannot benefit from such advocacy.

The English selectors had no problems. Statham was again fit, so that only Moss of the Bridgetown team stood down. Again one felt that the advantages, if the match were to produce a result, must lie overwhelmingly with the side winning the toss. Much, as far as England's chances were concerned, seemed to depend on Statham's recapturing of pace, and, if the wicket should take spin on the last two days, on Allen. On the evidence before us – with memories of Hall's fire and Watson's pace at Bridgetown, of Sobers' power and Worrell's relaxed certainty, of Singh's dipping flight and Ramadhin's accuracy – an English victory was a lot to expect.

FIRST DAY

The toss again to May, the promise of a pitch with 'pace like fire', from Edgar ('Man') Borde the groundsman, and long fretting queues outside the turnstiles. The samans were motionless in the heat: a few clouds like gunbursts lay above the hills.

Pullar leaned out to Hall's first ball and it was chased to the boundary edge and stopped. Cowdrey guided the next, short and sharply rising, into the grass squatters at third man and the pace of the outfield was apparent to all. A bouncer came next, then three through the short legs by Cowdrey, a couple to Pullar. An eventful opening over, which Watson, bowling to four slips, gully, and two backward short legs, balanced with a maiden to Pullar. Hall carried on with a wide and a no-ball, and the runs ticked up generously. But it was the feast before the fast.

Both bowlers, with their long arms and loose slinging actions, settled on a length – short and uppish – and the batsmen were kept back on their stumps fending the ball down. If the bowlers did not exactly hide the ball, they were not showing it earlier than essential.

After thirty-five minutes of such sparring Worrell bowled an over for Watson and Hall to change ends. Cowdrey cut him square for four, and the opening shift was resumed in different harness. Watson's fifth ball was well down the leg-side, Pullar followed it and Alexander was nicely across to take the catch.

If Hall and Watson looked quick at the start, they became positively ferocious now. Watson soon was in such a lather of sweat and dust that he might have come out of a coal mine. Barrington gave them any encouragement they might have needed. He felt blindly outside the off-stump, he scooped the ball dangerously near the short legs. Cowdrey, still digesting as it were, was kept on a diet of bouncers and short ones to the off. A nasty one off the seam took him amidships. Scarcely had he recovered breath when, trying to push down a rising ball from Hall, he deflected it off the inside edge. His off-stump cartwheeled over like a shot rabbit. They were dancing around now under the tulip tree.

May, kept permanently on the back foot, pottered for twenty minutes without scoring and one felt that the huge Coca-Cola sign announcing BATSMEN AT WICKET should have read BATSMEN AT WORK. Watson bowled the last over before lunch and May, having played at the fourth ball and missed, pushed tentatively at the next, pitched outside the off-stump and leaving him. The ball flew to Kanhai at second slip, knee-high, and that was that. May looked understandably sick. The score was 57 for 3.

Few fast bowlers could have kept up such pace over a whole morning. It was an onslaught much the same as they had produced at Bridgetown, and even more successful.

But Dexter wasn't having any of it. He drove Hall in his first over through mid-on and crashed him on the rise past cover. He appeared as cool and detached as a De Rezke cigarette advertisement. At 77 Singh bowled his first over in a Test match and it drew forth applause. Dexter picked his quicker one and beat the outstretched hand of mid-off. Next he placed Sobers under the saman at mid-wicket.

Barrington, whose answer to all this had hitherto been a streaky four between the shoulders of second and third slip, at last began to make headway. He swept Sobers repeatedly down to long leg, and lay back to carve him through the covers. Dexter having pushed the field out, short singles were there for the taking. Barrington hustled to his fifty, Dexter at his heels. Watson came back and Dexter lashed a short ball past extra cover for his own fifty. Next ball he flicked a half-volley off his legs that sped like lightning to the fence. At tea England were 170, Barrington 68, Dexter 61. Together they had scored a hundred in 105 minutes, and the West Indians this time were glad of the break.

Watson returned full of fire and Dexter, rapped on the knuckles, was soon in need of binding. Harold Dalton, M.C.C.'s masseur, bounded out and bound. Ramadhin bowled again, to five off-side fielders, and he pitched too consistently wide for anyone to be able to exercise them.

Solomon trundled up some crafty overs of leg spin, full of good-natured guile, until eventually Singh replaced him. In his first over Dexter, grown weary and frustrated at this enforced idleness, hit a shade early and half-heartedly at one well up to him and Singh pounced to his left, surprised at the gentleness of the offering. Again Dexter had dominated England's innings. He had, eschewing even the calculated risk, driven the fast bowlers off and the slow bowlers had become scared to attack him.

So Smith entered with the new ball due after one run; it was twenty-seven minutes later, with the new ball only two overs old, that he got off the mark. Barrington, ducking into a Hall bouncer, must have got the seam indelibly imprinted on his skull. He went down, looked as if he might stay down, but doggedly got to his feet.

Hall kept at it with a gusto wonderful to behold. Barrington, exhausted as well as stunned, no longer looked for runs. Smith, wisely, contented himself with seeing out the day. Since tea only 50 runs had been scored in ninety minutes, so it could be said that the batting rather than the bowling had lost its energy.

Yet it had been a notable recovery. From 57 for 3 to 220 for 4 speaks for itself. Barrington, with a great lump behind the ear, could lie back and take his ease, legs crossed as honourably as any Crusader's.

The attendance, 22,000, and the receipts, $19,000, were both records for the ground.

ENGLAND

First Innings

Pullar, c. Alexander, b. Watson.. 17
M. C. Cowdrey, b. Hall 18
Barrington, not out... 93
*P. B. H. May, c. Kanhai, b. Watson.. 0
E. R. Dexter, c. and b. Singh.. 77
M. J. K. Smith, not out 9
   Extras... 6

   Total (for 4 wkts.)..220

FALL OF WICKETS — 1–37, 2–42, 3–57, 4–199.

BOWLING (to date) — Hall, 17–5–50–1; Watson, 19–4–60–2; Worrell, 1–0–6–0; Singh, 14–5–27–1; Ramadhin, 17–6–36–0; Sobers, 3–0–16–0; Solomon, 7–0–19–0.

WEST INDIES — *F. C. M. Alexander, C. C. Hunte, J. Solomon, R. Kanhai, G. Sobers, F. M. Worrell, B. Butcher, K. T. Ramadhin, W. Hall, C. Watson and C. Singh.

SECOND DAY

The morning papers, in Trinidad and England, were full of the bouncer war. The news transpired that Hall had been spoken to by the umpires on the previous day and now Watson, after two bouncers in four balls, was cautioned in this second over. Barrington turned Hall off his legs to reach his hundred – 'Crash-helmets will be worn,' he said at break-fast – then was twice on his back ducking out of the way. Hall brought up a forward short leg and this was evidence of intention. Smith steered Watson between second and third slip, and Barrington, flinging his bat at a bouncer from Hall, scored four past gully. Hall and Watson were as fast as anything I have ever seen. When Smith faced Hall the forward short leg was joined by three others, fine of the umpire. Smith looked to have time in hand. Barrington got a slower full pitch from Hall and he spooned it just out of square leg's reach. He wasted full pitches woefully, as if suspicious of some late and latent devilry in them.

Hall, after three-quarters of an hour of assault, was spent, so Watson changed ends and Worrell, lazily lovely in action but quicker this time than usual, bowled over the wicket from the pavilion. The wind was behind him. He beat first Barrington, then Smith, both playing down the wrong line as the ball swung diagonally across them. The picking-up was brilliant, the throwing had the stumps going

35

down at all angles. The opening hour moved England along by only 34. Ramadhin had an exploratory bowl, rather with the air of a mining geologist carrying out an unpromising survey, but England went in, intact, at 275 for 4, Barrington 121, Smith 35.

Barrington was out immediately afterwards. He flicked at a good-length ball outside the off-stump from Hall and Alexander took a fine diving catch in front of first slip.

Smith began to drive Hall wide of mid-on, which meant that either Hall was slowing down or else that Smith was getting into focus. Illingworth sent up 300 with a no-nonsense square cut; Smith pulled a sudden long hop from Singh into a crowd of English sailors to reach 50. So Ramadhin bowled again, and Illingworth, having snicked him past slip for two, came too far out and across to the next ball, was beaten by the flight, and was bowled off his pads. Swetman went back to a half-volley from Watson and was only too plainly l.b.w. Trueman arrived and the Fast Bowlers' Union came into operation, Watson producing four slowish full tosses for him. Ramadhin threw them up on a teasing length but Trueman refused the bait with the obligatory self-denial of a Moslem during Ramadan.

Singh returned and Smith, with Worrell at silly mid-off looking into his eyes with an oculist's intensity, hit him straight back for six. Trueman, not to be outdone, followed suit next over. The stout lady selling cachou nuts all but dropped her load. Ramadhin changed ends and Smith at once pulled him into the stand at mid-wicket. It was becoming a question of six or nothing. After this, it was nothing for the best part of half an hour. Then Trueman, trying to turn Ramadhin, found himself l.b.w. But 35 useful runs had been added all the same.

Hall found enough energy to bounce one at Smith but was then savagely hooked under the pagoda-chalet at square leg. Ramadhin brought up three short legs for Allen and spun one between bat and pad.

Smith was 91 at tea, England 355 for 8. Smith, farming the bowling and scoring long singles, reached his 100 with a sizzling drive past mid-off. He had batted four and a half hours, baring his teeth at every ball, but building up his innings in a way Hutton would have approved. Once past fifty, his assurance had been complete.

Ramadhin, owing much to Worrell, finally got him. Smith drove hard to leg, we looked for the ball at long-on, but there was Worrell, his arms up at short mid-on, the ball in his hands. An over or two later Worrell knocked back Statham's off-stump. So England were all out 382, leaving Statham and Trueman thirty-five minutes' attack in the comparative cool.

No wicket fell. Trueman, much the quicker of the two, had Hunte weaving like a lightweight. But both Solomon and Hunte played Statham firmly in the middle of the bat. One had the feeling that Trueman, at least, with his opening spate of bouncers, had made his point. It seemed unlikely, not to say bad politics, that he would continue. But he had shown his hand and it had not been a bad one. No one could possibly criticize him for that.

ENGLAND

First Innings

Pullar, c. Alexander, b. Watson	17
M. C. Cowdrey, b. Hall	18
Barrington, c. Alexander, b. Hall	121
*P. B. H. May, c. Kanhai, b. Watson	0
E. R. Dexter, c. and b. Singh	77
M. J. K. Smith, c. Worrell, b. Ramadhin	108
Illingworth, b. Ramadhin	10
Swetman, l.b.w., b. Watson	1
Trueman, l.b.w., b. Ramadhin	7
Allen, not out	10
Statham, b. Worrell	1
Extras (l.b 3 w.1 n.b.8	12
Total	382

FALL OF WICKETS — 1–37, 2–42, 3–57, 4–199, 5–276, 6–307, 7–308, 8–343, 9–378, 10–382.

BOWLING — Hall, 33–9–92–2; Watson, 31–5–100–3; Worrell, 11.5–3–23–1; Singh, 23–6–59–1; Ramadhin, 35–12–61–3; Sobers, 3–0–16–0; Solomon, 7–0–19–0.

WEST INDIES

First Innings

C. C. Hunte, not out	8
J. Solomon, not out	14
Total (for 0 wkt.)	22

*F. C. M. Alexander, R. Kanhai, G. Sobers, F. Worrell, B. Butcher, K. T. Ramadhin, W. Hall, C. Watson and C. Singh to go in.

BOWLING (to date) — Statham, 4–1–11–0; Trueman, 5–2–10–0; Allen, 1–0–1–0.

THIRD DAY

It was immediately obvious this morning that whatever else Hall and Watson had done they had put Trueman and Statham properly on their mettle. Both kept the ball well up, varying their pace, and every now and then whipping in a really quick one. This was the intelligent tactic in the circumstances and it resulted in an immediate break-through. Statham, in his second over, had Hunte pushing forward on the leg-stump and the ball skidded off bat and pad to Trueman at backward short leg. Kanhai tried to drive a swinging full toss from Trueman three overs later; missed and was painfully l.b.w. Now this vast excitable crowd, 25,000 strong and like a spilled paintbox under the saman trees, was really humming. Sobers drove his first ball firmly to cover and the relief was audible. He tried then to crack a slightly wider one, the ball flying off the edge at decapitatory pace to third slip. May shot out a hand, the ball went almost vertically up and Barrington, at first slip, stood under it, caught it and threw it as high as the tulip tree. Not even Olivier before his Agincourt speech achieved as total a silence or suspension of emotion as existed while that ball was in the air. The bowlers stuck to it marvellously. Some of the magic green essences of youth seemed to well up in both, and Solomon, time after time, was left groping at Statham. The first hour produced 18 runs: three bouncers, as opposed to around fifteen by Hall and Watson during the comparable period, had been bowled. Worrell, too, was beaten off the seam more than once. Pullar at forward short leg made three point-blank stops in a row off powerful drives. Trueman's field at this stage was four short legs, four slips and only cover point in front of the wicket on the off-side. Statham's was roughly the same.

Ten minutes before lunch May gave Barrington a turn at Statham's end. Solomon slashed the last ball of the first over hard to Allen at cover and called. Worrell sent him back and Solomon, caught on the turn, was beautifully thrown out. He had struggled two hours for 23. Worrell now flung his bat at a ball well up to him from Trueman, got a thickish edge and Swetman scooped the ball up an inch from the ground. Worrell never even waited for the umpire's hand. West Indies were 45 for 5: Trueman's figures were 8 overs, 5 maidens, 12 runs, 3 wickets. It had been a fabulous morning's cricket, to which Statham, bowling with little luck, had contributed more than a fair share. He had not, compared with Hall, achieved anything like lethal pace, but he had moved the ball off the seam, he had made the batsmen feel for the ball outside the off-stump, and sometimes he brought one back to make them stab down at the last second. It was a model of controlled fast bowling. Trueman, to whom most of the wickets had gone, had varied his attack more, trying out swinging half-volleys and slower yorkers, using the crease and keeping the bouncer up his sleeve.

During lunch, pirate ladders were hoisted at strategic points outside the ground and admittance for the nippy became possible at ten cents a climb. The more orthodox rushed the gates or swarmed up the trees which quickly became festooned with blue trousers.

The afternoon in contrast was almost devoid of incident. Barrington, most valuably, bowled twelve overs of his leg-spinners for 3 runs and he will never do that again. Illingworth, taking over from Trueman after Alexander had turned him twice to the fine leg boundary, bowled seven overs for 8 runs. Butcher was an hour over 3. At 65 Statham came back at Trueman's end and Butcher gave a sharp chance to Trueman at backward short leg. He had been hurried all the time by the quick bowlers and soon, shuffling back to Statham, he was l.b.w.

May used Trueman and Allen after tea, Trueman bowling into a shifting wind. Alexander, who had batted stout-heartedly for over two hours without much trouble, suddenly left one alone on the off-stump from Trueman and was l.b.w. Four runs later Ramadhin called Singh for a sharp single to cover, the return from Dexter was quick to the top of the stumps, and Singh, not grounding his bat, and a yard short besides, was given out.

Hardly had umpire Lee Kow's finger gone up than it started. First an ugly, growing roar of protest, then a storm of boos, finally, from far back in the open stand to the right of the pavilion, the bottles.

Lobbed like hand-grenades the opening volleys bounced separately along the boundary edge. Within seconds these had grown into thick showers, not from this stand only, but from all round the ground. May called his boundary fielders in, and in no time at all only a tiny island round the pitch was free of bottles.

Gerry Alexander ran out through swarms of people who had now jumped the boundaries and were advancing menacingly on the middle. He talked briefly with May who had no alternative but to lead his players off the field. Flanked by police officers and with Trueman and Statham holding a stump each they managed to get safely through, the umpires, also with police escort, just behind them. A ricocheting stone struck Pullar on the elbow: otherwise they miraculously got through unscathed.

On the field it was another matter. The whole playing area was a confusion of darting figures, of gesticulating mobs, of isolated but brutal fights which the pathetically few police present – there were fifteen of them – could do nothing to break up.

Into all this the Governor of Trinidad and Tobago, Sir Edward Beetham, a bronzed, cool figure in a fawn suit, made his way, with Learie Constantine, now Minister of Works, at his side. Somewhere there, too, were the Premier, Dr Eric Williams and Sir Errol dos Santos, President of the West Indian Cricket Board, the man who more than any other put the Queen's Park Club on its feet.

But it was no good. The bottles, many of them deliberately broken beforehand, continued to rain and any one of these could have been nastily struck.

Blood was flowing now. In the middle of it a fire hose was hauled onto the field and trained on groups of bottle-throwers. The pressure was low and it merely sputtered out in pools at the firemen's feet like an elephant urinating. But it brought retribution. The bottles, which had shown signs of running out, descended with renewed force and this time the broadcasting box of Radio Trinidad on its glass-fronted perch came under fire. The glass was splintered and inside it the son of Sandy Lloyd, one of the umpires, was mildly hurt. Colonel Eric Beadon, Police Commissioner, who was on the field trying to marshal his miserably inadequate forces, got cut about the legs by flying glass. A policeman, almost impaled on the pavilion railings by a rum-crazed hooligan, had a great strip torn from his thighs.

Now, three-quarters of an hour after the first bottle had been thrown, a dozen mounted policemen, with a squad of tin-hatted reinforcements, appeared on the scene. Behind the wire-nettings of the stands the bottle-throwers, devoid of ammunition, scattered. On the field the brawlers gradually dispersed.

It was all over now, bar the shouting. The hospital cases, of which there were thirty, were removed; the sirens of the ambulances died away. The sixty who had been treated for cuts and wounds were given lifts home.

The flocks of white pigeons, on their endless, undeterred circuits, took the late sun on their wings as they dipped against the hills.

Darkness was falling as the players of both teams, who had been drinking fraternally together in the dressing-rooms, drove off back to the Queen's Park Hotel under police escort.

It had been a sorry, tragic and sadly shaming business.

In the bar of the Queen's Park pavilion there was the feeling of a national disaster – as indeed in its trivial way it had been. The members were stunned, shocked and ashamed. Such a thing had never before happened in Trinidad, an island renowned for its impartiality and sporting spirit. None of them had believed that, even under provocation – which there wasn't – it would have been possible. The general distress was touching to see, for a more well-meaning and hospitable group of members it would be difficult to find. After cabling to our papers, Woodcock, Roberts and I, plied with conciliatory whiskies, discussed the sad events with Gerry Gomez, Keith Edgehill, our admirable Press Liaison officer, and others of our Trinidad friends.

What had caused it? Pique, disappointment, totally irresponsible resentment at decisions by umpires who were respectively of British and Chinese origin? Or was it pre-planned, deep-lying racial prejudices, and political bitterness, finding, and seeking, a convenient outlet? Perhaps simply it was overcrowding, with irritation at West Indian failure boiling up in the packed stands that were hot as pressure cookers, sun, rum and whisky playing their part (dozens of bottles of spirits were discovered later among the piles of Coca-Cola and Seven-Up)? Added to this, gambling on every aspect of the play, as well as on mobile roulette tables, helps to create an atmosphere of fevered apprehension and excitement, sometimes bearing no relation to the state of the game.

Probably it was something of all these things. Mob reactions are hard to predict. But once the first bottles had been thrown (and there were too many of these, despite it being immediately after an interval, for it to have been quite spontaneous) anything could have happened. Unintentional killing and lynching, under the demon rum, were not out of the question. Women, many of whom had cowered with children under parasols, could have been disfigured for life.

Some five hundred people, out of 30,000 (the biggest crowd ever

41

to witness a sporting event in the West Indies), had, I imagine, actually fought or thrown, though several thousand had invaded the field. Yet the instigators may have been a mere couple of dozen.

That evening R. W. V. Robins, wearing the chocolate, pale-blue striped tie of the Queen's Park Club (an inspired touch of chivalry), issued this statement:

'It has come to my notice that rumours are being circulated that the M.C.C. intend to discontinue the Test match and go back to England.

Such a suggestion never entered any of our minds at all. We intend to go on with the game.

Our sympathies are entirely with the good people of Trinidad who have been let down by a few hooligans.'

It could not have been more conciliatorily put.

That night Sir Edward Beetham, the Governor, spoke on Radio Trinidad. He said:

'I may not be an active cricketer, but I am an extremely keen follower and indeed a real lover of the game. Before I ever arrived in the West Indies nearly seven years ago, after watching and enjoying cricket in many places in the world, I was always told that the West Indies was the real place to watch and enjoy cricket as cricket should be watched and enjoyed: a place where cricket was really considered to be what it is – the best game in the world.

'The West Indies had a tradition and an enviable reputation for sportsmanship and love of the game for the game's sake by both players and spectators, unsurpassed anywhere in the world where cricket is played. So far as the players are concerned, that reputation remains completely untarnished.

'This evening I have, however, witnessed a scene – I need not describe it, indeed it defies description – which would have been to me unbelievable – had I not seen it with my own eyes.

'As Governor of Trinidad, I wish to try somehow to convey to the M.C.C. team and also to the members of the West Indies team from other Territories, the apologies – which those who know me will know to be abject and completely sincere – of practically every single person in Trinidad for the most disgraceful behaviour which occurred amongst a certain section of the spectators this evening at the Queen's Park Oval.

'Members of both teams, I can only ask you to believe what I myself believe to be true – and that is that except for perhaps one person in a thousand, every man and woman, and any child old enough to understand, will condemn, as I do, the perpetrators of the disgraceful behaviour which we saw this afternoon.

'I sincerely hope that Mr Peter May and Mr Robins and Mr Alexander will accept that apology from Trinidad.

'To the guilty persons, I would say this: In a few reckless minutes you have not only disgraced yourselves, but disgraced the whole of Trinidad. You have thrown away Trinidad's good name for sportsmanship and, believe me, it will take many, many years to regain it.

'Tomorrow morning the whole world will read in the newspapers of your outrageous behaviour for which we all in Trinidad shall stand condemned.

'I have been with you in Trinidad for four and a half years. Until now I have been proud to have been your Governor. Tonight I am bitterly ashamed, more bitterly ashamed than you can imagine, for I can find no excuse whatever for your disgraceful acts.'

The Premier, Dr Eric Williams, who followed him, said:

'Ladies and gentlemen,

'After discussion with two of my colleagues – Dr Solomon and Mr Constantine – I have just sent off the following telegram:

"President M.C.C., Lord's, London, England.

"On behalf of the government and people of Trinidad and Tobago, I send my deepest regrets and apologies for incidents which caused disruption of the second Test Match today here in Port of Spain.

I am happy to inform you that there has not been the slightest hostility directed against the M.C.C. as a team or any individual player. We shall do our best to ensure that the happy connections on the field of cricket and other fields of sport which have always existed between us and you will not in any way be prejudiced by this occurrence.

"Learie Constantine, my Minister of Works and Transport, asks to be personally associated with this message. He and I have already expressed our personal apologies to Mr Peter May, Captain of the M.C.C.. and Mr R. W. V. Robins, Manager, and I am most glad to say that our regrets and apologies were most graciously received."

'Ladies and gentlemen,

'This afternoon I was a witness to one of the most disgraceful episodes I have ever seen or heard of on a cricket field. From as far back as I can remember, teams from England have come here to play. In recent years we have had visits from Australia, India and Pakistan, and I have no doubt that sooner or later New Zealand will come to us. The whole cricketing world in which we have played so great a part will be shocked, and rightly so, at what happened this afternoon.

'I have apologized to the captain and the manager of the M.C.C. team and also to the captain of the West Indies team, Mr Alexander.

'I understand that tomorrow the decision will be taken as to the future of this match. I can only express the hope, and I have reason to believe, that the decision will be in favour of continuation. In my view, the game must go on.

'Despite incidents over the last sixty years, the interchange of cricket visits between ourselves and the English people has given us such pleasure and has helped to form such deep and important ties that I do not think that, disgraceful as this incident is, it should be allowed to cut short a Test Match and thus affect a whole series and the relations which have been so securely established.

'I must ask each and every one of you, wherever you have the opportunity, to make it clear to all your friends and to all with whom you may come in contact that this incident has done the people of Trinidad and Tobago a great amount of harm and that we shall all have to do all we can to ensure that nothing of the kind ever takes place again.'

Mr Learie Constantine, the third to speak, said:

'I have played cricket in the five Continents and I have met sportsmen and gentlemen everywhere. I have played under circumstances and conditions which have not been always favourable.

'Never before have I seen nor did I believe it was possible to see the deplorable spectacle which blotted out the match and smeared our reputation as sportsmen as occurred at the Queen's Park Oval today.

'I have coached and played in India, Ceylon, Australia, England, Ireland and Wales. There are youngsters in those countries who have worked hard at their lessons. In their efforts, many have tried to emulate me in my attitude and approach to the game.

'There are others, too, who have come after me – Headley, Achong, the threw W's, Ramadhin, Valentine and the late, lamented Collie Smith, and they have exemplified West Indian sportsmanship wherever they have played in their own inimitable way.

'All this is now threatened by this irresponsible behaviour that we witnessed at the Queen's Park Oval today.'

After describing the Singh run-out, Constantine continued:

'The umpire's decision is final. Without that there is no cricket. What I want to do tonight is to appeal to my countrymen as sportsmen to accept the decisions of the umpires, to behave well during play, in victory and defeat, so that visitors to our country will realize that it matters not that we won or lost but that we played the game.'

The following report under the by-line of J. S. Barker, cricket writer and an Assistant Editor, appeared in next morning's *Sunday Guardian*:

'There is no way of adequately describing the disgraceful conduct of certain sections of yesterday's record crowd at Queen's Park Oval. How is it possible to convey the sense of defilement of the thousands of decent Trinidadians who watched with horror, and many through their tears, hundreds of their countrymen establishing an all-time low in sportsmanship?

'The principal targets of the mob's fury were Umpires Lee Kow and "Sandy" Lloyd. They were subjected to every descriptive obscenity the cess-pit minds of these "sportsmen" could conceive.

'In the dressing-room, Singh, shaken for once out of his customary impassivity, agreed that he was most certainly out. I put that on record, just in case any of the thugs who disagreed can read.

'The bottle-stones-and-sticks throwing, however, was only the disgusting climax. Umpire Lloyd had been booed from the moment he gave his decision against Conrad Hunte at the beginning of the day. When the players went into the pavilion at lunch, the booing and catcalling reached ominous proportions.

'There were rumours that the whole thing had been planned. I do not believe this, but it is a fact that a Mr W. Matthews, of Belmont, sold fifty cases of sweet drinks during the day – and did not get back a single bottle until he started to collect them from the ground.

'The nastiest aspect of the whole business was that many of the bottles hurled over had been broken before being thrown. But perhaps the sporting prize of the day should go to the goon who was chased off the wicket by the police whilst trying to mark the surface with the heel of his boot.'

The *Sunday Guardian* printed further statements, by the Deputy Commissioner of Police, by Sir Errol Dos Santos, and by former West Indian Test cricketers.

Major Sonny Carr, Deputy Commissioner of Police, said:

'It is the most disgraceful exhibition I have ever seen in my life. I do not speak of the attacks on the police as such, for policemen have been attacked already.

'But apart from the disgrace attached to Trinidad, the worst aspect of the incident is the fact that many innocent people, including one of Trinidad's leading sportsmen, Babsie Daniel, have been injured.'

In the Queen's Park Pavilion, where officials, sportsmen and spectators were discussing the afternoon's riots, Sir Errol Dos Santos sat, his head bowed, in one of the ante-rooms. He told the *Sunday Guardian*:

'I bow my head with shame. I never thought that I would live to the ripe old age of seventy to see my countrymen behave so disgracefully.'

Fears were also expressed that the incident might do untold harm to West Indian cricket. Two popular Trinidad cricketers, who have played for the West Indies in England, Australia, India, Pakistan and at home, commented:

Prior Jones: 'The West Indies is now emerging on the international cricket scene, and this incident might affect all future tours. It is a setback to cricket in Trinidad and the West Indies. Worse than that is the fact that it might be impossible to find umpires willing to stand in matches again.'

Gerry Gomez, a Trinidad and West Indian captain, had this to say: 'It is the blackest day in the history of Trinidad's sporting life. It is something that should make every self-respecting Trinidadian hang his head in shame. The effect can well be that the M.C.C. may ban Trinidad from all their future tours, and, in my opinion, should they decide to do so, they would be justified.'

One way and another, it had been quite a day.

ENGLAND

First Innings

Pullar, c. Alexander, b. Watson	17
M. C. Cowdrey, b. Hall	18
Barrington, c. Alexander, b. Hall	121
*P. B. H. May, c. Kanhai, b. Watson	0
E. R. Dexter, c. and b. Singh	77
M. J. K. Smith, c. Worrell, b. Ramadhin	108
Illingworth, b. Ramadhin	10
Swetman, l.b.w., b. Watson	1
Trueman, l.b.w., b. Ramadhin	7
Allen, not out	10
Statham, b. Worrell	1
Extras (l.b 3 w.1 n.b.8	12
Total	382

FALL OF WICKETS — 1–37, 2–42, 3–57, 4–199, 5–276, 6–307, 7–308, 8–343, 9–378, 10–382.

BOWLING — Hall, 33–9–92–2; Watson, 31–5–100–3; Worrell, 11.5–3–23–1; Singh, 23–6–59–1; Ramadhin, 35–12–61–3; Sobers, 3–0–16–0; Solomon, 7–0–19–0.

WEST INDIES

First Innings

C. C. Hunte, c. Trueman, b. Statham	8
J. Solomon, run not	23
R. Kanhai, l.b.w., b. Trueman	5
G. Sobers, c. Barrington, b. Trueman	0
F. Worrell, c. Swetman, b. Trueman	9
B. Butcher, l.b.w., b. Statham	9
*F. C. M. Alexander, l.b.w., b. Trueman	28
K. T. Ramadhin, not out	13
C. Singh, run out	0
Extras (l.b.2 w1)	3
Total (for 8 wkts.)	98

FALL OF WICKETS — 1–22, 2–31, 3–31, 4–45, 5–45, 6–73, 7–94, 8–98.

BOWLING (to date) — Statham, 18–8–31–2; Trueman, 19–10–32–4; Allen, 5–0–9–0; Barrington, 16–10–15–0; Illingworth, 7–3–8–0.

FOURTH DAY

After the long, long weekend, back to cricket. The day was hotter, the crowd appreciably less. Ramadhin, transformed nowadays into a neat batsman, formal as an outfitter's dummy, sent up the hundred and continued to cut with aplomb. But Trueman, with the first ball of his second over, a yorker, sent his middle stump spinning down to Swetman. Statham, in his next over, deposited Hall's off-stump like a bouquet at the feet of first slip. It had taken just twenty minutes. Trueman's figures were 21-11-35-5; Statham's 19.3-8-42-3.

So England, with a lead of 270, batted again. There were those who thought May should have done otherwise; but it was an even money gamble and I should have done the same. Pullar at once produced several lovely strokes off his legs and through the covers, and with Cowdrey making him run as if he'd taken a dose of salts England were quickly on the move. At 18, though, Cowdrey, looking for runs, dabbed at Watson, giving Alexander an easy catch. A few balls earlier he had cut at Watson and the ball, coming back at him, had shot over the off-stump. Alexander nearly took an astonishing catch a moment later. Pullar went to glance a ball on the leg-stump from Hall, imagining presumably that it would go with the arm. Instead it whipped in off the seam, Pullar got an outside edge, and Alexander, changing direction and flying at it, juggled, fell and finally dropped it.

Barrington was soon taking his familiar recumbent position under exploratory bouncers as Hall and Watson worked up a better pace.

The grass slope where all the trouble had started on Saturday gradually filled up. In front of the Press Box a woman, determined to take no chances, sported a parachutist's camouflaged helmet.

Alexander, concerned mainly with keeping the batsmen as quiet as possible, set defensive fields, only slip, gully and one backward short leg for the fast bowlers as against rings of four on either side in the first innings. Ramadhin and Worrell took over before lunch, damming the runs to less than a trickle.

Then Barrington, with that curious leaning-away stroke to the off – rather like waving away a footman and avoiding a fly at the same time – turned his attention to Watson. He took ten off his first over and, getting to Worrell's end, drove him past mid-off. Next he cut Watson very late for his fourth boundary in five minutes.

Ramadhin came back and again the stream dried up completely. The covers were set deep but Pullar, with somnambulist regularity, drove hard to them. The sun seemed very heavy. Heads were nodding like black tulips when suddenly Barrington swung cross-batted at Ramadhin and the ball bounced among them.

Pullar, seemingly unable to contrive such diversions, merely remained in occupation: until, after two and a quarter hours, he made a vaguish attempt to lift a flighted one from Ramadhin and was comfortably caught by Worrell at extra cover.

May, greeted with a warmth that must have touched his heart, received an immediate bonus of four when Sobers, with no run being even contemplated, flung hard and wide of Alexander. Barrington now got unaccountably stuck on 49. For twenty minutes he lingered, a man on the springboard pondering the nature of his dive. Then, flashing carelessly at Hall, he was safely gobbled up by Alexander. Hall, as always after a wicket, found sudden reserves of pace and a ball of tremendous speed quickly flattened Dexter's off-stump.

Alexander continued with Ramadhin after tea, Watson at length relieving the pounding Hall who had begun to pitch short again. Smith, having pulled Ramadhin from outside the off-stump high over mid-wicket, tried to force a straight one from Watson wide of mid-on. It kept lowish, he missed, and England were 122 for 5.

May, meanwhile, had been picking his way along, mostly in singles. He did not exactly look like getting out; at the same time his timing, whenever he went to drive, was such that one became conscious of an element of risk. So it turned out. For Singh, holding up the last ball of an over, had May driving the ball acquiescently back to him. In just such a way had he taken Dexter's wicket in the first innings.

To the first ball of Singh's next over, well up to him, Swetman shuffled back, missed and was l.b.w. 133 for 7, England 403 ahead, but with an air of unmistakable apprehension abroad.

Enter Jolly Jack Trueman, with rollicking gait, to face Singh. A highly-tossed one comes up, Trueman lunges, and the ball clears long-on standing by the boundary. The next two Trueman sweeps for four and two down to the desert areas at long leg. The last ball is on a length and this time Trueman, catching it on the rise, lands it in the last tier of spectators under the Radio Trinidad broadcasting box. The lead is 421, Singh looks chastened.

Illingworth, observing this, emerged from his deep interior conflict about Ramadhin and pulled him for four.

At 169, after exactly 75 overs, Alexander gave Hall the new ball. Trueman by now couldn't have cared less whether it was a golf ball. He played Watson firmly past the short legs three times in succession, then got a whisker-thin edge to the third man boundary. Worrell replaced the flagging Hall, and Illingworth, playing the two best strokes of the day, drove him twice in succession gorgeously through the covers. Sixty runs had flowed in thirty-five minutes.

So, at the last, England, who had appeared half an hour earlier to be intent on frittering the day away, finished 466 ahead.

West Indies, with Alexander again proving himself the quickest thing in pads – at least as far as chasing was concerned – had regained much ground, only to lose it again. Both Hall and Watson had once more flung themselves into battle, and Ramadhin, over a long, burning afternoon, with no help from the wicket, made of every ball a problem after his fashion.

ENGLAND

First Innings		*Second Innings*	
Pullar, c. Alexander, b. Watson	17	c. Worrell, b. Ramadhin	28
M. C. Cowdrey, b. Hall	18	c. Alexander, b. Watson	5
Barrington, c. Alexander, b. Hall	121	c. Alexander, b. Hall	49
*P. B. H. May, c. Kanhai, b. Watson	0	c. and b. Singh	28
E. R. Dexter, c. and b. Singh	77	b. Hall	0
M. J. K. Smith, c. Worrell, b. Ramadhin	108	l.b.w., b. Watson	12
Illingworth, b. Ramadhin	10	not out	28
Swetman, l.b.w., b. Watson	1	l.b.w., b. Singh	0
Trueman, l.b.w., b. Ramadhin	7	not out	32
Allen, not out	10		
Statham, b. Worrell	1		
Extras (l.b.3 w.1 n.b.8)	12	Extras	14
Total	382	Total (for 7 wkts.)	196

FALL OF WICKETS: *First Innings* — 1–37, 2–42, 3–57, 4–199, 5–276, 6–307, 7–308, 8–343, 9–378, 10–382. *Second Innings* — 1–18, 2–79, 3–97, 4–101, 5–122, 6–133, 7–133.

BOWLING: *First Innings* — Hall, 33–9–92–2; Watson, 31–5–100–3; Worrell, 11.5–3–23–1; Singh, 23–6–59–1; Ramadhin, 35–12–61–3; Sobers, 3–0–16–0; Solomon, 7–0–19–0. *Second Innings* — Hall, 18–3–34–2; Watson, 14–6–39–2; Worrell, 12–5–27–0; Ramadhin, 28–8–54–1; Singh, 8–3–28–2.

WEST INDIES

First Innings

C. C. Hunte, c. Trueman, b. Statham 8
J. Solomon, run not 23
R. Kanhai, l.b.w., b. Trueman 5
G. Sobers, c. Barrington, b. Trueman 0
F. Worrell, c. Swetman, b. Trueman 9
B. Butcher, l.b.w., b. Statham 9
*F. C. M. Alexander, l.b.w., b. Trueman 28
K. T. Ramadhin, b. Trueman 23
C. Singh, run out 0
W. Hall, b. Statham 4
C. Watson, not out 0
   Extras (l.b.2 w.1) 3
                                                                                    _____
   Total 112

FALL OF WICKETS — 1–22, 2–31, 3–31, 4–45, 5–45, 6–73, 7–94, 8–98, 9–108, 10–112.

BOWLING — Trueman, 21–11–35–5; Statham, 19.3–8–42–3; Allen, 5–0–9–0; Barrington, 16–10–15–0; Illingworth, 7–3–8–0.

FIFTH DAY

England batted on for another three-quarters of an hour; no one exactly threw their bats at the ball, but thirty-five fairly orderly runs, few of them off the edge, boosted England's lead to 500.

Trueman turned Watson off his legs to the square leg boundary, then was caught at the wicket. Illingworth, who tends to expose his leg-stump when pushing the fast bowlers to the on, scored prettily in the long-leg area. Allen, dropped at slip off Hall, snicked four fine of gully, glanced Hall to the boundary, and was caught next ball at the wicket. Alexander's four catches took his total to eleven in three innings.

May now called it a day, which meant that the West Indies had ten hours' batting to save the game. It also allowed the fast bowlers, each of whom bowled to four slips, and four short legs (one of the latter at silly mid-on), fifty minutes' attack before lunch.

Strangely, and rather sinisterly, Solomon managed to avoid Statham for the whole of this period. Hunte, who did the bulk of the scoring, was lucky more than once, but he saw the lifting one quickly and generally looked neat and compact. Allen bowled two overs before the interval and succeeded in keeping the short legs from thinking about food.

His first over of the afternoon did more. Solomon flashed at him and missed; he flashed again and this time Swetman held the ball aloft and screeched, successfully.

Illingworth bowled at the other end and Kanhai, quick to force anything a centimetre or two short, played him away for boundaries around square leg. Then he swept Allen first bounce to the scoreboard. Allen spun one past Hunte's off-stump and was late-cut in retribution. Fifty came and went.

Illingworth gave way to Statham. Kanhai continued on the rampage for a while, but gradually Statham and Allen shut him up. Allen, keeping a full length, had Trueman at leg slip, Cowdrey at short mid-on. Statham whistled one over Hunte's middle stump, had him flicking vainly at others. It was spirited, subtle bowling at both ends, the batsmen at full stretch.

The pitch was holding up; from England's point of view only too well. Statham, having bowled four desperately unlucky maidens in five, retired to nurse his grievances and Barrington had a spin. The middle hour of the afternoon produced ten runs. Hunte was stagnant and fallible, Kanhai cannily flawless. Barrington tossed them up and silly mid-off threw it back to him over after over. West Indies at tea were 76 for 1.

So it went on: Barrington at one end, Illingworth, now flighting it more, at the other. The ball hit the middle of the bat with predictable monotony. Then, within the space of ten minutes, Hunte gave short mid-on two brutal chances. First, he drove Barrington hard and low to Trueman's left. Trueman just got a hand to it. Then, with Allen on at Barrington's end, he drove no less hard through Cowdrey's outstretched hands.

Kanhai, long becalmed, contorted suddenly as if he'd been stung and the ball, from Allen, bounced off the corrugated-iron roof at mid-wicket. Allen, bowling round the wicket now, threw one up, widish, and Hunte, jumping out, got an inside edge which Swetman safely gathered. 107-2-47.

Kanhai, springing again with both feet off the ground, landed Allen a second time to mid-wicket. This second half of his fifty had taken three times as long as the first half.

Trueman came back after a rest of two hours and Sobers drove him with princely beauty through the covers. The new ball was six overs off, there was half an hour left of the day. Trueman bowled only one over, though, before Barrington returned in his place. Allen pitched one in the rough outside Sobers's off-stump and Sobers, visibly startled, went out to take soundings. This was something new.

Illingworth tried his luck there and made one jump ludicrously. Sobers lashed back a full toss and Illingworth, going for the catch, grazed his knuckles. He bowled one more ball then, wringing his hand, left for attention. An over later West Indies were safe for the night.

It had been a disappointing afternoon and evening. Few strokes, too few wickets. For three and a half hours Kanhai, with bat at forty-five degrees on the forward stroke against the spinners, had dropped the ball at his feet with the dutifulness of a gun-dog with a dead bird. Through him, mainly, the odds against West Indies saving the game had shortened to about evens. The new ball and the first hour of the morning would probably tell.

Allen had bowled well and threateningly: Illingworth and Barrington had been merely economical where economy had little meaning. Apart from that one rough spot outside the left-hander's off-stump the wicket had played with disarming ease. Or perhaps simply we lacked a spinner of sufficient violence.

ENGLAND

First Innings		Second Innings	
Pullar, c. Alexander, b. Watson	17	c. Worrell, b. Ramadhin	28
M. C. Cowdrey, b. Hall	18	c. Alexander, b. Watson	5
Barrington, c. Alexander, b. Hall	121	c. Alexander, b. Hall	49
*P. B. H. May, c. Kanhai, b. Watson	0	c. and b. Singh	28
E. R. Dexter, c. and b. Singh	77	b. Hall	0
M. J. K. Smith, c. Worrell, b. Ramadhin	108	l.b.w., b. Watson	12
Illingworth, b. Ramadhin	10	not out	41
Swetman, l.b.w., b. Watson	1	l.b.w., b. Singh	0
Trueman, l.b.w., b. Ramadhin	7	c. Alexander, b. Watson	37
Allen, not out	10	c. Alexander, b. Hall	16
Statham, b. Worrell	1		
Extras (l.b.3 w.1 n.b.8)	12	Extras (b.6 l.b.2 w.4 n.b.2)	14
Total	382	Total (for 9 wkts. dec.)	230

FALL OF WICKETS: *First Innings* — 1–37, 2–42, 3–57, 4–199, 5–276, 6–307, 7–308, 8–343, 9–378, 10–382. *Second Innings* — 1–18, 2–79, 3–97, 4–101, 5–122, 6–133, 7–133, 8–201, 9–230.

BOWLING: *First Innings* — Hall, 33–9–92–2; Watson, 31–5–100–3; Worrell, 11.5–3–23–1; Singh, 23–6–59–1; Ramadhin, 35–12–61–3; Sobers, 3–0–16–0; Solomon, 7–0–19–0. *Second Innings* — Hall, 23.4–4–50–3; Watson, 19–6–57–3; Worrell, 12–5–27–0; Ramadhin, 28–8–54–1; Singh, 8–3–28–2.

WEST INDIES

First Innings		*Second Innings*	
C. C. Hunte, c. Trueman, b. Statham	8	c. Swetman, b. Allen	47
J. Solomon, run out	23	c. Swetman, b. Allen	9
R. Kanhai, l.b.w., b. Trueman	5	not out	55
G. Sobers, c. Barrington, b. Trueman	0	not out	19
F. Worrell, c. Swetman, b. Trueman	9		
B. Butcher, l.b.w., b. Statham	9		
*F. C. M. Alexander, l.b.w., b. Trueman	28		
K. T. Ramadhin, b. Trueman	23		
C. Singh, run out	0		
W. Hall, b. Statham	4		
C. Watson, not out	0		
Extras (l.b.2 w.1)	3	Extras	4
Total	112	Total (for 2 wkts.)	134

FALL OF WICKETS: *First Innings* — 1–22, 2–31, 3–31, 4–45, 5–45, 6–73, 7–94, 8–98, 9–108, 10–112. *Second Innings* — 1–29, 2–107.

BOWLING: *First Innings* — Trueman, 21–11–35–5; Statham, 19.3–8–42–3; Allen, 5–0–9–0; Barrington, 16–10–15–0; Illingworth, 7–3–8–0. *Second Innings* (to date) — Statham, 12–4–23–0; Trueman, 8–3–18–0; Allen, 21–8–46–2; Illingworth, 21–11–28–0; Barrington, 18–12–15–0.

SIXTH DAY

Statham took the new ball almost at once, but as sometimes happens neither he nor Trueman worked up much pace with it. Sobers and Kanhai, far from being put on the defensive, took twenty runs off its first five overs. Sobers played Statham away off his legs and hooked a short one from Trueman with primitive savagery. He was, it seemed, already in purring mood. So Trueman went round the wicket to him and now, twice in an over, he hit him on the pads with ones that kept low. The first must have been preciously near; the second had Sobers walking. Statham and Trueman had picked up the scent. Statham flipped Worrell's pad in the next over and Worrell was out.

Butcher, arriving with a runner, jabbed his first ball down past the leg-stump: he pushed one just short of forward short leg; edged one inches over Smith's reach at backward short. Then Statham, in a marvellous series of deliveries, had him play and miss at seven in a row. The bowler looked pityingly forbearing.

May, after an hour of pace – Statham bowled seven overs – switched to Allen and Barrington. Illingworth, having shed most of a nail on one of his bowling fingers, was out of action. Allen was accurate, if not menacing. It became plain that the fast bowlers would have to do the work and, if England were to win, take the wickets.

At lunch West Indies were 184 for 4; three and three-quarter hours left.

Butcher was quite properly out to Statham, who'd changed ends, immediately afterwards. He played across the line and was almost rudely l.b.w.

Trueman, at a great pace for three overs, used a barrier of three short mid-ons – one more than Tayfield carries, and an unusual sight for a fast bowler. Two short legs were fine of the batsman's hip, and again only cover was forward of the bat on the off.

Suddenly, without warning, Kanhai struck back at Trueman. He crashed him off the back foot to the long-off boundary, drove the next ball to the sightscreen, pulled him into the crowd at square leg. A glance and a place for two each made it into sixteen off the over. Among all this was Kanhai's hundred: dogged, resourceful, finely calibrated.

Dexter bowled his first over of the match, a maiden. Illingworth at the other end beat Alexander with the first ball he'd flighted, and it must have been a hair's breadth.

Kanhai off-drove Dexter to the Coca-Cola board in his next over. The third ball of his third over was a full toss on the leg-stump and Kanhai, hitting it hard but a shade early, saw it curve right to Smith at mid-wicket. He banged his bat in understandable irritation.

This was the crucial wicket. Ramadhin was l.b.w. playing back next ball, so Dexter was suddenly, and fairly inexplicably, on a hat-trick. But he was doing a little off the seam and May could perhaps have found out about this earlier.

Singh, whose name will henceforth have local connotations comparable to the Archduke Ferdinand's at Sarajevo, was consider-ately treated. For over half an hour May asked him to face nothing fiercer than Dexter, Illingworth and Barrington, all of which he did with some assurance. Allen, the only spinner who might have paid off, was kept inexplicably idle.

As soon as he did come on, at a quarter past three, he took a wicket. Alexander, who had kept watchful vigil for over an hour and a half, pushed forward and the ball lobbed gently, off bat and pad, to Trueman at backward short leg. Trueman took it left-handed in a pose that would not have disgraced Nijinsky.

Singh dejectedly hit Barrington back and was gratefully caught by the bowler. Watson, last man in, played a leaping aboriginal kind of stroke to his first ball and Allen, lying deep at mid-off, took it safely.

Trueman leaped in the air, waving his floppy hat. It was smiles, handshakes all round. May waited for Statham to come in from the deep field and these two, through an avenue of sailors from the Royal Yacht *Britannia* – newly arrived with the Princess Royal – led England off.

There was, in the last resort, an hour and three-quarters in hand. That was the true measure of the victory, rather than the figure of 256 runs, crushing though the latter was.

It had been a great achievement by England's fast bowlers, a very great one, to bowl West Indies out twice on such a pitch. Singh at the very end, and Alexander, could have had no complaints about it. The wickets on this last day had been shared, Allen three, two each to Statham, Dexter and Barrington, one to Trueman, but the real threat had always come from Statham and Trueman.

Who could have envisaged this after the defeat by Barbados?

This was a match no one was going to forget in a hurry. The terrific opening barrage by Hall and Watson which brought England to 57 for 3, the perseverance of Barrington despite his clownish mishand-ling of the bouncer, the stirring driving of Dexter and the flowering assurance of Smith. Statham's and Trueman's beautiful use of seam and swing to sweep the cream of West Indies batting out of the way. The frittering away of time during England's second innings, Ramadhin's accuracy, Hall again, and then Trueman's lumbering onslaught with Illingworth.

Finally, the great questions of time, temperament and technique. In the end it was West Indian technique that ran out. But there remains Kanhai's courageous hundred – correct, poised methods adorned by sudden scarlet spreads of wing – that nearly held England up, the sustained attack of Statham on the last morning and afternoon, the ironic twist that brought the vital wicket to Dexter, and the rolling up of the innings by him and Barrington.

ENGLAND

First Innings		*Second Innings*	
Pullar, c. Alexander, b. Watson	17	c. Worrell, b. Ramadhin	28
M. C. Cowdrey, b. Hall	18	c. Alexander, b. Watson	5
Barrington, c. Alexander, b. Hall	121	c. Alexander, b. Hall	49
*P. B. H. May, c. Kanhai, b. Watson	0	c. and b. Singh	28
E. R. Dexter, c. and b. Singh	77	b. Hall	0
M. J. K. Smith, c. Worrell, b. Ramadhin	108	l.b.w., b. Watson	12
Illingworth, b. Ramadhin	10	not out	41
Swetman, l.b.w., b. Watson	1	l.b.w., b. Singh	0
Trueman, l.b.w., b. Ramadhin	7	c. Alexander, b. Watson	37
Allen, not out	10	c. Alexander, b. Hall	16
Statham, b. Worrell	1		
Extras (l.b.3 w.1 n.b.8)	12	Extras (b.6 l.b.2 w.4 n.b.2)	14
Total	382	Total (for 9 wkts. dec.)	230

FALL OF WICKETS: *First Innings* — 1–37, 2–42, 3–57, 4–199, 5–276, 6–307, 7–308, 8–343, 9–378, 10–382. *Second Innings* — 1–18, 2–79, 3–97, 4–101, 5–122, 6–133, 7–133, 8–201, 9–230.

BOWLING: *First Innings* — Hall, 33–9–92–2; Watson, 31–5–100–3; Worrell, 11.5–3–23–1; Singh, 23–6–59–1; Ramadhin, 35–12–61–3; Sobers, 3–0–16–0; Solomon, 7–0–19–0. *Second Innings* — Hall, 23.4–4–50–3; Watson, 19–6–57–3; Worrell, 12–5–27–0; Ramadhin, 28–8–54–1; Singh, 8–3–28–2.

WEST INDIES

First Innings		*Second Innings*	
C. C. Hunte, c. Trueman, b. Statham	8	c. Swetman, b. Allen	47
J. Solomon, run out	23	c. Swetman, b. Allen	9
R. Kanhai, l.b.w., b. Trueman	5	c. Smith, b. Dexter	110
G. Sobers, c. Barrington, b. Trueman	0	l.b.w., b. Trueman	31
F. Worrell, c. Swetman, b. Trueman	9	l.b.w., b. Statham	0
B. Butcher, l.b.w., b. Statham	9	l.b.w., b. Statham	9
*F. C. M. Alexander, l.b.w., b. Trueman	28	c. Trueman, b. Allen	7
K. T. Ramadhin, b. Trueman	23	l.b.w., b. Dexter	0
C. Singh, run out	0	c. and b. Barrington	11
W. Hall, b. Statham	4	not out	0
C. Watson, not out	0	c. Allen, b. Barrington	0
Extras (l.b.2 w.1)	3	Extras (b.11 l.b.6 w.2 n.b.1)	20
Total	112	Total	244

FALL OF WICKETS: *First Innings* — 1–22, 2–31, 3–31, 4–45, 5–45, 6–73, 7–94, 8–98, 9–108, 10–112. *Second Innings* — 1–29, 2–107, 3–158, 4–159, 5–188, 6–222, 7–222, 8–244, 9–244, 10–244.

BOWLING: *First Innings* — Trueman, 21–11–35–5; Statham, 19.3–8–42–3; Allen, 5–0–9–0; Barrington, 16–10–15–0; Illingworth, 7–3–8–0. *Second Innings* — Statham, 25–12–44–2; Trueman, 19–9–44–1; Allen, 31–13–57–3; Illingworth, 28–14–38–0; Barrington, 25.5–13–34–2; Dexter, 6–3–7–2.

For the first time ever England won a series in the Caribbean, the remaining Tests being drawn. All were hard fought and eventful, fine bowling by Hall and Ramadhin being countered by the batting of Dexter, Cowdrey and Barrington in particular. Six England batsmen made centuries, including Parks who replaced the ailing May and kept wicket. For West Indies Sobers made 709 runs in the series, averaging 101.

4th Test, England v Australia, Old Trafford, 1956

The Fourth Test was a crucial one for both sides: it turned out to be one of the unhappiest ever played between the two countries, and the rights and wrongs of it will be long debated. Whatever the speculation, however, the true result, one-sided as it was, was certainly arrived at: the toss, which England won, made difference in degree, not kind, and the pitch itself, the villain of the piece, was more one in charade than in reality. It is not often that one can say of a Test that, whichever side had batted first, the result would have been the same. It was so in this case, and it is important.

ENGLAND

First Innings

P. E. Richardson, c. Maddocks, b. Benaud	104
M. C. Cowdrey, c. Maddocks, b. Lindwall	80
Rev. D. S. Sheppard, b. Archer	113
*P. B. H. May, c. Archer, b. Benaud	43
T. E. Bailey, b. Johnson	20
Washbrook, l.b.w., b. Johnson	6
Oakman, c. Archer, b. Johnson	10
Evans, st. Maddocks, b. Johnson	47
Laker, run out	3
Lock, not out	25
Statham, c. Maddocks, b. Lindwall	0
Extras (b.2 l.b.5 w.1)	8
Total	459

FALL OF WICKETS — 1–174, 2–195, 3–288, 4–321, 5–327, 6–339, 7–401, 8–417, 9–458, 10–459.

BOWLING — Lindwall 21.3–6–63–2; Miller 21–6–41–0; Archer 22–6–73–1; Johnson 47–10–151–4; Benaud 47–17–123–2.

AUSTRALIA

First Innings		Second Innings	
C. C. McDonald, c. Lock, b. Laker	32	c. Oakman, b. Laker	89
J. W. Burke, c. Cowdrey, b. Lock	22	c. Lock, b. Laker	33
R. N. Harvey, b. Laker	0	c. Cowdrey, b. Laker	0
I. D. Craig, l.b.w., b. Laker	8	l.b.w., b. Laker	38
K. R. Miller, c. Oakman, b. Laker	6	b. Laker	0
K. D. Mackay, c. Oakman, b. Laker	0	c. Oakman, b. Laker	0
R. G. Archer, st. Evans, b. Laker	6	c. Oakman, b. Laker	0
R. Benaud, c. Statham, b. Laker	0	b. Laker	18
R. R. Lindwall, not out	6	c. Lock, b. Laker	8
L. V. Maddocks, b. Laker	4	l.b.w., b. Laker	2
*I. W. Johnson, b. Laker	0	not out	1
Extras	0	Extras (b.12 l.b.4)	16
Total	84	Total	205

FALL OF WICKETS: *First Innings* — 1–48, 2–48, 3–62, 4–62, 5–62, 6–73, 7–73, 8–78, 9–84, 10–84. *Second Innings* — 1–28, 2–55, 3–114, 4–124, 5–130, 6–130, 7–181, 8–198, 9–203, 10–205.

BOWLING: *First Innings* — Statham 6–3–6–0; Bailey 4–3–4–0; Laker 16.4–4–37–9; Lock 14–3–37–1. *Second Innings* — Statham 16–10–15–0; Bailey 20–8–31–0; Laker 51.2–23–53–10; Lock 55–30–69–0; Oakman 8–3–21–0.

ENGLAND WON BY AN INNINGS AND 170 RUNS.

FIRST DAY

A warm, cloudy morning, the toss to May, for the third time in four, and England for once making the best of a lovely batting wicket. No one at Old Trafford, this 26th day of July, could deny either the fine stroke-making of Richardson, Cowdrey, Sheppard and May, or the hopelessness of the task confronting the Australian bowlers. The pitch, far removed from the fast grassy one predicted the evening before by the groundsman, was shaven bare and marled: with the result that the fast bowlers could get the ball no more than stump high, a fact bitterly underlined by Miller bouncing the ball on it and ironically observing its total passivity. The outfield, in contrast to the red-brown, Suez Canal-coloured playing strip, was a rich oasis green.

Sheppard was down on the early scorecards at No. 2, but in fact it was Cowdrey who came out with Richardson to face Lindwall and Miller. So assured was the batting of both that Johnson folded up his close umbrella-field after only three overs. One could sense the Australians' disappointment in the pitch from almost the first ball: a strong crosswind, exaggerating Lindwall's inswing, was otherwise not of help either. The tension dispersed as quickly as the fielders. Archer was soon on, and Cowdrey, already given several pipe-openers by Richardson, who has as active an eye for the sharp single as has Cowdrey for the comfort of boundaries, disposed grandi-loquently of a full toss. Lindwall, Miller and Archer bowled in relay during this opening hour, and Cowdrey and Richardson, scoring 44 runs, played with such ease of attitude that they might have been club members reclining in favourite chairs, whisky and cigars in hand.

The introduction of Johnson and Benaud got them, as it were, to their feet: there was a smell of cheap runs in the air, as encouraging to effort as a judicious tip for the Stock Market. Johnson, bowling downwind, was especially inaccurate; Cowdrey swept him with the spin, waved him past mid-on; Richardson, leaning back, pulled and cut him. Next Richardson cut Benaud twice to the fence in an over, Cowdrey taking two fours off him also. At five to one Cowdrey, nine boundaries heavy, steamed to 50; at five past the 100 was hoisted; at twenty past Richardson's 50. One hundred and eleven before lunch, though meagre in comparison with Hutton and Barnett's 169 against Australia at Trent Bridge in 1938, was grate-fully received by 30,000 Mancunians, reinforcements for whom skirmished off every Old Trafford train.

Cowdrey mishooked Miller midway between square and long leg immediately after lunch, and for some while he had a job to reach any of the bowling. Miller, from round the wicket, aimed at third slip; Johnson floated ball after ball away as if the stumps did not exist. Richardson was luckier, being able to sweep Johnson twice for four, before inducing the bowler to such evasive measures that only the calling of a wide halted them.

Lindwall was given a spell in mid-afternoon: Richardson put his right foot across and, fairly letting the bat go, sent two widish good-length balls skimming past cover. One sensed the bridge telegraph ringing down for more speed, and Lindwall hurled down several at Cowdrey. The pitch softened them like a head sea and Cowdrey eased him twice to the mid-on boundary.

At twenty past three, the score 174, Cowdrey snicked a Lindwall half-volley, pitched well outside the off-stump, to Maddocks. He hurried away, as if to have gone on making runs would have been an abuse of charity.

Sheppard, with a youthful choir of his parishioners to cheer him on, strode out, a bare half-dozen innings behind him: with even less than that, MacLaren had once come to Lord's to play a historic innings. The journey was now reversed, but Sheppard, with equal lack of fuss and paraphernalia, soon showed it to have been worth while. Lindwall, putting amateurishness to immediate test, bounced a churlish first ball at Sheppard's head: then was played, with the bat far from the body, to the cover boundary.

Sheppard, chewing gum in the practice, no doubt relaxing, but sadly common to all from the two captains downward, was a little time taking his bearings; but two fours off Johnson, a square cut and a straight drive, put him on course. He moved down the pitch to the slow bowlers, judged their length quickly, hit hard: within minutes, the ice was broken, nerves were at ease. A new batsman approaches the crease as one lately come to a party where the others are already on familiar terms with each other: he has to make himself known before he can be accepted: and the period of acclimatization depends on his own authority.

Richardson, meanwhile, proceeded happily to his first Test century; he swung Benaud's first two balls of a new spell to the long leg boundary, was contained briefly on 98, and then pushed two sharp singles through the traditional cordon. The crowd stood, Richardson, flushing under his fair hair, raised his bat, the cheering drowned the shunting of a departing engine from Old Trafford station.

He hit one more four, chased a wide one from Benaud, and was caught at the wicket. May, accustomed to facing the first new ball, ironically entered with the second one only five runs off.

Sheppard, driving Johnson for successive fours, straight and through the covers, raised the 200: exactly 76 overs had been bowled. Lindwall took the new ball. Sheppard straightway stroked it through the covers, and Lindwall, not turning the other cheek, bowled a petulant bouncer.

Both before and after tea the new ball kept the batsmen comparatively quite: largely, though, because Lindwall and Archer bowled as wide as self-esteem allowed. When Lindwall pitched straight he was driven straight, first by May, then by Sheppard. At five o'clock Benaud had another bowl, and Sheppard hit him twice for four in three balls. Archer came on, spread his field defensively, began to bowl just short. May, however, placing with extraordinary skill and power off the back foot, merely bisected the gaps. Archer's three overs cost 29 runs, including a hook for six that shot Sheppard to his 50.

At half-past five drinks were brought out for the first, and only, time in the summer: weather apart, it was the only time the bowlers had been in need of encouragement.

With May hammering the ball past mid-on, and Sheppard, crouched squarer and lower over his bat, rising to brush it through the covers, the century partnership and the 300 were in nodding distance, when May was out. Benaud got several in a row to hustle a shade, and off one that turned and popped May, reaching out, was caught at arm's length by Archer at slip.

There was a Chekhovian twist to the day's end: the crowd, agog for Washbrook, found themselves applauding a grinning Bailey, sent in either to make a batting order record of five amateurs in a row, or to enable Washbrook to go home, or as a treat for Bailey. Anyway, Bailey decided to make it a treat for the crowd: having satisfied himself that his forward push was functioning, he pulled and cut 14 runs while Sheppard had time only to add 5. Three hundred and seven for 3 was a score at which a joke or two could well be afforded.

SECOND DAY

Again a warm, muggy morning, and without breeze. Johnson wasted no time on the faster bowlers, but began with himself and Benaud, each bowling to defensive fields. Sheppard, off both front and back foot, hammered the ball into the covers where, like circus performers, Harvey, Craig and McDonald, one after the other, brought off magnificent one-handed pick-ups. Thus do Cossack riders at brisk canters swoop from the saddle to snatch handkerchiefs from the sawdust.

At 321 Bailey, playing for Johnson's break – and he had turned several – was bowled by one that floated on through to hit the off stump. Washbrook played back and late to his first ball, which jumped past the handle of his bat: the second he slashed disdainfully past point for four. A moment or two later, going back to a well pitched-up ball from Johnson, he was beaten by the spin and rather guiltily l.b.w.

Oakman at once drove off Johnson's crouching short legs with an on-drive, a straight drive and a vast lean into the covers. Johnson therefore pitched wider and Oakman, going after him, was well caught at slip.

At 339 for 6 a little wind had gone from the sails: but Evans, seemingly propelled by a Merseyside gale, launched immediate onslaught: he hit Benaud on the rise for two ballooning sixes, ran up the pitch and sent the ball skimming over mid-off and mid-on. When Benaud pitched short he cut square or pulled: when Johnson had barely sidled up to the umpire, Evans was on his way to meet him, clattering him with percussive sweeps to long-on and mid-wicket and off the edge to square leg. It was a brassband interlude which, like most such, was of predictable duration. After half an hour Evans, practically at the bowler's end, was stumped for 47. Old Trafford is one of his most fancied batting pitches, the score and tempo of the bowling were just right, and like a music-hall star back amongst the plush and gilt of his favourite Palace, Evans had even the potted palms rocking.

Sheppard, advancing to a more formal music, now hit Johnson for three fours in an over: two of them cover drives, made on the move, were instinct with the controlled power of a Da Vinci cartoon. A stinging drive, half-stopped by Burke, however cost the newly arrived Laker his wicket: Harvey backed up and Laker, taking a second run with gentleman's gentleman's dignity, was run out.

Twenty minutes before lunch Sheppard, cutting Johnson late to the fence, reached his century: a fair weather innings, to be certain (he was to play the other sort a month later at The Oval), but one of

64

Liberal Member of Parliament, a career that might well have brought out the worst in him. What Fry nevertheless did write about in *Life Worth Living*, and surprisingly retain through two subsequent editions, was the account of his 1934 meeting with Hitler and his starry-eyed attitude to Nazi morality and intentions. There was something decidedly naïve about much of Fry's thinking, a residue perhaps of that early allegiance to classic ideals that retards many of its adherents, rendering them insensitive to contemporary life. Fry, it seems, devoted to the classics as he was, was otherwise appallingly read, ignorant of nineteenth-century and modern fiction and poetry equally. One of the reasons behind his failure as a politician and often as an after-dinner speaker, was that he failed to do his homework and, despite moments of brilliance, came over rambling, idiosyncratic and unprepared. This was the exact opposite to his approach to the technicalities and techniques of games.

Life Worth Living is the more interesting to read now if we are aware of these omissions from the narrative. The vulnerability and insecurity add extra dimensions to one who had so much ostensibly going for him. No one wrote more evocatively about the glamorous side of Fry than Denzil Batchelor, his friend and one-time secretary: 'It is half-past ten: time for the caravan to start from Brown's Hotel. The Bentley is at the door; Mr Brooks, the chauf-feur, is wise-cracking out of the side of his guttapercha mouth. Aboard are writing pads and binoculars and travelling rugs, a copy of Herodotus, a box of Henry Clay cigars and reserve hampers of hock and chicken sandwiches . . . A monocle glitters. A silver crest passes, high and haughty, above the cities of the plain. C. B. Fry is off to Lord's.'

About the composing of *Life Worth Living* Batchelor observed: 'Charles wrote it,' or more often than not, dictated it to me in his dressing gown and bedroom slippers between breakfast and lunch in his flat at Gloucester Place . . . He never re-cast the book, and he hardly re-wrote a sentence . . . The result was an autobiography in the round: more than a picture of its author – a glimpse or a touch of the living man in three dimensions. It gave to the world all he had done, all he had seen, much of what he enjoyed of the fun of the fair.'

Well, not quite all, as it turned out. But enough to be going on with for most people. 'You become a friend,' Batchelor observed, 'though not, I think, an intimate of the man who told the story.' That seems to me reasonable in the circumstances.

Fry, Gubby Allen observed, could be a very awkward man and he rubbed up enough people the wrong way to make enemies. He was never elected to the committee of the MCC, he quarrelled with his editors, publishers and agents, and he spent the greater part of his life in what most of his contemporaries considered to be, in relation to his gifts, a backwater. Yet, the missing dark moments aside, *Life Worth Living* gives off an air of immense well-being, the product of a mind consistently interested in the mechanics of grace – scientific, sporting, intellectual. Not for nothing did Fry know the engine of a car inside out, or all about wireless waves; it was entirely in keeping with his questing intellect that he should have taken lessons in dancing as a means of improving his footwork and at one stage toyed with training racehorses. For someone who turned down a Kingdom he was no snob when it came to rolling up his sleeves and learning a new trade.

The Presence of Ranji

IT IS, NATURALLY, at Jamnagar that the presence of Ranji remains most evident. Although the princes have long since been stripped of their titles and their privy purses – within a score of years all Ranji's predictions came to be fulfilled, though whether for the general good or ill is a matter of opinion – in many princely States the trappings, if not the reality, of power survive. Nawanagar was never anything but a minnow in the large pond of princely India but Ranji, by his own prestige and his progressive management of industry and agriculture, saw that it counted for far more than its size might have warranted. Fifty years after his death Jamnagar is still recognizably his city. Cattle may wander beside the bazaars or be parked like motorcars outside the arcades of Willingdon Crescent but the job of clearing and cleansing, that was Ranji's first priority when he became ruler, has not been undone.

The four main palaces of Jamnagar still remain, externally, much as Ranji left them. They may be the habitat of birds and bats, like the enclosed and highly decorated City Palace, or of pet animals, bucks, antelopes, gazelles, like Ranji's preferred Bhavindra Vilas, or simply shuttered and empty, except for the rare cold weather visitor, like the multi-domed Pratap Vilas Palace, or used as a government guest house like Vibha Vilas Palace; but whatever uses, or disuses, they are put to, they stand within their palace walls – the locked gates attended by Arab guards – as stately and resplendent as ever they did.

The grounds, alas, are scarcely kept up and gradually their handsome outbuildings – stables, garages, badminton and racquet courts – are

determination as well as charm, one of adventurousness as well as breeding.

The rest of the innings was merely a rapid tidying up. Lindwall bowled some elevating overs with the new ball, Sheppard and Lock both stroked boundaries off Miller through the covers, and ten minutes after lunch England were out for 459. The two hours before lunch had produced 142 runs.

The Australian innings, an account of which gives one the feeling of telling an absurdly tall story, began respectably enough. The light roller had been on – Johnson having learnt his lesson at Headingley – and it was an hour and a quarter before the pitch changed from waltz time to rock 'n' roll. During this period McDonald and Burke, without strain, scored 43 runs. McDonald, guiding Statham's second ball into the vacant covers for four, was generally the livelier, though Statham early on all but yorked him. Statham bowled six overs, Bailey three: at nine Laker came on from the railway end, and together he and Lock bowled seventeen overs without causing a flutter. At five to four May switched them round: the effect was akin to the sudden access of power after the repair of a faulty connection. McDonald, pushing forward, steered Laker heedlessly to Lock at leg slip: to his third ball, also from Laker, Harvey played back, and inside, and was bowled. Craig came in for the first time in a Test match in England, but though Lock now made the ball fizz up off a length, he stayed with Burke until tea: the score 62 for 2.

Lock's first ball of the evening spun sharply away, hit Burke on the glove, and Cowdrey at slip dived on it. Laker's first ball had Craig playing back, and, beaten by both break and pace off the pitch, l.b.w.

Mackay, as ill at ease as one playing Blind Man's Buff in a roomful of strangers, jabbed nervously at his second ball and was caught by Oakman at second slip. Miller drove Lock for a straight six: then, aiming to drive Laker, was held very close in by Oakman at short leg, the ball skidding off the inside edge. Two good catches these, at a shortness of range that makes any catching instinctive. Benaud, with unerring accuracy, delivered his second ball from Laker to Statham back by the fence at long-on: and Statham is as safe a catch as he is deadly a throw.

Archer, making a demented, Tube-station rush, was stumped by feet: Maddocks and Johnson, both playing back to off-breaks pitched well up, were convincingly bowled. In 3.4 overs since tea Laker had taken seven wickets for 8. Struggling to disguise the disbelief and pleasure that chased each other across his features he led England off the field for a rest and gossip.

At twenty past five they returned. Once more Statham and Bailey did the formalities: once more McDonald cut and Burke defended, for all the world as if it were the first innings. Twenty equable runs were scored, and then at a quarter to six, Laker, soon joined by Lock, resumed the exercise of his proprietary rights. McDonald, playing handsomely, now limped off for treatment to a knee.

Harvey, as if intent on instant reparation, made rapid ground to Laker's first ball; he hit it hard and low on the volley but, alas, straight to Cowdrey who, squatting like a Buddha in an odd position at shortish wide mid-on, threw the ball delightedly up. Harvey, in a rare moment of self-expression, tossed his bat in the air like a pipe-major, acknowledging with dismay one of the quickest 'pairs' in Test history.

Burke, with Craig as partner, played Lock and Laker in a manner to suggest that, if his example were followed, all was not yet lost. Of Australia's closing score of 53 for 1 he had made 33.

THIRD DAY

One has become accustomed now, at about the apéritif hour, to this ritual Saturday procession to the Test match wicket, as if a major operation were about to take place.

The captains proceeding first as grave as surgeons; umpires, like specialists in consultation, behind them, as though fearful of what examination might reveal; finally, the groundsman like an orderly awaiting their instructions.

Once at the pitch the prodding, undertaken with the ball of the thumb, begins. This is followed by closer visual scrutiny and depressions by the feet. If the pitch does not wince too audibly, the shaving process starts.

When completed, there is further laying on of hands, followed by a blanket bath, this morning's affair being particularly thorough. Next there is the formal disagreement between the captain-surgeons, further prolonged consultations between specialist-umpires, and finally, after agonizing deliberations, a verdict.

The crowd, who were today allowed in to witness these preparatory manoeuvres, from time to time offer vocal encouragement, though generally their attitude is that of students in an operating theatre, their manner hushed and respectful.

This time the preliminary verdict, offered after an hour's contemplation at 1.30 p.m., was that a second diagnosis would be made at a quarter to two. At ten past two the operation eventually got under way.

Statham, in his opening over of the afternoon, bowled from the Stretford end under recognizable sun, hit Burke twice on the legs, the first time painfully striking the instep with a full pitch.

Lock, from the railway, began with two maidens to Craig and was then replaced by Bailey, off whom, after twenty minutes, Craig scored the first run. At twenty to three Laker took over from Statham, using three short legs, no slip, and the rest of the field fairly deep. Burke immediately made an optimistic appeal against the light, which was rejected, and in the same over played an off-break stiffly and gently into Lock's hands at leg-slip. McDonald, continuing his overnight innings, lay back and cut Laker to the cover boundary, a stroke better than almost any played by an Australian on Friday.

Rain now came bustling up very fast out of a deluding sky, and, in no time at all, the water on the wicket was as clearly defined as on the Manchester Canal and about as muddy. The ground flooded, and a sizeable crowd returned to Old Trafford railway station as quickly as it had hurried in after lunch.

The match, ill-omened from the start, therefore made little progress.

Since 1905, no Test between England and Australia had resulted in a win for either side at Old Trafford, and the possibility of the present one breaking that gloomy record remained to be seen. Certainly, on their showing thus far, Australia did not deserve to escape: since making their disappointment at the wicket plain from the start, they had since scarcely bothered to put a face on it.

One has a right to expect from Test cricketers a certain degree of adaptability; the Australian batting, during their brief innings on Friday night, was bereft of all heart and skill.

The slowness of the pitch and its early dustiness were patently miscalculated; too much grass had been taken off it and it was from the beginning devoid of natural juice. The fast bowlers in turn showed it to hold nothing for them, and for Johnson, whose attack is essentially a pace one, losing the toss was a serious business.

Fortunately, cricket is not a game in which precise conditions can ever be stipulated, so that ill-balanced sides, able to perform only when weather and wicket are perfect, cannot hope to get away with it indefinitely against more versatile opponents.

Wickets on which a player like Mackay, by holding his bat straight and barely moving it, can bat for many hours, and even score runs, make nonsense of cricket as an art form. If one is going to discount completely its more subtle skills and graces, then let wickets be specially prepared by turf consultants to a uniform specification, and transported to all Test match grounds in suitable containers.

From lunch-time on Thursday the wicket had taken a certain amount of spin. Between the innings, the dust brushed off it was like a storm in the Sahara. No one could pretend that this was ideal; but preparing wickets is not an exact science, and, until it is, one has to deal in approximations.

The Australians, unfortunately, set off on the wrong foot. Their bowling, that of the spinners especially, was extraordinarily untidy on Thursday, and once the runs began to come they showed a definite decline in spirit. But fielding was of a high standard, and on Friday morning Johnson found something like his best form.

By then it was too late. The subsequent Australian collapse to Laker was a psychological one, a pure failure of nerve. England, faced by Australia's huge score at Brisbane in 1954, failed for exactly the same reason, though more nobly.

Technically, the Australian batting was extremely bad, veering between timid back play that allowed the spin its full value and despairing swings.

It is not unfair to suggest that a good English county side would have backed itself to make 250 runs in similar conditions. Burke was rarely in trouble and McDonald, until playing a careless stroke, looked full of runs. The remainder, faced by Laker, took their fate for granted.

England, of course, were particularly suited to the conditions. But, for once, we have bowlers equally capable of using any given wicket; and since the Selectors have stuck to the expedient principle of picking each team for the match in question, and of pinning their faith in class batsmen, whether in full practice or not, the batting, too, has acquired a width and distinction it had not possessed since the war.

Australians were commonly supposed to be immune to the off-spinner, but obviously they are now more at the mercy of the ball that turns into them than the one that leaves them. They get little practice against it, and the best spin bowler in Australia, Treanor, of New South Wales – who, one thought, should have made this trip – is a leg-breaker.

The truth is that since Hutton, setting complete store by Tyson and Statham in Australia, succeeded with an all-pace attack, the Australian Selectors, not unnaturally banking on England being largely dependent on these two again, laid their plans accordingly.

Conditional to this, with no spin bowler approaching the O'Reilly, Grimmett, or, for that matter, Laker–Lock class, they had small choice in the matter.

However one looks at it, the defects of the wicket were relative to the Australians' own inadequacy. On it, England made one of their largest Test scores for a long while, and, in doing so, showed how correct technique, based on forward play with the head down and the proper movement of the feet towards the pitch of the ball, can take care of most of the ball's movement after it has pitched.

The batting of May and Sheppard was of rare quality, and Cowdrey and Richardson, in easier circumstances, full of fluency and character.

Evans, literally by leaps and bounds, asserted that when there is a good score already on the board and the temperature is right, you cannot keep the cork in the bottle.

FOURTH DAY

For the second day in succession there was no play worth discussing: as a result the Australian reprieve verged on full pardon. Most remarkable was that any cricket took place at all: the rain was considerable over the week-end, and heavy overnight. However, a minor whirlwind sprang up during the morning, blowing the hats off Manchester citizens but also drying Old Trafford. The ground-staff worked unceasingly, and by a quarter to three Lock was able to bowl the first ball of the day. Heavy black bails, made from the lignum vitae wood used for bowls, successfully evaded the clutch of the gale, but Evans's cap sped off with a force that made it fortunate he had no need of wigs.

Lock bowled two maidens, Laker one: the drenched pitch was too dispirited to offer signs of life. Craig looked correct and poised, with a cap sitting baggily over a slim frame. Twice he played Lock splendidly off his legs for four: once he snicked a quicker ball fine of slip to the sightscreen. McDonald's bat and body were not always as close together as they might have been, but he looked rather safer than houses in this howling wind. A sudden squall after forty minutes sent everyone in for an early tea: but Bailey and Statham had not long been showing that the pitch still held nothing for them when a second, heavier shower finished it. Australia were 82 for 2.

FIFTH DAY

At twenty-seven minutes past five, after a day of constant anxiety and tension, England, by the apparently vast margin of an innings and 170 runs, made both the match and the Ashes safe. But an hour and five minutes in hand, in a five-day match is not much; not in Manchester. And today no Australian wicket fell before lunch. The pitch was saturated, and the wetness was not easily dispersed. But at lunch Leonard Hutton, not a foolhardy gambler, bet five shillings the match would be over by five o'clock: he lost his bet, but the premises on which he made it held good. At Old Trafford, once the drying process is properly under way, the sun takes instantaneous effect. It came out soon after one o'clock, and blazed with flapping wind from a clearing sky. An island or two of obscuring cloud, and the pitch becomes as devoid of life as a Victorian miss with the vapours. From a quarter past three until tea the sun withdrew, and again the bowlers were rendered helpless. But vital damage had been done. Finally the clouds sailed out of sight, and it was on a golden evening, with the wicket taking notice, if not exactly lively, that Laker bowled England to victory and his own way into the legends of the game. In 51 overs he took all 10 wickets for 53; making 19 wickets for 90 in the match, a feat unlikely ever to be equalled or surpassed. S. F. Barnes, on Johannesburg matting, took 17 wickets in 1913; the record hitherto.

The previous best in Tests between England and Australia were Verity's 15 at Lord's in 1934, and Rhodes' 15 at Melbourne in 1903.

The measure of Laker's achievement are the figures of Lock, who bowled three more overs in the match and took 1 for 106. At no time was the wicket truly a sticky; from time to time it quickened up and took varying amounts of spin, but Laker rarely, more rarely even than Lock, got the ball to pop. He took his wickets by unrelenting accuracy, by varying flight, length and intention with such imaginative skill that the batsmen were first hemmed in, then confused. They left shaking their heads.

After the usual tactical disagreement about the fitness of the wicket for play, Bailey began the bowling only ten minutes late. He immediately found the edge of Craig's bat, but the ball just failed to carry to Cowdrey at first slip. It was the nearest to a chance all morning. Neither batsman had either excuse for, or interest in, runs and they were content to push the ball gently down, with time and elbow room to do so. Bailey and Laker having made no impression, Oakman and Lock bowled until twenty past twelve, when May gave Statham the new ball. Statham made only one lift uncomfortably, and it was not long before Lock and Laker were renewing their blandishments with such violent flicking of the fingers that one felt only the most drink-sodden of pitches could resist them. Lock, trying perhaps for too much, began to pitch short and McDonald cut and pulled him. The last few balls of the morning from Lock showed a rising perkiness, but it was with 28 runs added, and no wickets lost, that Australia went in to lunch.

Craig, already over four hours at the crease, scored only 2 more: he went back to Laker, was beaten by the turn and plainly l.b.w. Lock's next over to McDonald cost 10 runs, including further cuts and a pull. Mackay had followed Craig, and, with seven men breathing down his neck, he stabbed a good-length ball into Oakman's stomach. Miller, having made up his mind to play every conceivable ball with his pads, floundered inelegantly, until, scooping belatedly at a yorker, he was bowled. Archer groped at his second ball, it spun off his bat, and Oakman snapped him up at short leg, low and a bare three yards square of the bat. Four wickets had fallen since lunch for 18 runs: Laker, who had reverted to the Stretford end, had taken 4 for 3 in nine overs. Lock, still hopelessly short, was repeatedly pulled by McDonald, so May tried Oakman from the railway, rested Laker and switched Lock to Laker's end in an effort to improve his morale. The sun being temporarily hidden, the pitch was again devitalized, and Benaud, taking guard twice an over, flattening divots with the slow ponderousness of a Shakespearian grave digger, found as little to trouble him in the bowling as McDonald. Together, with Australia 181 for 6, they made their way in to tea, having been in composed partnership for eighty long minutes.

The sun, and the interval, unsettling for them and refreshing for Laker, brushed them quickly from the scene. Laker's second ball turned very sharply, McDonald was hurried in his stroke and Oakman took the crucial catch, his fifth of the match, at short leg. McDonald, out only eleven short of a hundred, had shown wariness and resource for five and a half hours: his feet were not always in the right place, but, unlike several more illustrious colleagues, his heart was. It was a warm persistent innings, one which, considering its context, had surprisingly few dull passages.

Laker's first two balls to Lindwall, turning enough to surprise both batsman and wicketkeeper, went for four byes each: but Lindwall stuck, growing more adhesive every over, and by five o'clock he and Benaud were once more causing apprehensive glances at wrist-watches and furtive scurryings to the bar. Benaud's was the essential wicket and it came unexpectedly: having played consistently at the pitch of the ball, he suddenly misjudged the flight, went back to almost a half-volley, and was bowled.

Lindwall and Johnson offered token resistance for twenty minutes, then Lindwall edged an off-break to Lock at leg-slip. Maddocks, shuffling back as in his first innings, was at once l.b.w. It had by now become almost as important to the crowd that he be out to Laker, as be dismissed at all. Lock had sensibly not slackened effort at the other end.

Laker, in response to a chanting crowd, appeared on the balcony, pink and pleased, a glass of beer in his hand: so modest a drink can rarely have been as richly deserved.

It is with relief that one leaves Manchester: the memories of captive days in hotel bars and bedrooms, rain streaming over the Piccadilly buses, and umbrellas rearing through the drizzle like shiny, jostling seals, are too strong for affection ever to take hold. To appreciate

Manchester one needs to have been born there: and never to have moved from it.

Yet once the sprawling suburbs, the rubbery tentacles of Altrincham, Cheadle and Stockport, are shed, one is suddenly on the high edge of the Peaks. On a granitic switchback goats pick their way along the roadside beneath arching woods. The smoke of Manchester begins to sway behind you as flimsily as a parasol against the sun. Dwellings are hewn into the rock, isolated and solid, the clustering, parasitic building estates brushed off like crumbs into the grey circle of industrial gloom.

Making my way out on the Buxton road, the evening was as clear as a bell. A week earlier I had been sitting in the warm, riverside darkness of the Trout at Wolvercote, fireflies cruising the banks, and the crowned lion on the island thrusting through the poppies at the marauding peacock. In hot sun, the hood down, I drove out of Oxford northwards through Warwick and Lichfield, skirting the sunken and smoking arena of the Potteries – the signpost to Burslem crowding in scenes from Arnold Bennett, urging one to drop in on Denry Machin perhaps, and see how things were with 'the Card'.

Then, beyond Macclesfield, like a sign of storm, the smoke cone of industry was hoisted on the horizon. On a windless morning, the yellow fields brimming with light and the cattle swishing their tails at flies, each mile brought a reduction in freshness and clarity. Long before I reached Old Trafford the sun was dimming on soiled streets and struggling patches of grass.

Now it was behind one, attached only by its trail of images: storm, and wind, and Laker spinning his way through the drier moments, gnawing slowly into the wormwood of the Australian batting: Lock, hands on hips, hissing in pure disbelief at the temerity of any batsman who opposed him (and they did): Richardson cover-driving Lindwall with an orchard sweetness of sound: Sheppard coltish in his leggy stridings, stroking Johnson away in gorgeous liberty: McDonald propping up, hour after hour, the frail card-house that every over threatened to tumble about him.

South: and villages of grey stone, with streams running under curved walls and people strolling out under overhanging rocks. A region of caves and great country houses: the ruins of Peveril on the cracked hill above Castleton: Haddon, Hardwick and the sham Norman eccentricities of Bolsover: Melbourne Hall, with its lime alleys and great yew tunnel, Chatsworth, Kedleston; and Alton, its towers, turrets and battlements a monument to the nineteenth-century Gothic imagination at its most riotous, soaring over a wild horticultural landscape of cascades and woods dreamed into existence by Capability Brown.

Buxton, a rock-enfolded Bath, with the lights from the Palace Hotel flicking on above the railway, and the road slipping down beneath a huge, green-domed Pavilion and out again past its grey arcaded crescent, opposite which, in the well of St Ann, bubble the blue thermal waters that draw those who have lived too immoderately to this healing, Portland-stone spa.

Down into Matlock, through wooded gorges with the dusk seeming to drift out of cracks in the rock, river and road entwined under limestone tors, and the Derwent polishing its pebbles at the entrances of dragon-held caves.

By Ripley, the headlamps were probing the scaly barks of trees stalking the darkness; and soon Nottingham was a great shield of light familiarly flung over the hidden collieries and waters of the Trent.

The Fourth Test acted, metaphorically as well as literally, as a kind of watershed to the season: the main issues were decided, and though it was still possible for the Australians to level the rubber, no one expected them to do so at The Oval. For the next three weeks they toured in an atmosphere of approaching farewell and mild anti-climax.

2nd Test, South Africa v England, Cape Town, 1957

The first Test of this series, played in Johannesburg over Christmas, went to England by 131 runs. England, batting first, made 268, Richardson 117, Cowdrey 59, and 150, South Africa 215 and 72. Bailey took 5 for 20 in South Africa's second innings.

ENGLAND

First Innings		*Second Innings*	
P. E. Richardson, l.b.w., b. Heine	45	c. Endean, b. Goddard	44
T. E. Bailey, c. Waite, b. Tayfield	34	b. Heine	28
Compton, c McLean, b. Tayfield	58	c. and b. Goddard	64
*P. B. H. May, c. Waite, b. Tayfield	8	c. Waite, b. Heine	15
M. C. Cowdrey, l.b.w., b. Adcock	101	c. Waite, b. Tayfield	61
D. J. Insole, c. Goddard, b. Adcock	29	not out	3
Evans, c. McGlew, b. Goddard	62	c. Endean, b. Goddard	1
Wardle, st. Waite, b. Tayfield	3		
Laker, b. Adcock	0		
Loader, c. Keith, b. Tayfield	10		
Statham, not out	2		
Extras	17	Extras	4
Total	369	Total (for 6 wkts. dec.)	220

FALL OF WICKETS: *First Innings* — 1–76, 2–88, 3–116, 4–183, 5–233, 6–326, 7–334, 8–335, 9–346. *Second Innings* — 1–74, 2–74, 3–109, 4–196, 5–208, 6–220.

BOWLING: *First Innings* — Heine 19–0–78–1; Adcock 22.2–2–54–3; Tayfield 53–21–130–5; Goddard 38–12–74–1; van Ryneveld 3–0–16–0. *Second Innings* — Adcock 3–0–8–0; Heine 21–1–67–2; Goddard 17.5–1–62–3; Tayfield 12–4–33–1; Watkins 10–2–46–0.

SOUTH AFRICA

First Innings			*Second Innings*	
*D. McGlew, c. Cowdrey, b. Laker	14	b. Wardle		7
T. Goddard, c. Evans, b. Loader	18	c. Bailey, b. Wardle		26
H. Keith, c. Evans, b. Loader	14	c. May, b. Wardle		4
C. B. van Ryneveld, b. Wardle	25	not out		0
H. Tayfield, run out	5	c. Evans, b. Wardle		4
R. A. McLean, c. May, b. Statham	42	l.b.w., b. Laker		22
J. Waite, c. Evans, b. Wardle	49	c. Cowdrey, b. Wardle		2
W. R. Endean, b. Wardle	17	handled ball		3
J. Watkins, not out	7	c. and b. Wardle		0
P. Heine, b. Wardle	0	b. Wardle		0
N. Adcock, c. Evans, b. Wardle	11	b. Laker		1
Extras	3	Extras		3
Total	205	Total		72

FALL OF WICKETS: *First Innings* — 1–23, 2–39, 3–48, 4–63, 5–110, 6–126, 7–178, 8–191, 9–191. *Second Innings* — 1–21, 2–28, 3–42, 4–56, 5–67, 6–67, 7–67, 8–67, 9–71.

BOWLING: *First Innings* — Statham 16–0–38–1; Loader 21–5–33–2; Laker 28–8–65–1; Bailey 11–5–13–0; Wardle 23.6–9–53–5. *Second Innings* — Statham 8–2–12–0; Loader 7–2–11–0; Laker 14.1–9–7–2; Wardle 19–3–36–7; Compton 2–1–3–0.

ENGLAND WON BY 312 RUNS.

FIRST DAY

Runs were in the air and a lot of dust, too, from a swirling south-easter that whipped the spray over the jetties and rocked the fishing boats in Table Bay. The town was full of coons, dressed up in striped silk tail coats and coloured toppers, parading to banjos and guitars in bright rehearsal for their New Year's carnival. At Newlands the wind was confined by the sprawling signature of Devils Peak that seemed to give out heat like a radiator from its mauve ravines.

May left out Lock, from the twelve named, won a good toss, his sixth out of seven against South Africa, and England were quickly away to a hare-like start. The tortoise hours were to come later with afternoon torpor and the sedative leg-side attack of Goddard. Richardson snicked Heine's first ball of the day a foot short of the slips, hit the second, which was a full toss, through the covers for four, and took a single. Bailey was surprised by a late inswinger and glided 4 runs inches fine of leg slip. Heine was dangerous but variable, Adcock more accurate but less menacing. Bailey played some nice strokes off his legs, lifted a no-ball from Adcock to mid-wicket for 3 and drove Heine to the sightscreen with almost a flourish.

At noon Tayfield came on with 35 runs scored, most of them by Bailey. Richardson began now to show the benefit of his long innings at Johannesburg. He forced a good-length ball past mid-on with a serenity bred of content, swung a full toss to the oaks at square leg and twice swept Tayfield against the spin to long leg. When Tayfield dropped shorter he cut him or hit him past extra with bat held well away from his body. Goddard kept Bailey playing stiffly as a robot at the other end and in the last over before lunch succeeded in bowling five outside the leg stump and three on it. England went in with 73 runs scored.

Heine changed ends in the afternoon, also aimed at Richardson's leg stump and was rewarded by an l.b.w. decision, Richardson mistiming a flick off the pads. Tayfield, bowling with his two mid-ons rather closer than usual, had Bailey almost dropping off to sleep, so exact was his length and so limited Bailey's intentions. After forty minutes he had Bailey playing inside one that went straight through and Waite took the appropriate catch. Tayfield had the wind coming from wide mid-on and now and again he threw one well up and the breeze took it across.

In this way did he get May, who hit him once beautifully through the covers, tried it again and was well caught at the wicket. Compton, meanwhile, had taken 12 off an over from Heine, two peremptory off-drives and a hook that had the finality of an auctioneer's hammer. Twice Heine was unlucky, getting enough bounce to hit the shoulder of Compton's bat and clear the slips. Tayfield bowled fifteen overs at a stretch for 16 runs, no one square or at mid-wicket or behind the bowler, and Compton was content, or at any rate prepared, to push him gently back. Cowdrey was mellifluous and controlled as Flagstad singing *Isolde*, but he was not willing to sacrifice grace to force, with the result that he took twenty minutes to score, took an hour over 6 and remained on 10 for three-quarters of an hour. At last Compton swept and connected at Tayfield, and then Cowdrey hooked Adcock, who bowled fairly fast after tea, twice to the oaks. Compton reached 50 out of 150, and he then relaxed to the extent of 6 runs in forty-five minutes. Cowdrey was hedged in with three short legs by Tayfield, but he placed Goddard so fruitfully with the swing to mid-wicket that, height of Goddard's humiliation, one of the leg-slips had to be withdrawn.

By five-thirty the sun was reaching far into the stands and England coasting along in the hundred and eighties. Partisans from the oaks called for van Ryneveld, the provincial captain, to be called into action, but it was Tayfield who went spinning tirelessly on. And he got Compton too: a weary sweep, and McLean had not an inch to move at fine leg half-way to the boundary. It was a wicket to fatigue as much as to the bowler. But there were moments of happiness in Compton's innings, of nostalgic charm as well as the familiar struggle and constraints of recent weeks.

With a fishtail breeze now blowing almost straight down the pitch van Ryneveld was finally brought on to bowl against it at Insole, who had yielded to him with a Wildean lack of resistance to temptation at the Wanderers. Cowdrey leaned away and bisected the covers, Insole swung Tayfield for the first time in the whole day over the short legs and then between them, and in fact scored 20 runs himself in twenty minutes. Not since Edrich set about the Australians in the last half-hour one evening in the second Test at Sydney had one seen a fresh batsman make such practical use of flagging bowlers.

Tayfield bowled forty-one overs during the day for 69 runs, and he bowled them well, knowing the hesitation of English batsmen, Evans apart, to go after him. But 214 for 4 was for England a satisfactory score, especially with the Trade wind blowing and abetting the natural wear of the pitch. The toss had been worth more than a fifty from May, even if less personally gratifying.

SECOND DAY

Again the streets were full of dancing coons, their silks flashing in the sun like jockeys on their way to the start. At Newlands there was less wind, but what there was blew over Adcock's left shoulder when he bowled the first over of the day with the new ball. Insole and Cowdrey placed nicely off their legs, Cowdrey reaching 50 with a deflection so smoothly steered past square leg that it seemed the bat had no part in it. Goddard bowled for Heine after half an hour, and his first three overs were aimed exactly half outside and half on the wicket, an improvement on the day before. Twenty-two runs came quietly, a huge mongrel Great Dane made a ruminatory perambulation of the pitch, and then Insole, making the first indifferent stroke of his innings, failed to get over a half-volley from Adcock and was caught low down by Goddard at gully. Adcock, a full hour downwind, twice found the edge of Cowdrey's bat but no fielder to hand. When Adcock rested, Goddard came on and was guided by Cowdrey between the leg fielders to the plane trees that shade the grass banks below the railway line. He pitched straighter, and Cowdrey drove him to the screen. Evans meanwhile had brightened up the running, twice evaded cover's grasp with curling drives, and settled to strokes off more honest parts of the bat.

The myth of Goddard's invulnerability to the pulled drive was now shattered by Evans, who banged him twice to the mid-wicket boundary, removed the leg-slips and rendered long-on more than an ornament. Ten minutes before lunch Tayfield, who had been rotating his shoulders hopefully under the scoreboard, was permitted to bowl. Evans glanced him almost out of the wicket-keeper's gloves for 4 and 3, and gingered singles out of Cowdrey that brought three lots of overthrows in as many minutes. The score at lunch was 300, Cowdrey 72, Evans 40.

The first hour of the afternoon provided 8 runs for Cowdrey, dopey a little perhaps, after victualling, but Evans lashed Tayfield with such force that extra cover's cap shifted in its wake. He pulled Goddard again, drove him straight and had scored 22 in no time at all before he landed a very high one into McGlew at long-on. Wardle played several overs with a bat dead as a poker face, but getting no help from Cowdrey in the business of scoring runs, rushed down the pitch to Tayfield and was stumped. Laker entered, McGlew brought on Adcock, and by the time Laker had got his bat down via the Inner Circle route from point and slip his leg stump was down.

Loader took 10 off an over from Tayfield and was caught at cover. Four wickets had gone for 23 while Cowdrey pushed forward at Tayfield as if practising in front of a mirror. So when Statham, the last man, came in he looked like being left stranded in the upper reaches of a century he should have got long ago. Statham, however, played Adcock with meticulous care and at last Cowdrey returned to life. He stepped out and lifted Tayfield with no perceptible follow-through to McLean on the boundary edge at long-on: a six it looked, then a catch, but McLean, treading on the toes of small boys, could not quite hold it as it drifted away from him. Having got range and direction Cowdrey hit the next half-volley straight into the crowd behind mid-off. A beefy drive then beat McGlew at cover and he was 100. It was an innings immaculately executed but conceived through strange periods of inhibition. In the next over, turning Adcock to leg, he was estimated l.b.w., the umpire presumably having had enough of a good thing.

Among blowing dust McGlew faced Statham around three-twenty and at once found they were keeping pretty low. He moved, as he always does, right into the line of the ball and looked neat and secure. Loader and Statham, however, were given not much more than a token bowl and at 16 Laker, with something like animation, set two forward and one backward short leg and began spinning them to McGlew. Bailey came on at 23 and, attacking Goddard's off-stump with what were to him away-swingers, gave him a gentle dose of his own medicine. He bowled six overs for 5 runs and Goddard contained himself and, one hoped, profited spiritually. McGlew played Laker with a thoughtful air and some difficulty: then, moving down the pitch, was beaten in the air, got an inside edge and was caught by Cowdrey at leg-slip. May curiously replaced Laker almost immediately with Wardle, who was exceedingly sparing with the chinaman, and brought on Loader to bowl with the dust instead of Bailey. Goddard and Keith were more continent outside the off-stump than at Johannesburg, but at 39 Loader got Goddard to play, swung late and Evans took a high catch. Nine runs later Keith, in precise fashion, followed him in.

Laker came on again for the last quarter of an hour and van Ryneveld was crowded in as if it had been the last, not the second day. Low white clouds drifted in and draped the mountain, the 'table cloth' that forms on hot evenings towards sundown.

THIRD DAY

Almost from the first it was a question of the follow-on, but it was five to five, with the turtle-doves gargling noisily in the oaks, before

South Africa finally were out for 205, fifteen runs short of saving it. But May by then had decided his lead was not enough and he took the circuitous, what one might call the Cape route, to victory. Throughout the day, in fact, May had adopted a defensive policy: he wanted the bowlers to get wickets, certainly, but he was not prepared to barter any for time, and the field was set to guard against the bowler's errors rather than to make the most of his successes. From the moment Wardle came on, at a quarter to one, it was plain that, with a score of 369 to bowl with, he was a more than fair insurance risk. One would have liked to have seen him begin the bowling with Laker to an attacking field, but May's way was to open with Statham and Bailey for forty minutes, replace Bailey with Laker and then at noon Statham with Loader, and keep a quick bowler going continually at one end. It was five to three before spinners were used at both ends, and then it only needed two chancy boundaries off Wardle for Loader to be immediately recalled.

For thirty-five minutes or so Tayfield, the night watchman, and van Ryneveld played on a hot, cloudless morning like opening batsmen. Tayfield, as he usually does, needed luck against Statham, for he is slow at moving into the line of quick bowling, but he weathered the worst and was looking fairly settled when Laker was brought on. Van Ryneveld glanced Laker's first ball wide of Cowdrey at leg-slip and set off for what appeared a comfortable two. Statham chased it and van Ryneveld, seeing him pick up, checked and then came on. Tayfield, noticing him check, turned back and both batsmen arrived at the same end just as the ball arrived in Evans's gloves. Evans rolled the ball up the pitch with the dainty bias of a lady bowls champion and broke the far wicket. So the unhappy van Ryneveld had been involved in three run outs in a row.

Statham had a long accurate bowl at McLean, who was hard put to keep out several that skidded through fast, raising a panful of dust. McLean relaxed at the other end, cutting Laker square, gliding him, and then hitting him effortlessly over mid-off. A sweep to mid-wicket brought him another 4 runs and so Wardle had his bowl, but only a quarter of an hour before lunch. He began round the wicket and at once had van Ryneveld reaching forward like a blind man. McLean drove him hard on the half-volley whenever he could, but the ball, though it was sailing off the middle of the bat, was never predictably off the course of several fieldsmen. Just before lunch McLean, curbing enthusiasm, pushed forward modestly.

But in the afternoon he made fine strokes off the back foot, hitting Statham past cover and conveying by his ease of manner that batsmen, whatever anyone might think to the contrary, were really adventurous beings. Van Ryneveld, perfectly safe all morning against Laker and the quick bowlers, now first made complete nonsense of Wardle's googly and was then bowled behind his legs playing no stroke. McLean was once more contained by Statham, but a square cut to the plane trees encouraged too sanguine a hook at the next ball, barely short of a length, and he spooned up a simple catch to May at mid-on.

At five to three Wardle was required to change ends for Laker to get the benefit of a slightly worn patch. This seemed a concession too generous both to Laker and the batsmen, who were altogether happier to have Wardle at the pavilion end. Waite, in now with Endean, is probably the best player of Laker among the South Africans, bat coming forward together with pad, and wrists dropped loosely on the spin. Anything short he pulled with a decisive crack, and by using his feet he was able to call in due course his share of short ones. For two hours in the full heat of the afternoon, with bush fires smoking amongst the scrub of Table Mountain, he batted with firmness and discrimination. Endean, after rather an old bachelorish start, swept once or twice with surprising vehemence to mid-wicket and Wardle was returned to the dog-house and replaced by Loader. Loader in fact bowled aggressively and he twice found the inside edge of both Waite's and Endean's bats with short ones that Cowdrey at leg-slip flicked so smartly back to Evans that the unsuspecting batsmen were all but run out. But Wardle, with so many runs to play with, was the man and this was marking time.

When Wardle did come back after tea he soon polished off the innings. He threw his chinaman up to Endean, who blinked at it and was bowled. He threw several more up to Waite, bowled him one that went the other way and had him caught by Evans, pushing forward. Heine got in a knot and was bowled first ball, also by the chinaman. So at 191 Adcock arrived with the task, subsequently proved unnecessary, of making 29 in conjunction with Watkins to save the follow-on. He smacked 10 without a moment's thought, but trying to clear Devil's Peak misjudged the wind and was caught in mid-pitch by Evans, who waited under a skier long enough to have called for dark glasses against the glare. It was splendid bowling by Wardle and he should have been encouraged to do it much earlier.

Richardson and Bailey batted seven minutes under the hour for 21 runs. Neither was in the slightest trouble against Heine, Adcock and Goddard, but, financial considerations of the last day's gate apart, it seemed rather slow going. Not, of course, that there was not a fair amount to be said, in terms of a wearing pitch, for occupying the crease, and the security of making South Africa bat fourth.

FOURTH DAY

A scorching, windless day. England's target was as many runs over 200 by tea as could be managed with or without safety. McGlew, who was without Adcock, suffering from an inflamed toe, set as defensive fields as honour allowed, no slip for either Heine or Goddard, and no one nearer to the bat than twenty-five yards. Heine and Goddard were kept going like pack-horses all morning, and Heine again in the afternoon with the new ball was bowled until he almost dropped. Watkins, presumably in the side as an all-rounder, had to wait till the English aggregate was 500 for his first bowl. Tayfield was not allowed an over till two o'clock, by which time England were 125 for 3. He then bowled economically and well.

The tea and declaration score was 220 for 6. Bailey and Richardson scored 46 in the first hour, May and Compton 37 in the second. After lunch Compton took over an hour for 14, while Cowdrey made 50 in the same time. Because of this, for the first time in the series, the batting side averaged a run a minute for the two hours of the afternoon.

Generally, however, it was cautious cricket, along lines to which any follower of contemporary Test matches has long been used.

Cautious, but not without flavour, particularly while Cowdrey was batting, for his was an innings as matured and full of body as a Club port. It was as if during the hours of darkness some latent, but persistent anxiety had been sieved away. He drove to the off with easy swing, left shoulder aimed at mid-off as few now do, placed to the on boundary with a turn of the wrists as sensitive to calibration as a radio tuner, and flicked Watkins and Heine square of cover with an economy of movement that allowed no fielder to trouble himself. And the South African fielding was magnificent in its persistence, in its disregard for the expenses of effort when runs had virtually ceased to matter. At the very end they were diving in the dust to turn fours into twos, Tayfield and Watkins each making saves more memorable than hosts of catches.

Richardson for forty minutes enjoyed himself, as he had done at Trent Bridge against Australia with similar latitude. He is not a fluent cover driver, but off the back foot he cuts square with fore-arms thrown right out and places effectively, with a jerky thrust made far from the body, between cover and extra. Off his legs he is a controlled nudger of singles, and he runs very fast between the wickets. An addition to his repertoire on this occasion was an almost vertical straight drive for 2, the ball dropping dead like a mashie shot on pitching. Bailey, faced by Goddard with a crescent of five men on the leg side, hit one ancient cross-bat stroke past mid-on to raise their second 50 partnership of the match. He swept Goddard with a will and drove the half-volley with a force that, had his bat been human, would certainly have caused it to raise eyebrows.

At 74 they were out to successive balls. Richardson was nicely taken by Endean at mid-wicket off a firm hit, and with the next ball at the other end Heine brought one back to bowl Bailey off his elbow. Heine, with his arm rather than body action, continued, despite his weariness, to get lift, and even late in the afternoon he bounced one up to give Cowdrey a nasty crack on the head. Compton began with a square cut and a hook that reached the pickets before Heine had properly followed through, but his inability to take evident singles made him for some while something of a liability. May and he took it so gently from noon till lunch that the cleanness of Waite's taking on the leg side was of more positive interest than either.

May, going for runs, was soon out after lunch, caught at the wicket off Heine, who thus made it four times in six innings. Then came Cowdrey, scoring 61 out of the 87 made in the next eighty-seven minutes, with Compton long unable to beat the field. Watkins bowled short and straight to him, Tayfield straight and a good length, and Compton shook his head as stroke after stroke went straight to a fieldsman. At 196 Cowdrey was caught at the wicket off Tayfield, who had been turning one or two. The new ball was given to the footsore Heine, and Compton now made some lovely strokes through the covers and finally a sweep that must have restored his sagging confidence and affection for that shot. On the dot of tea he gave a tired return catch to Goddard.

For an hour and a quarter McGlew and Goddard played Statham, Loader and Laker with comparative calm. McGlew got down on one knee to smother Laker's spin and Goddard turned up his nose at anything outside the off-stump. Runs were not much in the offing and by a quarter past five, when Wardle came on, only 20 had been squeezed through May's defensive cordon.

Wardle, though he badly looked in need of an extra slip and silly mid-off, at once had McGlew straining. In his second over McGlew, sweeping at almost a full toss, was bowled round his legs in a cloud of dust by the googly. He had batted an hour and a quarter for 7. Keith soon danced down the pitch, missed, and Evans, unsighted, missed also, the ball lifting. It was of no account, for a moment later Keith a second time came out, lifted his head and was caught by May at extra cover. Goddard was beaten more than once by the chinaman, but with Endean stuttering a little against Laker, he stuck. Cowdrey fielded some very good ones at deepish leg-slip, but the English throwing was indolently wide.

FIFTH DAY

Probably it was the hottest morning of the Cape summer, the flat reclaimed land of the port area in a carbon haze and Table Mountain giving off a powdery blue heat. Driving to Newlands over the De Waal highway, with the bush buck and zebra grazing in the shade of flowering gums, one estimated the time of the South African surrender at around three o'clock. But, as at Johannesburg, it took only ninety minutes, the South African second innings realizing the same dismal total of 72 runs. The procession began immediately and never was halted. By one o'clock one was back in the sweltering city, with England two Test matches up, and winners this time by 312 runs.

May for once began the day with Wardle. Goddard leaned, full stretch, forward to the chinaman in his second over, got an edge and was snapped up by Bailey at slip. McLean drove Wardle handsomely straight and through the covers, and when Laker came on for Statham at the other end, was for the first time faced by two spinners. Endean played as much with his pads as he could, having these days the regard for his bat of one who fancies it to be made of porcelain. Playing thus to Laker, the ball popped vertically up off his pads, and was in danger of dropping on his stumps. Suddenly realizing this, and oblivious to the efficacy of bat or even head, Endean swatted the ball off as if it had been a fly. Evans and Laker appealed, and Endean was rightly given out 'handling ball'. For some obscure reason, it does not count to the bowler.

McLean next went to scoop a ball from Laker off his leg stump, found it coming through quicker than he expected, and was l.b.w. Waite, who on Thursday played Laker so very well, was then completely foxed by Wardle's googly and caught at slip by Cowdrey. Watkins went to pull the googly and was caught off a hard return hit by Wardle. Heine was bowled second ball by a straight quicker one, which meant that four wickets had fallen at 67. Tayfield was dropped first ball by May, who just failed to hold a fierce hit left-handed at mid-wicket. Three runs later he was given out, caught at the wicket, when Evans could have stumped him off the same ball but missed the bails as he whipped the ball across. Laker bowled Adcock with his first ball to him.

As certainly as the Johannesburg Test was Bailey's, so was this one Wardle's. He took 12 wickets for 89 and no one, with the possible exception of McLean, had the foggiest idea of how to deal with him. Latterly he bowled almost exclusively chinamen and googlies, and his control over them was astonishing. Against probably any other bowler, or combination of bowlers, in the world, South Africa could have been expected to save the match. Laker bowled with his now customary accuracy and intelligence, but he got only occasional turn and was rarely beating the bat. The pitch was fairly worn at the end to which Wardle was bowling, but even he could only get the ball to break slowly. But he threw it well up and the batsmen, quite unable to fathom which way it would spin, pushed hopefully out. They were just good enough now and again to get a touch.

A fortnight ago the present situation, England two up and the South Africans completely demoralized, would have been a pipedream. May, who has now won ten tosses out of twelve since becoming Captain, was certainly lucky to win these two, but the fact is that despite four successive scores of under 20 by himself, England have slowly, but surely, grafted their way into being a powerful batting side. Richardson and Bailey batted extremely well in both innings, Compton twice scored over 50, with application rather than genius, while Cowdrey, for long batting in a hair shirt, on Friday donned robes of magnificence. Evans, as at Johannesburg, cut and drove with an extrovert abandon that made the negative leg-side bowling of Goddard, so frustrating to all others, merely seem insipid.

By and large, of course, England's is a bowlers' team, as varied and strong probably as we have ever had. In Australia it was the pure speed of Tyson and Statham, in England over two seasons the orthodox spin of Laker and Lock: now it is the googlies and chinamen of Wardle. The batsmen have no respite, for scarcely a bad ball is bowled at either end in the day. Moreover, May has enough and varied bowlers to prevent a batsman settling against any one kind.

The South Africans, even more than England, have found these ten, almost uninterrupted, days of Test cricket both mentally and physically exhausting. In England, as a touring side, they were tuned up, in full practice, and led with inspiration and generous zest by Cheetham. Here they are a team of individual, separated, week-end cricketers, not in full practice against Test standard bowling, and evidently finding it a strain. This last week Heine and Goddard have been bowled practically into the ground by McGlew, who, for all his grim determination, has so far not seemed able to draw from his players that extra blending of keenness and relaxation that is necessary if the total endeavours are to add up to more than the sum of the individual contributions.

There are nearly three weeks now before the Third Test begins at Durban, but there appears little on the face of it that the South African selectors can do meanwhile, unless they can bribe Wardle to come and bowl in the nets from now until then. They will probably bring in one new batsmen at least, and the most likely one is Funston.

But there is only one match of consequence before the Test, that between M.C.C. and Natal at Pietermaritzburg, and Funston comes from the Transvaal. M.C.C. on the other hand have not for years been so happily placed as a touring side. This week they have minor games at Queenstown and East London, the week after, a four-day match against Natal, and then, on the twenty-fifth, the Test. They can, without complacency, take the New Year easy.

Jan. 7th. Cape Town. Newlands is so certainly, in the popular imagination, the most beautiful Test ground in the world that one half hopes to disagree. But in honesty one cannot. Separated from the sea and the city by Table Mountain, it lies deep under the rocks of Devil's Peak. The mountain line is no distant prospect, but an immediate backdrop up to which one has to raise one's head. The pavilion is full of flowers, the stands painted the blue of the sightscreens at Lord's. If you sit among the plane trees, with your back to Table Mountain and the railway, you look across at a thick line of oaks, the people under them stippled with light as in a painting by Pissarro or Seurat. From every other position Table Mountain flowing into its foothills dominates the eye. The playing surface is excellent, the weather these last days flawless – hot but not humid.

Driving the five miles to Newlands from the City there are two routes: along Main Road and through District 6, the Malay quarter, where from the corner of one's eye one gets a quick glimpse of most lovely profiles, or up over De Waal Drive, past the University, surely one of the most spectacularly situated in the world. Usually I drove in one way and back the other. At night, up on the hill, the air was full of pine scent: below, lights came on all over Cape Town, flat as a board below. Riding lights sprinkled the anchorages, and at Sea Point the long Atlantic waves poured themselves up the beach like soda. From Signal Hill and Constantia Nek the lights flicker in new perspectives, rolling down steep declivities or following the wide breasts of the hills.

Constantia, in daylight, trails its vineyards up to the rockline of the mountain, the beautiful Dutch Colonial farmsteads embedded in Morning Glory and their gardens blazing with huge Cannas. But at night, driving along the looping hill roads to Hout Bay or out to the sea at Muizenberg, one senses, the headlamps nosing the oaks on the edge of devastating precipices, only the release from detail of the dark. Mountain and sea are merely intensifications of darkness, diurnal human problems are discussed, far out of sight, at the bar of the Kelvin Grove Club or in the tiny balustraded dwellings of District 6, and one is absorbed by the nocturnal noises of the woods, of the cool rushing air, of the long wake of the moon broadening over Table Bay.

2nd Test, England v West Indies, Lord's, 1963

Dexter's Innings

Every so often there comes a Test match which, without reference to what precedes it or comes after, exists in its own right. It acquires the inevitability of a work of art, it gives off the aroma of a choice bloom, the soil for which has been long and lovingly tended, and the lesser, swarming shoots cut back to make way for it. There have been many glorious and sweeping victories in Test cricket, achieved sometimes against all odds, but it is the essence of this particular kind of match, the 'sport' bred of two cultures, that at the finish it should be precisely balanced. The Brisbane tie between West Indies and Australia in 1960 was plainly of this order, hurrying to its fantastic climax; the drawn match, immortalized by Bailey and Watson, at Lord's against Australia in 1953 was another; but neither throughout its length quite compared with the Lord's Test of this year, in which England and West Indies, having fought each other to a standstill, ended up six runs and one wicket short respectively. It was not only a match of constantly fluctuating fortune and advantage, flaming to sudden heights of drama, but one in which half a dozen performances remain indelibly printed on the collective memory of those lucky enough to see them. Dexter's first innings, scornfully achieved against the world's two fastest bowlers, both on the rampage, produced one of the most astonishing hours of cricket ever seen at Lord's. Butcher, on the Saturday, and Close, on the final afternoon, played in their different ways innings of heroic stature. Cowdrey's catching, the bowling of Hall and Griffith, and above all that of Trueman, who took eleven wickets, were such as to make any match memorable. There were as many subsidiary performances, each integral to the final result. Over and above this, Lord's was packed to overflowing, disappointed queues stretching to all parts of St John's Wood, the crowd inside every bit as West Indian as English. Every ball bowled produced a reaction of some sort and, in between, the hubbub died away to an electric stillness. It was as if the sound had been orchestrated, identifying melodies emerging from the mass to elaborate private themes. For three days, after the gloomiest of forecasts, the sun shone; when, after the week-end, the rain returned, it was able to intrude, not to deter. How precisely it affected the result is incalculable; possibly England might have won on the fourth evening, despite Cowdrey's blow, but then again they might not.

West Indies, since the war, have enjoyed mixed fortunes at Lord's. In 1950, the original Calypso Test, Ramadhin and Valentine, on their first visit, reduced England to scrambling incompetents. In 1957, despite an astonishing innings of 90 by Everton Weekes on a brutish pitch, they went down in three days. Since then they had been beaten by England in the West Indies, losing only at Port of Spain, the bottle-throwing affair, after having rather the better of four drawn games. The following winter they had set all Australia alight, losing the last Test by the smallest of margins in a thrilling series.

As a result they arrived in England in April 1963 with a team containing more justly renowned players than any other country could boast. In Worrell they had a captain, in his heyday one of the century's great all-rounders, who under an exterior casual to the point of sleepiness led them with a subtlety and skill as persuasive as it was soothing. Many thought Kanhai the best batsman in the world, Sobers the best all-rounder. Few would quarrel with that, or dispute the pre-eminence of Gibbs as an off-spinner. Hall and Griffith as fast bowlers had no rivals in speed, stamina and general hostility. The fielding, often their undoing in the past, was uniformly safe and frequently brilliant. There seemed no evident weakness, with Hunte as a commanding opening batsman, and Butcher and Solomon stabilizing the middle batting. Worrell, still a batsman of classical ease and delicacy, came in at number seven. There was Sobers to bowl at fast-medium or out of the back of his hand as required. Murray, initially the understudy wicket-keeper, developed so rapidly that by the time of the first Test he suffered nothing in comparison with any contemporary Test rival.

England, since their last meeting, had surrendered the Ashes to Australia, losing at home to Benaud in 1961 – just – but holding their own in the tough, relentless, but finally drab series played to a draw during the winter of 1962–63. They had returned from Australia with much fighting credit, but with the image of Test cricket sadly tarnished. From that series only four players – Dexter, Trueman, Barrington and Titmus – emerged with reputations enhanced and places secure. They were short of an opening pair, lacking in a leg-spinner and left-arm bowler, while Statham was visibly wilting. Much reorganization was going to be necessary.

There were twenty-five minutes to go before lunch*. Stewart took two runs from Hall's opening over from the nursery end, and then Edrich, the first ball he received, was caught by the wicket-keeper on the leg side off Griffith. It was the old story. Dexter, one was glad to see, came next, hurrying down the steps as if unable to contain himself, but the prospect was intimidating. At once, though, he asserted himself, turning Griffith to leg, and then hitting off the back foot with something like anger. Bareheaded, his hair cut unusually short, he suggested no nonsense. If something of the romantic had been shorn away, so, one hoped, had folly. Stewart, however, made negligible headway; he parried and stabbed, and it was no great surprise when, off the last ball before lunch, Griffith had him well taken by Kanhai at first slip. Griffith, no-balled four times already, had in the same over all but bowled Dexter, a sharp break-back skidding off the inside edge to long leg.

During lunch, with 2 wickets down for 20, it was hard not to feel that 301 was an impossibly long way off. Hall had barely got a sweat up; Griffith, still encumbered in thick wool, had taken no more out of himself than a man yawning and stretching before starting the day's work.

Round the boundary the West Indians, chattering like magpies, poured beer down their throats and exuded huge pleasures. English picnickers, remembering the batting disasters of the Australian winter, ate with foreboding, reconciled to a long, uphill slog, if not a

---

* The situation on this second morning was that West Indies had been bowled out for 301. England replied with 297. In their second innings West Indies made 226, leaving England to make 230 to win. They were 228 for 9 at the close, having needed 8 off the last over.

92

slithery and steep descent. What nobody could suspect was that in the next hour they would be present at one of the greatest innings seen at Lord's since anyone could remember.

It is never easy to compare innings, for the context and the opposition vary as much as do individual styles. Dexter, all told, batted for only eighty minutes, receiving some 70 balls. Off these he scored 70 runs, being out to Sobers at 102, the scoreboard at his dismissal bearing a cock-eyed aspect. One could imagine City gentlemen, not hurrying overmuch after hearing the lunch-time score, or well-lunched members of clubs reluctantly bestirring themselves from comfortable armchairs, arriving at Lord's around three o'clock to find England past the hundred, last man already mystifyingly out for 70. It happened so quickly that even watching it going on, the scale was difficult to comprehend. Suddenly Dexter was 50, the innings not in ruins, but classically erect, like pillars soaring with eagles. One remembered Hutton's 145 here against Australia in 1953, Benaud's dashing 97 three years later, Weekes's 90 in 1957, all innings of brilliance and quality. Yet each of these was somehow more in the expected order of things, part of a consistently evolving match. Dexter, in no more than an hour after lunch, reversed the whole pattern, defying nature itself. The tide swarming in was inexplicably put on the ebb.

Unfortunately, one cannot anticipate events, the historic rapidly belonging to memory rather than to reality. All that in the way of framework needs establishing is that at 2.10 p.m. England were 20 for 2, with the world's two fastest bowlers pounding in for the kill. An hour later the hundred was up, Hall and Griffith long since put to flight.

It was Griffith, with two wickets already in the bag, whom Dexter first set himself to destroy. The surfeit of no-balls continued, it is true, enabling him to test the propitiousness of the omens, but very soon it was impossible to distinguish between legality and impropriety, so violently did Dexter hit.

Griffith, coming in at the start with that noble, upright run, cradling and rocking the ball, a love-child to be sacrificed before the great leap of the delivery, continued from the pavilion, where against the dark brick and glass the hand is never easy to focus. But at once he was stopped in his tracks, Dexter twice in an over crashing half-volleys to the palings before Griffith had properly followed through. The report like gunshot made it unnecessary for him to look.

He turned and walked back, a shade stunned, but with the assurance of one who can afford a certain indulgence. In the next over, it happened again. So he pitched short, slanting the ball in from the full width of the crease. Dexter hooked on the rise, not upwards but with a cross-batted ferocity that rattled the glasses in the Tavern bar. He bowled fuller and Dexter drove beautifully either side of cover. Griffith dug one viciously in and Dexter slammed it to mid-wicket. Occasionally he flicked off his legs, or cut caressively with the abstracted tenderness that is the reverse side of violence.

Barrington, not always the most sensitive player to the needs of the moment, accommodatingly pushed singles to give Dexter the strike. Never other than hurried, with frequent removal of the right hand at the moment of contact, he stabbed Hall out of his stumps or off his ribs at what seemed the last possible second. One had the illusion that both Hall and Griffith were twice as quick against Barrington, but it was simply that when they bowled to Dexter the ball shot back past them faster than it was propelled. Soon Barrington was cutting and glancing with something like affability.

Dexter reached fifty, and the applause, echoing round St John's Wood, did him justice. He held up his bat as if quieting it, an intimation that more was to come. Hall now trudged back without eagerness; Griffith was somnambulist, enveloped in fogs of disbelief.

At 83 Worrell replaced Hall with Gibbs, who began a stint of 27 overs interrupted only by tea. Sobers took over from Griffith. Wagnerian thunder gave way to Mozartian melody, the cut and the deflection more evident than the drive.

Dexter, as nervously spent as the fast bowlers, recouped his energies, getting a second wind. So often, at such times, has one seen him get out in the fatal seventies. At once Sobers, varying the inswinger with the leg cutter, began to hit him about the pads. Dexter grew edgy, robbed of momentum and flourish. Sobers, using the crease, whipped one past the off stump; an over later he brought one in with the arm and Dexter, playing slightly across, was l.b.w. In precise fashion at Hove a week earlier had Sobers dismissed him. At Edgbaston a fortnight later he got him again, this time with one darting in from leg to flatten the off stump.

All the way in, the whole crowd of 30,000 stood and applauded. The successive tiers of the Pavilion rose to him, stilled only when Cowdrey, almost unrecognizably slimmed, picked his way out. Such was the sense of anti-climax, the dispersal of tension, that further play seemed almost an affront, mere routine after satiation.

Innings Chart – Dexter l.b.w. b. Sobers, 70

Duration 83 minutes. Starting score 2 for 1; score at end 102 for 3. [Total runs 100 – Dexter 70 (75 balls), Barrington 20 (44 balls), Stewart 0 (13 balls), extras 10.]

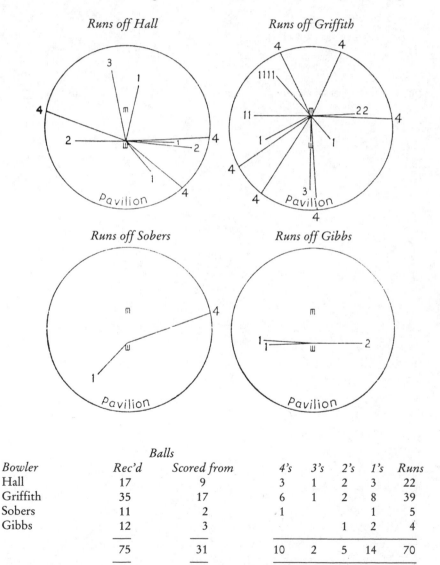

Bowler	Balls Rec'd	Scored from	4's	3's	2's	1's	Runs
Hall	17	9	3	1	2	3	22
Griffith	35	17	6	1	2	8	39
Sobers	11	2	1			1	5
Gibbs	12	3			1	2	4
	75	31	10	2	5	14	70

The series began with West Indies demolishing England at Old Trafford. At Edgbaston England won almost as decisively, Trueman taking twelve wickets in the match. West Indies went one up at Headingley, by over 200 runs. They won again at The Oval, by eight wickets, with Griffith taking 6 for 71 in the first innings. Trueman took 34 wickets in the series, Griffith 32. Three West Indians made centuries, against none by the English.

PART II

The Poetry of Sport

Cricket at Brighton

At night the Front like coloured barley-sugar; but now
Soft blue, all soda, the air goes flat over flower-beds,
Blue railings and beaches. Below, half-painted boats, bow
Up, settle in sand, names like Moss-Rose and Dolphin
Drying in a breeze that flicks at the ribs of the tide.
The chalk coastline folds up its wings of Beachy Head
And Worthing, fluttering white over water like brides.
Regency squares, the Pavilion, oysters and mussels and gin.

Piers like wading confectionery, esplanades of striped tulip.
Cricket began here yesterday, the air heavy, suitable
For medium-paced bowlers. Deck-chairs, though, mostly
                                        were vacant,
Faces white over startling green. Later, trains will decant
People with baskets, litter and opinions, the seaside's staple
Ingredients. To-day Langridge pushes the ball for unfussed
Singles; ladies clap from check rugs, talk to retired colonels.
On tomato-red verandas the scoring rate is discussed.

Sussex *v.* Lancashire, the air birded and green after rain,
Dew on syringa and cherry. Seaward the water
Is satin, pale emerald, fretted with lace at the edges,
The whole sky rinsed easy like nerves after pain.
May here is childhood, lost somewhere between and never
Recovered, but again moved nearer, as a lever
Turned on the pier flickers the Past into pictures.
A time of immediacy, optimism, without stricture.

Postcards and bathing-machines and old prints.
Something comes back, the inkling, the momentary hint
Of what we had wanted to be, though differently now,
For the conditions are different and what we had wanted
We wanted as we were then, without conscience,

                                       unhaunted,
And given the chance must refuse to want it again.
Only, occasionally, we escape, we return where we were:
Watching cricket at Brighton, Tate bowling through

                                    sea-scented air.

A Cricketer in Retirement

For George Cox

The marine and the regency, sea frets,
And somewhere the Downs backing a station
Like a Victorian conservatory. I come upon
A scorecard yellow as old flannels and suddenly
I see him, smilingly prowling the covers
In soft shoes, shirt rolled to the forearm,
Light as a yacht swaying at its moorings,
Deceptively courteous. An element
Of silk, of ease, with none of the old dutiful
Sense of the regiment, the parade-ground
Posture that gave even the best of them the air of retainers.
Instead, a kind of compassion linking top hats
With turnips, the traditional turning to devilry.
One apart, yet part all the same,
Of that familiar pattern of families,
Parkses and Langridges, Tates and Oakes and Gilligans,
Griffiths and Busses, Sussex is rich in,
The soft air phrased by their fickleness.

Never one for half-measures, as generous
With ducks as half-centuries, he seemed
To calculate extravagance, waywardly spendthrift
With the cold calculators, Yorkshire, the Australians,
Hove and the Saffrons ablaze with his fireworks,
Dad wincing in his grave. With others,
Less challenging, he was often vulnerable,
Giving his wicket to those who were glad of it,
Indulgently negligent against parachuting spinners.
Now there are no scorecards, just pulled hamstrings
In village cricket and instead of fancy-free

Strokes in festival arenas the soothing
Of successors. The forearms make gardens,
And the journeys have lengthened, a sunset
Of orchards and vineyards, where reclining in a bath
Of imperial proportions he observes a wife
As delicate with pastry as he was at the wicket.

J. M. Parks at Tunbridge Wells

Parks takes ten off two successive balls from Wright,
A cut to the rhododendrons and a hook for six.
And memory begins suddenly to play its tricks:
I see his father batting, as, if here, he might.

Now Tunbridge Wells, 1951; the hair far lighter,
And body boyish, flesh strung across thin bone,
And arms sinewy as the wrists are thrown
At the spinning ball, the stance much straighter.

Now it is June full of heaped petals,
The day steamy, tropical; rain glistens
On the pavilion, shining on corrugated metal,
The closeness has an air that listens.

Then it was Eastbourne, 1935; a date
Phrased like a vintage, sea-fret on the windscreen.
And Parks, rubicund and squat, busily sedate,
Pushing Verity square, moving his score to nineteen.

Images of Then, so neatly parcelled and tied
By ribbons of war – but now through a chance
Resemblance re-opened; a son's stance
At the wicket opens the closed years wide.

And it is no good resisting the interior
Assessment, the fusion of memory and hope
That comes flooding to impose on inferior
Attainment – yesterday, today, twisted like a rope.

Parks drives Wright under dripping green trees,
The images compare and a father waves away
Applause, pale sea like a rug over the knees,
Covering him, the son burying his day

With charmed strokes. And abstractedly watching,
Drowning, I struggle to shake off the Past
Whose arms clasp like a mother, catching
Up with me, summer at half-mast.

The silent inquisitors subside. The crowd,
Curiously unreal in this regency spa, clap,
A confectionery line under bushes heavily bowed
In the damp. Then Parks pierces Wright's leg-trap.

And we come through, back to the present.
Sussex 300 for 2. Moss roses on the hill.
A dry taste in the mouth, but the moment
Sufficient, being what we are, ourselves still.

Test Match at Lord's

Bailey bowling, McLean cuts him late for one.
I walk from the Long Room into slanting sun.
Two ancients halt as Statham starts his run.
Then, elbows linked, but straight as sailors
On a tilting deck, they move. One, square-shouldered as a tailor's
Model, leans over, whispering in the other's ear:
'Go easy. Steps here. This end bowling.'
Turning, I watch Barnes guide Rhodes into fresher air,
As if to continue an innings, though Rhodes may only play by ear.

On an Engraving of
Alfred Mynn Esq (1852)

Grasped like a twig in his enormous hands,
The crude bat is a measure, as now his expanding
Frame places him in Time – a Victorian,
Whose engraved features yellow while a band
Plays in the distance, and a gulf of pleasure
Yawns. Now, as we watch his careful
Studied posture, we imagine the bowler rolling up his sleeve.

Beneath the solemn black-quiffed forehead
The eyes, like cameras, study us – developments
Of their passive gaze; and what is said
Nobody knows, as all we see is part
Of our costumed Past – the stomach bellying like a sail,
Pale-blue sash, and narrow, faded flannels.
And what is hidden is the art
That made his name a byword in a social age,
The brilliant speed and swinging flight
No portrait can suggest, words recreate or disparage.

A Portrait of Hammond

Even at 1/500th you can't freeze him,
Make his image quite static.
He remains more mobile than diagrammatic.

Take compass, protractor. However
You dismantle him, the parts
Remain true, suggest velocity.

Leonardo would have made him fly,
This batsman so revving with power
He seems airborne.

Like some prototype birdman
Straining at silk moorings, he conveys
Ambiguity, both imprisonment and release.

Never mind the earthbound heaviness
Of hip, of shoulders, his cover-drive
Evokes airiness, an effortless take-off.

A study in anatomy, circa 1930. Anonymous.
But there, nonchalantly stuffed
In his pocket, that blue handkerchief signs it.

Remembering Hutton

Leonard, I see you as by Rodin, head in hand,
Leaning on a rail. The chipped blue ocean
Repeats the colour of your eyes.

Your usual air was that of one
Whose gaze was inward, storing images
Like paper flowers yet to open.

Your art as batsman was ever one that leaned,
Its secret timing. In conversation
Jokes came without flourish, dry as dust.

A classical method, sideways on,
Head still and left arm high. Parchment pale,
You flourished according to event.

Eloquent as sculpture in your driving, you fended down
Bouncers as you might unruly dogs,
Distracted almost. Now, ruminant on high,

I imagine your ethereal presence,
Feet slightly splayed, left forearm incised,
All heaven in wonder at your repertoire.

Watching Benaud Bowl

Leg-spinners pose problems much like love,
Requiring commitment, the taking of a chance.
Half-way deludes; the bold advance.

Right back, there's time to watch
Developments, though perhaps too late.
It's not spectacular, but can conciliate.

Instinctively romantics move towards,
Preventing complexities by their embrace,
Batsman and lover embarked as overlords.

Late Gower

Arm confined below shoulder level
As if winged, the slight
Lopsided air of a seabird
Caught in an oilslick. 'Late' Gower,
As of a painting by Monet, a 'serial'
Whose shuffled images delight
Through inconstancy, variety of light.

Giambattista Tiepolo
In his 'Continence of Scipio' created
Just such a head and halo.
For this descendant no confines
Of canvas, but increasing worry lines,
Low gravity of a burglar.

Stance, posture, combine
To suggest a feline
Not cerebral intelligence. A hedonist
In his autumn, romance lightly worn,
And now first signs of *tristesse*,
Faint strains of a hunting horn.

Stanley Matthews

Not often *con brio*, but *andante, andante,*
    horseless, though jockey-like and jaunty,
Straddling the touchline, live margin
    not out of the game, nor quite in,
Made by him green and magnetic, stroller
    Indifferent as a cat dissembling, rolling
A little as on deck, till the mouse, the ball,
    slides palely to him,
And shyly, almost with deprecatory cough, he is off.

Head of a Perugino, with faint flare
Of the nostrils, as though Lipizzaner-like,
    he sniffed at the air,
And finding the way open, uncluttered, draws
Defenders towards him, the ball a bait
They refuse like a poisoned chocolate,
    retreating, till he slows his gait
To a walk, inviting the tackle, inciting it.

At last, unrefusable, dangling the ball at the instep
He is charged – and stiffening so slowly
It is barely perceptible, he executes with a squirm
Of the hips, a twist more suggestive than apparent,
    that lazily disdainful move *toreros* term
        a Veronica – it's enough.
Only emptiness following him, pursuing some scent
Of his own, he weaves in towards,
    not away from, fresh tacklers,
Who, turning about to gain time, are by him
    harried, pursued not pursuers.

Now gathers speed, nursing the ball as he cruises,
Eyes judging distance, noting the gaps, the spaces
Vital for colleagues to move to, slowing a trace,
As from Vivaldi to Dibdin, pausing,
        and leisurely, leisurely, swings
To the left upright his centre, on hips
His hands, observing the goalkeeper spring,
        heads rising vainly to the ball's curve
just as it's plucked from them; and dispassionately
Back to his mark he trots, whistling through closed lips.

Trim as a yacht, with similar lightness
        – of keel, of reaction to surface – with salt air
Tanned, this incomparable player, in decline fair
                to look at, nor in decline either,
Improving like wine with age, has come far –
        born to one, a barber, who boxed
Not with such filial magnificence, but well.
'The greatest of all time,' *meraviglioso*, Matthews –
        Stoke City, Blackpool and England.
Expressionless enchanter, weaving as on strings
Conceptual patterns to a private music, heard
Only by him, to whose slowly emerging theme
He rehearses steps, soloist in compulsions of a dream.

World Cup

    It is, after all, a kind
Of music, an elaborating of themes
That swell and subside, which
In the converting of open spaces
Take on a clean edge.
    A throw, a chip,
A flick, Wilson to Charlton,
To Moore, to Hunt, to Greaves –
The diagonals cross, green space is charmed.

A precise movement, balletic in ordained
Agility, with the players as if magnetised
Moving into places seemingly allotted them
– They seem from above to be pushed like counters
And only the fluffed pass, the momentary
Crudity disconcerting as a clerical oath,
Destroys the illusion. A goal restores it.

Arms raised like gladiators, they embrace.
Human emotions swamp them, childishly even
For such protagonists of perfection.
    And involved in this mixture
Of the fallible and the dreamy,
The percussive and the lilting, they demonstrate
How art exists on many levels, spirit
And matter close-knit as strangling lianas.

Football Grounds of the Riviera

Rock-cut, railway-flanked, with sea edging its flat
Surface, Monaco hangs top-heavy over dwarfed white posts:
Casinos and aquariums bulge above the crenellated coast,
Arc-lights strung along the Stadium like cloche hats.
Below, the pitch is smooth as green Casino baize
Whose wheels spin over water pink with haze.
Coated in sunset, the harbour's neat, dark palms,
Like roulette players, keep stiff their salt-drenched arms.

Scrambling over bald, dusty but flower-scented ground,
Cactus gesticulating, olive-edged, makeshift and public-
    owned,
Ventimiglia's forwards fan out round Bordighera's goal,
Jerseys striped like fishes in a noisy shoal.
Mountains bisect the sky with rocky signature
And sea-air modifies the players' temperature.
Mauve waves grow taut and spray the piazza pines,
As fishing boats trail their lamps in golden lines.

Menton at home to Nice, the French League leaders,
Sun only a rind squeezed dry of its heat,
And below us the voices of bathers scratch
At the cellophane air, airing ignorance of the match.
The tide recedes, drawing yachts in gentle retreat.
Outlined against mackerel sky, rock-bound readers
Golden indulgent flesh, absorbed in their books' spilled
    flush:
The frontier, insentient, hardens, the coastline in ambush.

G. Lineker

A style suggested by a name,
A way of comportment, of playing –
In the merging of 'line' and 'glint'
Necessary elusiveness, hint
Of mother of pearl, 'nacreous',
As in the opening, knife-edged,
Of two halves of an oyster.

In the music of Satie there is
Similar opportunism, echoes
And chances taken up, exploited –
'Striker' and 'lion', a 'cur'
Hanging around on the off-chance.
Something dabbled, as in a painting
By Seurat, linked dots
That on good days veer towards fable.

F. D. Amr Bey

Open Squash Rackets Champion 1933–38
Former Egyptian Ambassador to the Court of St James

There, in his name, a desert
Lordliness, this expert
Of the backhand volley:
            his on-court manners
In keeping with his status.

Dropshots were tender as butterflies
Alighting, wrist and racket
Taut as cello strings. Deceptively
            impassive
He wrong-footed even as he smiled.

Nile, feluccas, sand,
Ingredients of style
Adaptable as sails to wind
            or currents,
The masking of a stroke.

He floated his returns
To hang like parachutes,
Lobs dying in corners.
            An exquisite
Geometry made Mondrians of his game.

Caressive, with the touch
Of cat or pianist, an aloof
Interloper in his sidewall boasts;
            his rallies
Made dialectics out of dialogue.

116

Warmed up by this practising
Of scales, these conversational martini-dry
Exchanges, there came a time
           to end them.
A flick like a full-stop finished it.

Yearlings

A string of horses black against the snow,
December light already beginning to go

And the beeches absorbing them, a rust
Tunnel through which like mist

They jog, shadowy invaders.
Caparisoned, they suggest courtliness

And lineage, heirs
To historic names whose sires

Gaze through hooded eyes,
Innocent of pride or surprise.

Before Racing

Pink layer of icing sugar,
Till the straw sun dissolves it,
And the Downs, drained by the cold
Of their green, sweep grey
To grey sea. Trees are mastheads.

Elements of blue like eyelids
And the lanes lathered with breath.
Clink of steel and stealth of hooves
As they return in Indian file,
An air of innocence about them.

As yet it is anybody's
Morning, a slate clouded
With nothing; but gradually,
Under the cold, something's
Moving, beginning to conspire
Towards a finish flushed with silver.

At the Races, Germany 1945

Smells of cigar straw dung
That odour of unleavened bread
Germans hump around with them
– a stink of defeat, alienating.
Only the silks ripple, are exciting.

After winter, so much pastiness
Smeared over everything, contaminating
As gas, as debilitating,
These jockeys incite senses to riot.
Which number will come up?

It is like old times. Girls
In fur boots, willowy and entrancing,
Horses glistening like metal,
And the country, all greenness and blossom,
Reflective and glancing.

By the Tote refugees in long coats gossip
Politics, fumble their betting slips.

Left: W. G. Grace, whose lengthy career ran from 1865 to 1908.
HULTON GETTY

Right: K. S. Ranjitsinjhi, known by all as 'Ranji' who played for Sussex and England.
HULTON GETTY

Left: Amr Bey, Open Squash Rackets Champion 1933–8. Hulton Getty

Right: C. B. Fry, all-rounder without equal. Hulton Getty

Above: Bill Woodfull (Australia) ducks to a ball from Harold Larwood at Brisbane, 1933. HULTON GETTY

Below: Wally Hammond (left) and Don Bradman going out to toss. England versus Australia, Nottingham, 1938. HULTON GETTY

Above: Stanley
Matthews (left)
playing for Stoke City,
1938. HULTON GETTY

Left: Joe Davis, the
World Professional
Snooker Champion
from 1927 until he
retired unbeaten in
1946. HULTON GETTY

Above: Colin Cowdrey batting
during the the third Test against the
Australians at Melbourne. Cowdrey
went on to score 102 in his first Test
century, 6 January 1955. HULTON GETTY

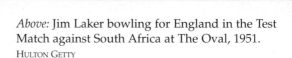

Above: Jim Laker bowling for England in the Test
Match against South Africa at The Oval, 1951.
HULTON GETTY

Left: Alec Bedser, who led England's attack in the
struggling decade after the war. HULTON GETTY

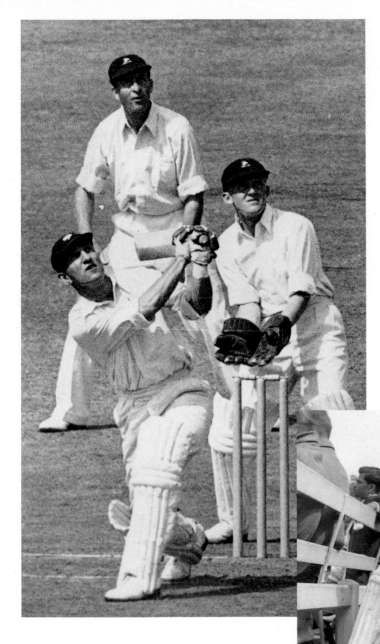

Left: Leonard Hutton
batting during the final
Test Match at The Oval,
16 August 1947.
HULTON GETTY

Right: Frank Worrell,
10 June 1950.
HULTON GETTY

Sussex County greats.
Left: George Cox (1947),
Below left: Hugh Bartlett (1948)
Below: John Langridge (1949).
HULTON GETTY

Right: Peter May, one of the greatest batsmen of the post-war period June 1955. HULTON GETTY

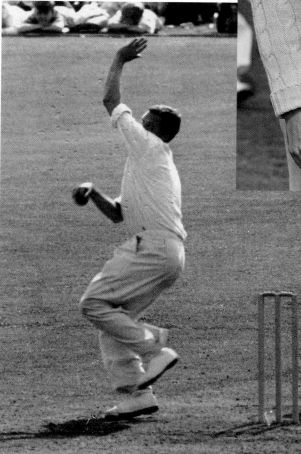

Left: Australian captain Richie Benaud in action against England at Old Trafford, where the Australians won the fourth Test to retain the Ashes, 1 August 1961. HULTON GETTY

Left: J. M. Parks, one of the most talented among the great Sussex families of cricketers. His father, J. H. Parks, also played for England and holds the unique record of 3,000 runs and 100 wickets in a season. HULTON GETTY

Below: Gary Sobers, possibly the greatest all-rounder in the history of the game. HULTON GETTY

Right: Geoffrey Boycott, who amassed vast quantities of runs for Yorkshire and England in the 1970s, 25 July 1970.
HULTON GETTY

Below right: David Gower, arguably the most graceful batsman of his generation, 1978. HULTON GETTY

Below: No one since Ted Dexter has hit the ball as hard as Ian Botham or so electrified a Test crowd, May 1983.
ALLSPORT

Left: Curtly Ambrose bowling in the third Test against England in Trinidad, 13 February 1998. ALLSPORT

Below: Brian Lara in 1994, during his innings of 501 not out against Durham. ALLSPORT

Racing at Kassar Säid

The limp palms coated with dust.
And the coaxed horses, thin about the rump,
Swishing at flies. A stink
Of cigars and dung, through which,
Oily and lubricious, tussore taut over plump
Thighs, women talk as they stalk.
Elaborate this language of the eyes,
Such as belongs to the once-veiled, ink
In their glances, an ambiguous communiqué
Meaning everything or nothing.
               In the sandhopper paddock
The Favourite balefully urinates, steam
Rising from fizz. On tall heels,
Hair marbled under nylon, metallic legs gleam.

       Movement and pecuniary lust,
Where the expense-account faces, olive-smooth,
Suggest what cannot be transacted, a mere
Flicker of eyelids in exchange of prophesies.
And each on his way rejoicing,
Binoculars slung, a gloved woman hung
At the elbow, as if the real purpose
Were social. Silks opening and closing,
A conjuror's slick shuffle, and a hooped
Outsider snaps the fan into focus, nosing
Through the dust.
            High on the neck, French-style,
Oblivious jockeys goggle at the sun
In a murderous finish. Meanwhile,
Unobtrusively, elsewhere, real murder is done.

Death of a Trainer

In Memory of Alan Oughton

Among fellow jockeys bandy and small
He was straight as a board and tall,
So long to the knees
He could pick up and squeeze
Novices and old rogues round all sorts of courses.
Neither bred to the sea nor horses,
The son of a Pompey tailor,
He walked with brisk roll of a sailor,
Tilted, as by saddle or quarter deck,
A curve from hipbone to neck.

Falls caught up with him, of the kind habitual
To riders over sticks, but he seemed at last
Safe in his Findon stables, at his disposal
A handful of jumpers not especially fast
Nor clever, but amenable to discipline
And patience, ridden out on a skyline
Of downland and sea, in lime dawn
Or half darkness, clouds torn
By gales blistering the channel,
Mist thickening beechwoods to flannel.

Busy as a ship, smelling of hay
And leather, of mash and linseed,
The yard seemed that ideal harbour
In which work has the essence of play,
Day-long, night-long, obedient to need,
The summer's sweetness, winter's bleak labour.
But season following season, winner

Following winner, so did pain circle,
Eyes grow strained and the thin body thinner,
Until there was only the long hell.

What I still see is a skeletal guy
Half imagined, half real, between races at Fontwell,
Saddle under one arm, threading his way
Through the weighing room, or wiping jellied eel
From his lips, sawdust running out of him
As he drops in the distance, each limb
Jerky as if on a string, patch
Over one eye, trilby dead straight,
And a gelding quickening to snatch
Up the verdict, just leaving it too late.

Blue Grass

Stubble stretches to the horizon,
Reservoir of sunlight,
Transparent as eyelids, tree-fringed.

But 'blue' only at certain
Communions of light and season,
In contrary breezes.

Dawn-stained, dusk-shadowed,
A blue of memory, invisible.

Racehorses at Gulfstream

Turning for home, at last off the bridle,
They seem as they lengthen their strides

Almost to falter. Beneath them, green thickens,
Goes drowsy, as though a film

Were being slowed, the frame frozen.
They have for a second the air

Of somnambulists, moving loosely
In envelopes of water. An uphill element

Is against them. They break free,
And their actions, recovering, turn languorous,

Muscles slithering in quarters
Transparent under sweat, their veins swollen.

Palmettos and flags become fixed blurs,
And towing in their slipstreams long shadows

They dent distance as it dwindles,
Air, earth conniving, eyes limitless.

Stallion and Teaser

For him, who is above preliminaries,
It is no more than the seigneurial
Raising of hooves round a mane,
A brief thrusting. He strolls off,
Lordly as the sun, indifferent now
To the mare, her bride's eyes dying.
But for that other, amiable,
Grey around the lip, who never
Quite made it, civilities
Of courtship are what he must settle for –
Eyes hazy with love-light, the nuzzle
Of arched necks, legs quivering
As if caressed by cool breezes. She bridles,
Looses her urine. And removed from her,
Pawing stubble in the distance,
He must comfort himself with a suitor's
Dwindling euphoria, remembering
Her shiver, sweat drying on his skin.

The Big 'A'

Heading for the old IND Special Race Track Express from
   42nd Street and 8th Avenue
'Right to Big A's own subway' I take in error the regular 'A'
   train
Loaded with students and messengers and kids
With black gollywog hair and fur collars, and I sit opposite a
   neat fellow
Of about seventy in goldrimmed specs, nose an inch from the
   racing page
Which he keeps there from 34th Street
To well past Delancey, crossing a spatted foot
Over another or coughing into a silk muffler and making
   marks
With a gold pencil. He is embedded
In Form, the elimination of irrelevance.
Shuttling the tightrope between Brooklyn
And Queens, Myrtle Avenue, Chauncey Street, we are back
   above ground
At Euclid, on the straight run to Rockaway
And Aqueduct, shedding the straphangers,
Clerks and business men and reps on their rounds, only
Racegoers, collusive as addicts on the
Last stretch to the hide-out.

Shuffling behind Goldrims and a mate
Picked up at Kosciusko, a lard-faced limping
Hungarian park-keeper from Coney Island,
His lunch wrapped in brown paper
Like a parcel of underwear, we dig our toes in
On the steep ramp linking subway to racetrack,
The air crisp over flowerbeds and paddocks,

A sense of the sea, with gulls wheeling,
The vapour trails of 747s taking off
From JFK airport dissolving like smoke rings
In blue bronzed by Fall foliage, and on the track
Itself, under great overhanging beaks of steel,
An air of the Stock Exchange, bits of paper
Like confetti scattered everywhere, men
With newspapers for faces, coke bottles, cigars,
Swans cruising the ponds stiffnecked as old
Boston matrons, the starter riding out
In hunting pink, horns blowing for jockeys
To get mounted, the parade to begin.

And once begun these nine-race meetings
Held under the auspices of the New York
Racing Association, President John H. Krumpe,
Have something of the automated monotony
Of the dogtrack, an endless succession
Of 6-furlong sprints following each other
On an absolutely level dirt surface, the horses
Curiously insignificant, the jockeys mostly Mexican
But with extravagant names – Jorge Velasquez,
Jesus Guadalupe, Jacinto Vasquez, Angel
Sandiago, Brasila Baeza (celebrated in England
For his riding of Roberto), Daryl Montoya, John Ruane,
Laffet Pincoy Jr. Expressionless in their silks
They themselves seem rather a let-down,
Idling to the start as if going to the gallows.
The purses are enviable, but once under way
It's the betting that matters, exactas and doubles,
Wins and show, and the final getting-out stakes
On the last race when Arum Lily, the favourite,
Saves everyone's bacon, and the crowd of mainly
European origin, Spanish, German and Italian,
With a sprinkling of negro, pads through the debris,
Past the soup and chowder bars, exalted
Or listless, scuffing leaves from the tarmac,
Shuh-shuh, back up the ramp
To the subway, the return to the grindstone.

128

Golfers at Savannah

Flush to the Wilmington these greens,
Deepening under sprinklers, take on
A velvet frostiness, a sheer bloom.
Areas of worship conjured from plainness
In a huge country, pampered
And caressed they lie placid
As lake-water in landscapes quiet as convents.
These are the nature reserves
Of America, the competitive
Harnessed to the orderly, the lion
Lying down with the lamb, the rattler.

In Illinois and Oregon they rehearse
These dream territories, briefed
For the cedarwoods and doglegs,
Lush fairways cleaving through blue sea-frets,
The river interrupted by palm trees,
Chipmunks shinning up oaks,
Green phased out in magnolias.

Through long winters they go through
Imaginary rituals, take warmth
From playgrounds made legendary by Nicklaus
And de Vicenzo, Palmer, Player,
Trevino, on sleepless nights
Study angles with navigators' eyes,
Debate irons and woods, run through repertories.

And I watch the jets circling Savannah
In tropical thunderstorms, decanting them
On their four-day packages, surprised
By the Spring and the steaminess,
But ready to take on anything,
To put a good face on it.
Soon they are out in lumberjackets
And peaked caps, bright sweatshirts,
Sunburn coming up on them like birthmarks,
The wind fresh off the Wilmington.

At dusk, shrimpboats slither for the Sound,
The river become a bolt
Of silver spiked by reeds.

In hotel rooms they shower bodies
Ringed at neck and elbow,
The nude flesh in long mirrors
White as if singletted.
And later, at a teak bar
Tended by black barmen they rarely notice,
Their characteristic roughness
Drops from them like skin, whisky
And exercise working their wonders.
Through cigarsmoke they recall old heroes,
Harry Vardon, Walter Hagen,
Compare Johnny Miller and Tom Weiskopf.

Their women, used to segregation,
Have the bleached air
Of marigolds left too long in the sun.

But next day, some before breakfast,
Eggs sunny side up, waffles and syrup,
They are out on their trolleys,
Sniffing the freshness, lakes incised
As half moons, fairways immaculate –
A ball fades in the blueness,
Hanging as if parachuted, then plops
Like a pheasant dropped by a gun-dog.

In the pro-shop and club room
Rummaging through displays
Of equipment, starched whites,
Spiked shoes, check pants,
They take imaginary swings
With new clubs, over cokes
And coffee linger among accessories.

High noon and lawnmowers like cicadas,
Abundance of blue. Then, punctually,
In late afternoon, the build-up
Of clouds over the Atlantic,
A conspiratorial whisper of bamboos.
Thunder breaks the sky open.

An hour later, slopes
And gullies streaming, the sun
As if nothing had happened
Draws off the water.
But it's over for the day,
And they retire under rainbows
Bright as candy
For the comfort of Bourbon and brandy,
Easy after their endeavours.

In the last dusk of hibiscus
And lilac, the air enamoured of itself,
I watch them stream north
In their jets, back to winter
Or what's left of it,
Something of the South rubbed off
On them, an association of images,
Spring with a shimmer of irons,
The bamboos still after thunder,
The languorous couches of greens.

PART III
A Scrapbook

C. B. Fry

LIFE WORTH LIVING, his auto-biography, shows the best of C. B. Fry, because, unlike its garrulous author, it can be picked up and put down when you feel like it. For most of Charles Fry's long life he was a genial, hospitable and cultivated companion, able to talk knowledgeably on a variety of subjects and eccentrically on a number of others. He had a classically trained, inquiring, adventurous mind and he lived a life full of physical and, up to a point, intellectual challenge. He was magnificently built and noble in bearing and as an all-round athlete – at cricket, soccer, athletics and rugby especially – he was without equal in this century and probably in any other.

From *Life Worth Living* you will learn, in generally relaxed and entertaining fashion, all that Fry wished to tell you or could remember about a legendary existence from the early days of the century up to the outbreak of the Second World War. These 'phases of an Englishman', as he subtitled his book, take in such matters as public school and Oxford, cricket for Sussex and England, soccer for the Corinthians, his friendship and travels with Ranji in India and Geneva, hunting and shooting with Maharajahs, the running of the training ship *Mercury*, journalism, a meeting with Hitler, and a visit to Hollywood.

The style is fluent and anecdotal, the tone varying between the modest and self-deprecatory and the faintly hectoring. Fry's head was full of odd notions but he was a genuine enthusiast, a student in the real sense of the term. He could also be opinionated to a degree, high-handed and self-centred.

Grandees do not always wear well in real life, and Fry, a grandee in his heyday if there ever was one – Ranji called him 'Carlo' – was often considerably more wearing to listen to than to read.

There is no one alive now, I imagine, whose cricketing career overlapped with Fry's, though Gubby Allen got his blue at Cambridge the year after Fry, at the age of fifty, played his last first-class match. We have to take his stature therefore on trust and see him through the eyes of others. His performances, however, speak for themselves, especially in the golden summers with Ranji for Sussex. In comparison, though, with the Prince, he seems to have been a manufactured rather than a natural batsman, and as a bowler he was soon outlawed for throwing.

Life Worth Living appeared in 1939, since when two recent books have been published that tell one a great deal more about Fry than he chose to reveal himself. Clive Ellis's biography *C.B.* (1984) and Ronald Morris's *The Captain's Lady* (1985). In addition, there is Denzil Batchelor's *C. B. Fry*, written during Fry's lifetime.

Ellis's admirably sane and balanced account and Morris's extraordinary story of life as a *Mercury* cadet corroborate each other in essentials. The salient facts seem to be that Fry was little more than an amiable figurehead at *Mercury* during the fifty years that he was nominally in charge and that to all intents and purposes this training school for naval cadets was ruled, in the most austere and tyrannical fashion, by his wife Beatie.

Fry makes only the most fleeting references to his wife in *Life Worth Living*, usually of the order that 'my Madame', as he calls her, bowled to him in the garden or accompanied him to matches in which he was playing. What seems extraordinary about the relationship is that Fry, at the age of twenty-six, one of the most handsome and promising men in England, the possessor of a First in classics at Oxford, a future Test cricketer, with the world apparently at his feet, should have embarked on so strange an arrangement. Beatie Sumner, at the age of fifteen, had fallen in love with a dashing

horseman and banker, Charles Hoare, married and twice her age. She eventually ran off with him after the expiration of a court order forbidding their relationship. They lived together for some years and had two children, perhaps even a third (the last officially credited to Fry). Hoare meanwhile had bought the *Mercury*, a renovated China tea-clipper, and turned it into a training ship. It would appear that when the sexual element between the High Anglican Hoare and Beatie waned it was replaced by religious fervour. Hoare was unable or unwilling to get a divorce, and Fry, then teaching at Charterhouse, took up with Beatie, marrying her in 1898. For some years Beatie moved between Fry and Hoare, but after Hoare's death in 1908 Fry moved permanently to the Hamble river and *Mercury*. At the time of their marriage, Beatie was thirty-six, ten years Fry's senior. Her early beauty was now camouflaged under unbecoming masculine clothes and the demeanour of a martinet. However, though their relationship was never judged romantic, she bore Fry two children, the last at the age of forty-eight.

In 1929, Fry experienced a severe nervous breakdown, 'thwarted genius' Beatie put it down to, which lasted nearly five years and reduced him to a pitiable state, often paranoiac and given to periods of wildly irrational behaviour. *Life Worth Living* makes no reference to any of this either, nor indeed to several unsuccessful attempts to become a

being disposed of or converted. It is ironic that the huge and magnificently ornate Pratap Vilas Palace, which Ranji himself had built, should have received as its first guests his own mourners.

Within, the palaces reek of desertion, though their long corridors are still swept and a residue of ancient palace servants, a dozen or so in all, emerge sleepily from compounds or pantries to preserve the illusion of occupancy.

It is in Ranji's own room in the Jam Palace – the room in which he died – that the illusion is most devotedly fostered. Nothing here has been disturbed since Ranji's body was carried from it. The bed with its silver headboard is made up, and propped against the pillow lies a portrait of the Jam Saheb in ceremonial dress. On a bedside table Sir Pelham Warner's photograph, inscribed 'To Ranji, the greatest batsman of my time, from his sincere admirer and friend "Plum", December 1912', bears witness to Ranij's farewell season in English cricket. Popsey's cage is there, and many portraits; a row of cricket bats the colour of rich tobacco; old uniforms and turbans.

The heart of the room is not the bed but the locked glass cabinet beside which, on a shelf, stands the romantic alabaster head, in the *art nouveau* style, of a beautiful young woman. The cabinet itself contains such items as a letter from George V's secretary commiserating on the King's behalf on the loss of Ranji's

eye; Ranji's glasses and cigarette case; his medals and Orders; his half-hunter on its gold chain, a miniature silver bat, a lighter; rings and cuff-links and pins; pieces of jewellery.

On the highest of the three shelves Ranji's passport, the photograph in Indian dress with turban and eye-glass, lies open: Caste/Rajput; Religion/Hindoo; Indian home/Nawanagar; Profession/Ruling Prince; Place and date of birth/Sarodar 10 Sept 1872; Domicile/Nawanagar; Height 5ft 9; Colour of eyes/Dark brown; Colour of hair/Black/grey; Visible distinguishing marks/Smallpox marks on the face.

On the right of this, the six glass eyes which took their turn in Ranji's face are lodged in two satin-lined cases, marked 'G. Muller, 8 New Oxford Street'. For nearly a third of his life the socket of Ranji's eye had each night to be bathed by his doctor. During his years at Jamnagar, Dr Prosser Thomas later recalled, he had made efforts to establish a clinic in the city. Always, though, Ranji would mischievously summon him from his work to make up a four at bridge. Until the last days the ritual of replacing the eye and washing the eye-socket were the only tasks the doctor was allowed to perform.

There are still two servants alive at Jamnagar who have looked after the Jam Saheb. In their old age they carry out their shadow duties, materializing silently on bare feet, much as if His Highness were still alive.

They attend and guard his room as if it were a shrine, allowing nothing to be moved.

For all that, Ranji's room is not a solemn place, simply the bedroom of a much loved and revered ruler who, in his day, happened to be a great cricketer. His trophies and personal effects are all around and though the sun streams through the shutters over the marble corridors outside and the hyenas and peacocks screech, within all is shuttered cool.

'When a person dies who does any one thing better than anyone else in the world,' wrote Hazlitt, discussing the fives player John Cavanagh in his famous essay 'Indian Jugglers', 'it leaves a gap in society.' That was certainly true of Ranji. Elsewhere in the same essay Hazlitt wrote, again about Cavanagh: 'He could not have shown himself in any ground in England, but he would have been immediately surrounded with inquisitive gazers, trying to find out in what part of his frame his unri-valled skill lay' – and that was true of Ranji too.

His effect on people was not confined to cricketers. The sculptor Eric Gill observed in his *Autobiography*, published seven years after Ranji's death:

And while I am thus writing about the beauty and impressiveness of technical prowess I cannot, for it made an immense difference to my mind, omit the famous name of Ranjitsinhji. Even now, when I want to have a little quiet wallow in the thought of something wholly delightful and perfect, I think of Ranji on the county ground at Hove ... There were many minor stars, each with his special and beloved technique, but nothing on earth could approach the special quality of Ranji's batting or fielding ... I only place it on record that such craftsmanship and grace entered into my very soul.

Ranji in Australia, 1897

WITH *Stoddart's Team in Australia* is a fascinating book about a disappointing tour. 'The team left England in September, 1897,' *Wisden* records, 'full of hope that the triumph of three years before would be repeated, but came home a thoroughly beaten side.' The 'English Team' as *Wisden* refers to them, won the first Test by nine wickets but were beaten in the remaining four, twice by an innings, once by eight wickets, and finally by six wickets.

There were various reasons for this unexpected failure. Several players failed to adapt to Australian light and pitches, there was an influenza epidemic among the English players that had lasting effects, and Richardson was badly incapacitated by rheumatism, unbalancing the attack. Ranji himself, one of the few successes of the tour, was frequently ill. As a result, the comparative figures for the two sides make sad reading. Seven Australians averaged over 35 as against three English, and while six Australians shared the wickets, only Hearne and Richardson at appreciably greater cost did any damage at all. Hirst took 2 for 304, Hayward 4 for 164, and Briggs 9 for 485. Against this compare Noble's 19 wickets at 20.26,

Ernest Jones's 22 at 25 and Trumble's 19 at 28.

In batting, there was less difference at the top, Darling, McLeod and Hill averaging 67, 58 and 56 as against MacLaren's average of 54 and Ranji's of 50, but whereas the Australians batted consistently down the order, the English did not. Once the Australians had squared the series in the second Test in Melbourne there was only one side in it.

The present book, based on a diary kept by Ranji, was published by James Bowden and went into at least four editions the same year. It is unlikely that Ranji wrote every word, more probable that he passed over his notes and gave his opinions in conversation to a practising journalist, a practice not unknown today. He was contributing articles on the tour to the Australian *Review of Reviews* and these evidently form the basis of certain chapters.

The result, however contrived, is unmistakably Ranji, the technical and tactical observations displaying the same simple authority as those in *The Jubilee Book of Cricket*. The viewpoint is essentially that of a player writing at first hand, rather than that of a critically detached observer. The immense gain is that we get a vivid, fresh and informed account of what it actually felt like to be on that particular tour, whether on the voyage out, travelling the country, or on the field of play. Ranji's observations, whether on wickets, the dubious action of Jones, crowd behaviour, or the differences in technique between the players of either side, are tersely to the point. Naturally, he is courteous to his own colleagues, discussing failure sympathetically, though without indulgence.

The main loss is that about Ranji himself there is almost nothing. Were he on the sidelines this would scarcely have mattered but with MacLaren he was one of the two stars of the side. Not only that, but he acquired a notoriety that resulted in bats, matchboxes, hair-restorers and chairs being named after him. He was courted by Australian society, celebrated by cartoonists, and on occasion, largely due to his criticism of the fairness of Jones's delivery, fiercely barracked.

Ranji began in great style, matching a brilliant double century by Clem Hill in the opening game at Adelaide with 189 by himself. In the first Test at Sydney, Ranji, suffering badly from a throat infection and not long out of bed, went in at number seven, scoring 175. He was in at the death with MacLaren, who made 109

and 50 not out, when England won the match with the loss of only one second innings wicket.

At Melbourne, when England faced a daunting total of 520, Ranji batted handsomely to make top score of 71 and on a broken wicket in the second innings 27 out of 150. At Adelaide Australia again topped 500, Ranji making 6 and 77, the latter with a badly bruised finger, in England's second successive innings defeat.

At Melbourne, in the fourth Test, when England lost the toss for the third time running, Ranji made more than anyone else for his side, though only 24 and 55. At Sydney, in the final Test, Ranji was out to a brilliant catch for 2 in the first innings and to a bad decision for 12 in the second. Altogether he made 457 runs in the Tests, and 1,157 runs in all matches, with an average of 60.89. Only MacLaren, who had a fine tour, approached him with 1,037 runs at 54.57.

After leaving the *Ormuz* at Colombo on the return voyage Ranji, still some way from being assured of succession to the throne of Nawanagar, spent over a year in India. In his next meeting with the Australians, at Trent Bridge in 1899, he played one of his greatest innings, making 93 not out and saving the game.

An Indian Playing for England

WHAT IS REMARKABLE about Ranji, among many other things, is how quickly he became a 'character'; before the end even of his first season he had acquired a following. Few people outside Sussex, except perhaps the regulars at Lord's, can have seen him more than half a dozen times at most, yet already he was a star. It was by no means only because he was Indian, a bloom of the tropics; not all Indian cricketers have caught the public fancy. Nor was it because, like the Aga Khan, for instance, in matters of the Turf, he was a great swell. He became that, too. But in these earliest of days it was simply because of his prowess. He batted, as he looked, like no one else. 'Prince Ranjitsinhji being now the people's darling, everyone who follows cricket can conjure up his form in the field, at point or short slip – alert and intent, ever poised ready to spring on the ball like a panther. Everyone knows how his hands find each other behind his back between the delivery of ball and ball, how the back of his gossamer shirt flutters in the wind while tremors ripple down to the wristbands which he keeps always so tightly fastened. And everyone knows how, during the interval between a wicket and 'man in', no one is so keen upon the ball as the Indian Prince, no one has so many subtle ways of throwing it, or is a greater adept at catching it – now a hair's breadth almost from the Turf, now a yard above his head.'

The mannerisms, the attire, had become public knowledge, but they were merely extensions of the player. In 1896, only his second season in the first-class game, the rumour of Ranji was to become living legend.

It was, once again, an Australian summer, Harry Trott leading a side whose attack included Griffen, Jones and Trumble. Ranji was so soon into his stride for Sussex, 30 and 74 against MCC at Lord's, 64 and 33 against Lancashire at Old Trafford, hundreds in successive matches against Yorkshire, Gloucestershire and Somerset, that by the beginning of June he had established himself as the most exciting batsman in the country. In addition, at Sheffield Park, that most lush of Sussex estates, he made 79 and 42 for Lord Sheffield's eleven in the Australians' opening fixture.

Despite all Ranji's runs Sussex had not prospered. Lancashire, largely through Mold's ferocity on a lively wicket, beat them comfortably, and Yorkshire by ten wickets. Grace's double century at Hove enabled

Gloucestershire to hold out for a draw, and Somerset in the next match were rescued by Lionel Palairet.

There was no doubt, though, that if he were considered, Ranji must be a certainty for the first Test, to start at Lord's on 22 June. He had made his runs, often in difficult conditions, against the best bowlers in England.

But the circumstances of an Indian playing for England were ones never before considered. In 1896, and it was the last year in which this was the case, Test teams were not chosen by an independent selection committee, but by the county at whose ground the match was to be played. Thus MCC, whose President was the Lord Harris, six years previously Governor of Bombay, were responsible for the team for Lord's, Lancashire for the Old Trafford side, Surrey for the final Test at The Oval.

Lord Harris was not, in fact, in favour of playing what he called 'birds of passage', and Ranji, though asked to make himself available, was not chosen for the Lord's Test, an omission that resulted in public and press outcry. Some thirty years later Duleepsinhji, Ranji's much cherished nephew and little less a player, played in the first Test against South Africa but, objected to by the South Africans, agreed to stand down for the rest of the series.

The Australians, when Ranji was selected to play in the second Test at Old Trafford three weeks later, raised no such objections. Ranji, on being invited, insisted that the Australians should be consulted. They were,

Trott expressed his delight, and no more was heard of the matter.

As sometimes happens when selectors miss the tide, Ranji went through an indifferent patch after his wonderful May. Indeed, between 30 May, when he made 107 in the second innings against Somerset at Hove, and 27 June, when he scored 171 not out against Oxford at Hove, Ranji batted seven times for Sussex at an average of 16. He did, however, make 7, 146 and 30 for MCC, and 47 and 51 not out for the Gentlemen. The Gentlemen v. Players match took place at Lord's immediately before the Old Trafford Test. This was Ranji's first appearance in the Lord's fixture and he entertained everyone in a crowd of ten thousand with his batting on the opening morning. 'One of the most brilliant and delightful pieces of batting seen at Lord's last season' was how *Wisden* described it. The Gentlemen, despite their weak bowling, beat the Players by seven wickets, Woods and Grace taking five wickets in the first and second innings respectively, and Ranji and Jackson making 98 and 97 in the match for once out. Ranji, incidentally, batted only ten minutes for his 47, hitting a boundary off each of the twelve balls he received except one, which he put away for three. The Players' bowling included Richardson, of whom Ranji was contemptuously dismissive, Briggs, Lohmann and Hearne. Not surprisingly the packed pavilion, then only six years old in its present form, rose to him.

After the Lord's Test, which England won by six wickets, Richardson and Lohmann bowling Australia out before lunch on the first day for 53 – Ranji came back to form for Sussex, putting together 69 and 73 against Kent at Hastings. Two and 36 against Surrey at The Oval – rarely a happy ground – was one of his quieter games, but by then he had received A. N. Hornby's invitation to take the place of William Gunn at Old Trafford. Gunn, though now thirty-eight, was a trifle unlucky to be dropped, having made 25 and 13 not out at Lord's. He played again for England against Australia three years later, on his home ground of Trent Bridge, and this time with Ranji. Jones bowled him for low scores in each innings and he was never picked for England again.

Since their defeat at Lord's the Australians had thrived. England made some odd changes, MacLaren, who had scarcely played at all, replacing Tom Hayward, and Briggs coming in at the last moment for Lohmann, who reported unwell on the morning of the match.

Old Trafford tends to have extremes of weather, pouring rain or tropical heat. On this occasion it was the latter, and once Trott had won the toss and chosen to bat, England were soon rueing the absence of a fourth regular bowler. The Australians got off to a good start in ideal batting conditions. Iredale, left out of the first Test, made a handsome hundred, Giffen 80 and Trott 53. With Australia 240 for 2 at one stage, Grace was in some trouble, calling on seven bowlers without much success. In the end Richardson, despite bowling 68 overs in the innings, all with the same ball as was then the custom, found a second wind, taking the last five wickets and finishing with 7 for 168. Australia were all out for 412, a good deal less than at one time seemed likely.

England, with weather and wicket still excellent, made a dreadful start. Trott, surprisingly opening the bowling himself with Jones – at Lord's it had been Jones and Giffen – had both Grace and Stoddart stumped with only 23 on the board. Ranji, batting at number three, took the score to 104 with Abel, but wickets fell steadily thereafter, despite the fact that Jones strained a muscle and could only bowl five overs. Ranji was caught by Trott off McKibbin for 62, and only a bold 65 not out by Lilley, going in at number eight, took England past the 200.

Ranji alone of the earlier batsmen had shown anything. His and Lilley's efforts were not, however, enough to save the follow-on. By the second evening England, 109 for 4, seemed to have been cornered. Ranji was still there, but Grace had failed for the second time in the match, Stoddart had been bowled by McKibbin for 41, and just before close of play Giffen had removed Abel and Jackson in quick succession.

The large crowds of the first two days, sensing an early defeat for England, declined to part with their money a third time. England, after all, were still 72 behind and the main batting had gone.

They missed something for although Brown was out for 19 at 132 and MacLaren for 15 at 179, Ranji, as *Wisden* put it, 'rose to the occasion, playing an innings that could, without exaggeration, be fairly described as marvellous.'

Wisden is not usually remarkable for other than the plainest of descriptive prose. In this instance their account rises to the occasion, too.

'Ranjitsinhji very quickly got set again, and punished the Australian bowlers in a style that, up to that period of the season, no other English batsman had approached. He repeatedly brought off his wonderful strokes on the leg-side, and for a while had the Australian bowlers quite at his mercy ... Ranjitsinhji's remarkable batting, and the prospect of the Englishmen after all running their opponents close, worked the spectators up to a high pitch of excitement, and the scene of enthusiasm was something to be remembered when the Indian cricketer completed the first hundred against the Australians ... It is safe to say that a finer or more finished display has never been seen on a great occasion, for he never gave anything like a chance, and during his long stay the worst that could be urged against him was that he made a couple of lucky snicks. He was at the wicket for three hours ten minutes, and among his hits were twenty-three 4s, five 3s and nine 2s.'

No one could write handsomer than that. Ranji carried his bat for 154, the next highest score of the innings on the last day was 19, and England were all out 305.

The Australians, needing only 125 to win, put on 20 without sign of unease. At this point Richardson, beginning a fantastic spell of fast, hostile bowling, bowled Iredale, century-maker in the first innings, for 11. Six runs later he had Darling caught at the wicket. At 28 Ranji caught Giffen off him at slip, and at 45 Trott was taken behind the wicket.

Suddenly the outcome seemed far from being a foregone conclusion, though the pitch was still playing as well as at any time in the match. Gregory and Donnan, however, inched their way forward, until at 79 Gregory was caught by Ranji at short leg off Briggs. Donnan was out at 95, Hill at 100, both to Richardson who had bowled unchanged.

With three wickets left Australia needed 25. With only nine more needed Lilley dropped Kelly off Richardson. Trumble and Kelly, however, hanging on by the skin of their teeth, saw Australia safely home. The last 25 runs, every one of which had to be fought for, took an hour to make and were made in absolute silence.

Once victorious, the Australians were given a great reception by the Manchester crowd, swelled in the sultry afternoon by a steady flow of those in the city who had picked up the signals.

If it was Ranji who initially set up

the finish for one of the most dramatic of Test matches, Tom Richardson's performance was one of the greatest by a fast bowler. Altogether Richardson bowled 110 overs in the match, taking 13 wickets for 244. Neville Cardus wrote about Richardson: 'He looked the part: tall, splendidly built and proportioned, with a long – not too long – striding run culminating in a beautifully poised leap, left shoulder and side pointing down the wicket, the right arm swinging over, then finishing near or behind the left hip.'

Richardson, in his prime 'as handsome a sight as was ever seen in a cricket field, dark, black-haired, black-moustached', was famous for his break-back. Cardus wrote that when he came up to the wicket to release the ball he called to mind a great wave of the sea about to break.

This was the same Richardson, among the greatest in the long line of English fast bowlers, whom Ranji had despatched so cruelly at Lord's a week before. Richardson, in 1894–95 in Australia, had taken 69 wickets at 23.42, and in the season after this one, pounding down on the lifeless Surrey pitch, he was to take 273 wickets. He died mysteriously in the Swiss mountains – allegedly of his own volition, aged only forty-one.

After this, the next few weeks were inevitably something of an anti-climax. Ranji, in the Bank Holiday match at Hove against Middlesex, disappointed the huge seaside crowd that had come to see him bat, making only 2 and 18 in a 9-wickets Sussex defeat. He made up for this, though, in the very next match, going in at seven in the first innings against Nottinghamshire and making 52 out of 177, and in the second innings 100 not out. Sussex, as so often in the summer of 1896, failed in the first innings and then recovered so well in the second that hopeless causes were often redeemed. The innocuousness of their bowling, nevertheless, meant that though they often saved matches they rarely won them.

Sussex, with Ranji's eye on fishing possibilities and the grouse season coming up, now set off on their West Country tour. Ranji enjoyed himself with 38 and 54 in a losing cause at Bristol, where Grace made 301. Grace having already taken 243 not out off the Sussex bowling at Hove, every hair on his beard must have now been familiar to them. Gloucestershire only got home in the Bristol match with a quarter of an hour to spare, Ranji making them fight to the last, though with negligible support.

The match against Somerset at Taunton was a freak affair. When rain caused the match to be abandoned Sussex had made 559 and Somerset 476 for 6 wickets. Ranji scored 54, most of them in company with Fry, while the left-handed Killick batted over six hours for 191. Somerset lost an early wicket to Fred Tate, after which the Palairet brothers put on 249, both scoring over 150. A year earlier they had made hundreds in the same innings against Middlesex.

ALAN ROSS

AUSTRALIA

F. A. Iredale, b. Briggs	108	b. Richardson	11
J. Darling, c. Lilley, b. Richardson	27	c. Lilley, b. Richardson	16
G. Giffen, c. and b. Richardson	80	c. Ranjitsinhji, b. Richardson	6
*G. H. S. Trott, c. Brown, b. Lilley	53	c. Lilley, b. Richardson	2
S. E. Gregory, c. Stoddart, b. Briggs	25	c. Ranjitsinhji, b. Briggs	33
H. Donnan, b. Richardson	12	c. Jackson, b. Richardson	15
C. Hill, c. – Jackson, b. Richardson	9	c. Lilley, b. Richardson	14
H. Trumble, b. Richardson	24	not out	17
†J. J. Kelly, c. Lilley, b. Richardson	27	not out	8
T. R. McKibbin not out	28		
E. Jones, b. Richardson	4		
Extras b. 6, l.b. 8, w. 1	15	Extras (l.b. 3)	3
Total	412	Total (7 wkts.)	125

FALL OF WICKETS: *First Innings* — 1–41, 2–172, 3–242, 4–294, 5–294, 6–314, 7–325, 8–362, 9–403, 10–412. *Second Innings* — 1–20, 2–26, 3–28, 4–45, 5–79, 6–95, 7–100.

BOWLING: *First Innings* — Richardson, 68–23–168–7; Briggs, 40–18–99–2; Jackson, 16–6–34–0; Hearne, 28–11–53–0; Grace, 7–3–11–0; Stoddart, 6–2–9–0; Lilley, 5–1–23–1. *Second Innings* — Richardson, 42.3–16–76–6; Briggs, 18–8–24–1; Hearne, 24–13–22–0.

ENGLAND

*W. G. Grace, st. Kelly, b. Trott	2	c. Trott, b. Jones	11
A. E. Stoddart st Kelly b Trott	15	b. McKibbin	41
K. S. Ranjitsinhji, c. Trott, b. McKibbin	62	not out	154
R. Abel, c. Trumble, b. McKibbin	26	c. McKibbin, b. Giffen	13
F. S. Jackson run out	18	c. McKibbin, b. Giffen	1
J. T. Brown, c. Kelly, b. Trumble	22	c. Iredale, b. Jones	19
A. C. MacLaren, c. Trumble, b. McKibbin	0	c. Jones, b. Trumble	15
†A. F. A. Lilley not out	65	c. Trott, b. Giffen	19
J. Briggs, b. Trumble	0	st. Kelly, b. McKibbin	16
J. T. Hearne, c. Trumble, b. Giffen	18	c. Kelly, b. McKibbin	9
T. Richardson run out	2	c. Jones, b. Trumble	1
Extras (b. 1)	1	Extras (b. 2, l.b. 3, w. 1)	6
Total	231	Total	305

FALL OF WICKETS: *First Innings* — 1–2, 2–23, 3–104, 4–111, 5–140, 6–140, 7–154, 8–166, 9–219, 10–213. *Second Innings* — 1–33, 2–76, 3–97, 4–109, 5–132, 6–179, 7–232, 8-268, 9-304, 10-305.

BOWLING: *First Innings* — Jones, 5–2–11–0; Trott, 10–0–46–2; Giffen, 19–3–48–1; Trumble, 37–14–80–2; McKibbin, 19–8–45–3. *Second Innings* — Jones, 17–0–78–2; Trott, 7–1–17–0; Giffen, 16–1–65–3; Trumble, 29.1–12–78–2; McKibbin, 21–4–61–3.

UMPIRES: J. Phillips, A. Chester. *Captain †Wicket keeper

W. G. Grace

I SUPPOSE WE HAVE to admit that W. G. Grace, if not the most appealing, was, as Robert Low puts it in his excellent new biography,* 'the greatest cricketer England has ever seen'. His career certainly lasted the longest (1865–1908), and his physical presence and authoritarian manner dwarfed most of his contemporaries. In runs scored on often dreadful pitches he was on his own, until a ripe middle age, and he nine times took over 100 wickets in a season. Until he became too stout to bend over he was a safe, if not agile, fielder.

Yet no one thought him an attractive batsman, any more than Bradman was. They were a pair of acquisitive squirrels, ungainly in Grace's case, but confident in method, hawk-eyed, determined, eschewers of the fancy. As a captain Grace was self-indulgent to his own bowling and appeared to lose interest when others were in action. He was not an imaginative leader or a thoughtful tactician. I wonder, if he had been a smaller man, whether he would have seemed so heroic and remarkable.

All agree that he was a 'mighty Victorian', in an age that produced what now seem great men, but he was disappointingly limited. Clifford Bax, in his elegant monograph of 1952, which Low appears not to have read, remarked of the Grace brothers that they were 'among Matthew Arnold's philistines'. They knew nothing of their towering contemporaries, inhabiting a world that at no point touched that of the great writers, artists, and political figures of their day. It seems a pity.

There have been a number of biographies of Grace, even more books in which he is a leading figure, but Robert Low's is the fullest and probably the best written. Grace, never one to hold back, of course wrote about himself but not very enterprisingly. Ranji, with the aid of C. B. Fry, dissected Grace's methods the most revealingly: 'by making forward and back play of equal importance . . . he turned an old one-stringed instrument into a many-chorded lyre'. Polite as ever, Ranji observed that 'what W. G. did was to make utility the criterion of style,' a remark that applies equally to Bradman.

As I discovered only too quickly

W. G.

149

when I embarked on my biography of Ranji, the actual playing details of long ago matches, scores, results, averages, statistics, are difficult to keep interesting. Not surprisingly the performances in Grace's career are the least lively part of Low's book. After all, you can follow these in *Wisden*.

There is, though, an excellent chapter on Grace the cricketer as seen by his contemporaries and Low's 12-page introduction is so masterly a piece of compression that, in a sense, what follows is almost superfluous. He doesn't answer the question about why Grace grew so bushy a beard, surely a hindrance when taking guard, but he deals succinctly with everything else, his appetite for money, his occasional doctoring, his sharp practices, his kindnesses, his outbursts of temper, his autocratic behaviour.

C. L. R. James saw Grace as 'pre-Victorian', despite the fact that Victoria had been Queen for 11 years before Grace was born. Neville Cardus more accurately found him archetypally 'Eminent Victorian', instantly recognisable by the common man.

Robert Low convincingly sees him as intrinsically modern, a professional through and through. Grace's colleagues resented his comparatively large earnings from the game, which greatly exceeded those of everyone else, including the professionals, though he was nominally an amateur. But he was a star, who added thousands to the gate.

A West Country man, who ended his days in southeast London beagling and golfing, a legendary figure as a cricketer, a family man – Low gives all aspects of this monumental figure just about the right amount of space. By recent standards his biography of 295 pages is modest. There are excellent photographs, including early ones of Grace tall and slender, but none beardless.

Harold Larwood

IT IS HARD TO think of a character less suited to the limelight, even less to being the centre of notorious controversy, than Harold Larwood. The main protagonist in 1932–33 of Bodyline, the bowling of fast, short-pitched balls on the line of the body to a legside field, Larwood was never more responsible than the infantry-man who is ordered to go over the top. The theory was conceived by others and the orders given by the captain D. R. Jardine. In his previous Test series against England, that of 1930, Bradman had made scores of 8, 131, 254, 1, 334, 14, 232 – an average of 139.14. Larwood in that series had taken 4 for 292, and was dropped for one Test. Australia won the series.

Something needed to be done. Larwood had already played a series in Australia, that of 1928–29, when he took 18 wickets for 728 – including 6 for 32 in the first Test at Brisbane. He bowled then to a conventional fast bowler's field. Bradman averaged 66.85. At the end of the Bodyline series Bradman averaged 56, Larwood had taken 33 wickets at an average of 19.51, and England had won by four Tests to one.

Bodyline, then, could be desig-nated, in practical terms, a success. But the feelings it aroused did great damage to the relationship between England and Australia, and Larwood himself was so upset by the criticism that he declined to play against Australia when they next appeared in England in 1934. Larwood, who had demonstrated such phenomenal speed and accuracy in carrying out instruc-tions, was never again a Test bowler of consequence. He was obliged, as a result of the strain imposed on his left leg, to cut down his run and to bowl at nowhere near his original pace.

Neville Cardus, watching this secondary Larwood bowl in his last season, was moved to write: 'Fast bowling is dying out. Alf Gover runs on the flat of his feet, and bowls not much faster off the pitch than the Larwood of today; Larwood who now is compelled to use the canter of compromise instead of his old lovely gallop over the earth, head down, like a young colt chafing his bit.'

Cardus was rather too keen to write off the modern player. 'Larwood was the last of the classical bowlers,' he wrote. 'He showed his left side to the batsman, as Tom Richardson did. His body swung over the right hip, and his follow-through was thrilling.' But Lindwall, a decade or so later, bowled with the same lovely flowing action. Bedser and Lillee showed their left shoulders to the batsman, and certainly Frank Tyson, in 1954–55, must have been as fast.

Ian Peebles has given the most evocative description of Larwood in action: 'He ran about 18 yards, accelerating with controlled rhythmical strides, on the last of which his shoulders opened with a long swing of his fully extended arms. His right hand described a great arc starting from near the calf of his leg, and, at full pressure, his knuckles would touch the pitch on his follow-through. Co-ordination was perfect, so that the whole concerted effort was applied to the moment of delivery.'

Larwood came from mining stock and mining country. He was rather less than medium height, but in any photograph his head was raised an inch or two by the thick shock of hair cut flat across the top. He was stocky in the manner of Fred Trueman, and he had to contend for far too much of his playing life with unresponsive, doped pitches. In the circumstances it was surprising that he lasted as long as he did, 1924–1938, even though the last four seasons were at half-cock.

In Larwood's time, the 1920s and 30s, professional cricketers did not on the whole ask for much and they did not get much. They had, most of them, the manner and speech of countrymen. Larwood may have been exceptional, but only in his bowling. All those who knew him and played with him remarked on his unassuming character, his domestic nature. 'In cricket between the wars,' Robertson-Glasgow once wrote, 'the two most magnificent sights that I have seen were Hammond batting and Larwood bowling ... in both these cricketers I have found something heroic, something of immortal fire, which conquers argument.'

The career of Larwood, 'who blew like a gale and bent the flower of Australia', Robertson-Glasgow puts as a mere eight years. It was a fact that, even more than most fast bowlers, Larwood had to be nursed. He was in the real sense a 'strike' bowler, best used in short, lethal spells. Despite the long arms and strong back the frame could only stand so much. It is not recorded that Harold Larwood had much to say outside cricket. While the Gods once lifted him to something like immortality they put him down again, gently and soon, when they had no more use for him.

So Larwood by the age of 30 had bowled his last ball in a Test match and returned to the unspectacular circuit of the county grounds. He never lost his Nottinghamshire accent, he took up shopkeeping, and he and his wife produced five daughters. The times in England were not good to him and he made the long voyage to Australia with his family. He settled peacefully in what had once been enemy territory and he spoke sometimes with visiting English cricketers who felt honoured to be able to call on him. He was, after all, the man with whose name fast bowling was synonymous.

H. LARWOOD NOTTINGHAMSHIRE
BORN 14.11.04, NUNCARGATE, NOTTS

BATTING

	Matches	Innings	Not out	Runs	Highest score	Avg	100
Test	21	28	3	485	98	19.40	0
First-class	361	438	72	7,290	102*	19.91	3

BOWLING AND FIELDING

	Runs	Wickets	Avg	5 W/I	10 W/M	BB	Ct	St
Test	2,212	78	28.35	4	1	6/32	15	0
First-class	24,994	1,427	17.51	98	20	9/41	234	0

Crusoe

IT SEEMS TO ME important, for the pleasure of his contemporaries, for the use of cricket historians and addicts, for future cricket correspondents and for students of good prose generally, that a one-volume edition of Raymond Robertson-Glasgow's writing on cricket should exist. It has not been an easy book to compile, for Crusoe wrote for newspapers for over thirty years and much of his best work has a necessarily ephemeral context. That this should be so, however, is the fate of every journalist; sub-editors usually get at the most telling and vivid images anyway, and those that survive go down into obscurity with the incidents that produced them. In Robertson-Glasgow's case this was the more serious, since, unlike Cardus, he was not really an essayist, nor did he publish any accounts of overseas tours, such as would have been testimony to his evocative skill and overall tactical shrewdness. In this last respect he was unlucky, for he had planned a book about the 1950–51 MCC tour of Australia, which he was covering for *The Observer*; unfortunately *The Times* correspondent fell ill, Robertson-Glasgow did his job, and his own book, which he had nearly finished, was made obsolete by *The Times* publishing all the match reports he had done for them in a booklet of their own. It was a great disappointment to him and the waste of a lot of work. As a result, his professional brilliance as a daily journalist must be taken largely on trust. About 1953, when I succeeded him on *The Observer*, he felt he had done enough about cricket and turned to other things. He was not very well at the time and he preferred in future to write from the security of his cottage at Pangbourne rather than to report from the field of play. He suffered most of his life from severe and recurrent bouts of depression and in the circumstances the tone and charity of his writing was astonishing.

This present volume, *Crusoe on Cricket*, as it stands, contains the cream of the half-dozen or so books that he produced. By 'cream' I mean most of the milk too, for when I came to select I found that there was little, for one reason or another, that seemed to me superfluous or dated. He got as much out of the obscure as out of the famous, and I think he preferred them. He saw cricketers as characters, not as robots, and I have found it necessary to jettison less than half out of the two full volumes of Sporting Prints that he collected during his life and on which his fame deservedly rests. There may be occasional repetitions, and sometimes other games creep in, particularly golf, but even when he described the same players twice, at different moments of their careers, he imposed a fresh vision of them.

He was a miniaturist, a master of compression, concise, elegant, witty.

The form of much of his writing was dictated by the exigencies of the 700–800 word 'print' but I think in any case that he could say all he wanted in that space. His style was the result equally of a classical education and of a romantic temperament, and he had the real cricketer's indifference to statistics. Where Cardus, in Crusoe's own phrase, was 'master of the rhapsodical style, cutting his sharp epigrams from the most amorphous material', Robertson-Glasgow was the gentle but high-spirited deflater. 'On the great moments and the great cricketers, he has no equal,' Crusoe observed about Cardus, 'but, amid his copiousness, he is eclectic.' He himself was eclectic but not copious. Cardus's materials were the Lancashire and England teams of the twenties and thirties; Crusoe was at his happiest with Oxford and Somerset, with schools and villages. He wrote about Test matches as if they took place in the Parks, as no doubt he wished they did. This does not mean he was disinterested in high drama or the legendary players. He merely recoiled from the boring, the self-centred, the thoroughly ordinary, even when these brought results. Between 1920 and 1950 he still managed to dissect the technique and convey the character of nearly all of those who played out the essential history of their time. No one else did so quite as well.

I have thought it sensible here to print first an extract from *46 Not*

Out, the autobiography Crusoe published in 1948. This covers the years 1920–24, that is to say the Oxford and Somerset period during which he was, as he calls it, a 'practising cricketer' rather than an 'intervener'. It sets the background and, as it were, establishes the credentials, though this seems scarcely necessary. For the rest of his life Crusoe played at weekends or in the summer holidays. He must, with his high, rollicking action, have been a formidable bowler in 1924, able to get the inswinger to straighten out at a lively pace, and occasionally veer late the other way, and fifteen years or so later he had not lost the knack, though some of the zip. My own appearances with or against him were long after he had given up regular first-class cricket, but I remember at Oxford in 1941, when he played against us before we went to Lord's, being astonished at his pace from the pitch. He was even able, in the Authors v. Publishers matches of the early fifties, to get some bounce off the Westminster School wicket at Vincent's Square and anyone who can do that at the age of 50 is no mean bowler.

Next, in order, comes *The Brighter Side of Cricket*, almost in its entirety. This was published in 1938, and was Crusoe's first book. It has always been an especial favourite of mine, not only because it was given to me as a reward for captaining an eccentric but unbeaten preparatory school team, but because it opened my eyes to what cricket was really

about, its discipline and grace, its jokey comedy, its rich nostalgias and fantasies. I have read it a score of times and know much of it by heart.

The third section contains a selection from the two volumes of *Cricket Prints* published initially in 1943 and 1948. Most of these appeared in *The Observer* and though some of their subjects are now little more than names they form part of a unique gallery of portraits. They came into being because someone died or retired or emigrated or scored a hundred hundreds, or perhaps just because a space had to be filled. I intended to cut out the more obviously topical, but in the end I could hardly bear to. In any faded old team photograph the humbler have, after all, as much right to their place as the others.

The three last sections, taken from *Rain Stopped Play*, 1948, *Cricket Prints*, 1948, and *All in the Game*, 1952, are, on the whole, more frivolous, written when Crusoe was edging away from the dialectics of the Press box and back towards the village match. I have included nothing from *How to Become a Test Cricketer*, 1962, because there is nothing in it he had not done better before and also because in any case it is obtainable. Nearly everything else in this book has long been out of print. I don't think anything of consequence is missing, nor that any of it is irrelevant.

I need say no more here about the writer, at home equally with the great and the insignificant, able as fluently to suggest Tate bowling and Sutcliffe batting, the blacksmith slogging and the curate taking one on the shins. From his prose the smell of linseed oil and ancient pads, of village dressing rooms and of the Long Room at Lord's, come over with equal vividness. It is always a cricketer writing.

But the man was no less remarkable. The thing you noticed about him first, apart from a resemblance to the actor Alastair Sim, was his reverberating laugh. He had, when speaking, a disconcerting habit of thrusting his face right up close to yours, never moving his eyes off you, and then, swaying away out of reach like a boxer, of throwing back his head and roaring. It was a laugh that penetrated all corners of a pavilion and there was no gainsaying it.

He was a fabulous talker, a restless match for Fry and Cardus in invention, anecdote and energy, and he wore his learning very lightly. He was tremendous company, unless you were feeling frail, though his infectious conviviality must often have been an effort. But behind the jovialness and the joking there was a considerateness, a gravity that rarely got into his writing. Above all, he was a man of great sweetness and charm, of abiding loyalties and surprising compassion. With Cardus, he helped to raise cricket reporting from journalism into an art. Those who never saw him bowl or heard his laugh will, I hope, get something of his real flavour from these pages.

Farewell to Alec Bedser

ALEC BEDSER'S retirement after the end of this season marks the last retreat of the great players who, mainly on the losing side, held England together in the struggling decade after the war. Hutton, Washbrook, Compton, Edrich, Evans, and now Bedser, who for the best part of ten years *was* England's bowling.

For most of this time he had no regular fast bowler at the other end.

He was never favoured like Statham, Tyson and Trueman, who have always known the comforting presence of each other, besides commanding their own real pace. Bedser had to do it the hard way, unsupported by reliable batting, or at his peak, by top-class spin or fast bowling.

By the time Statham was ready, he himself was on the unwitting edge of his Test career, for out of the blue a year later the brief tornado of Frank

Tyson toppled him over. That was in Australia, in 1955. Bedser had gone out as our leading bowler, but early on he developed shingles and never really recovered on that tour. At Sydney, on a wicket made for him, Hutton took what seemed the sensational and unjustifiable gamble of leaving him out.

In that Test and the next one Tyson made history. Alec seemed scarcely able to comprehend it. 'I don't know, I don't know,' he kept on repeating, with the bewilderment of one whose hair had been turned white overnight by some incomprehensible and uncalled for vision. Only it was real enough. Bedser played once more, against South Africa in 1955, but his Test career, one that had brought him more wickets than any English bowler, was suddenly over. In future, the knife would still cut, but it no longer drew blood.

He was never more than a lively fast medium, though the ball fizzed off the pitch into Evans's gloves with an exhilarating thud. He was a bowler, one felt, by *métier*, as some are locksmiths, or bootmakers or violinists. An over by him with the ball cut viciously from leg, or dipping in late to have the short legs diving, was the end product of years of training and devoted application. He practised a noble art, in which diligence, skill and cunning were reinforced by honest toil.

An ungainly mover when not bowling – I remember him complaining once in Lennon's Hotel, Brisbane, 'I don't know about all this talk of beautiful movers. What difference does it make how people move as long as they get there?' – he had an ease of delivery that came very near, through its perfect suitability for the purpose, to being beautiful.

He walked back with an authority that made his stature, in every sense, plain. His run-up was both relaxed and to the point, exactly preparatory in its steady gaining of tension to that final devastating swing of the massive shoulders. At the crucial pivoting moment the left arm was extended and high, the hand with the ball low and diagonally almost in line. The hips rotated, the left foot came down with a thud to jar the Antipodes, and the ball was let loose as if catapulted.

Bedser's, far more than a fast bowler's, was an art of variety. He was as absorbing to study, with his changes of pace, of swing and cut, as Laker. Watching him through glasses on his way back to bowl, his brow beaded with sweat, his brain thinking dark thoughts, was an exercise in prediction. What was it to be this time? One on the off, darting away at the last second; one on the leg stump but ready to spring towards the off if not stunned; or the one lazily swinging in from off to leg with a late acceleration that, with Lock round the corner, made any stroke a hazard? It was impossible to tell, for his mastery over them all was near complete, his instinct unique and infallible.

Infallible? Well, as infallible as it is possible for a swing bowler to be. Sometimes, it is true, the ostensible leg-cutter went the other way, the inswinger without permission straightened out. If you hold the seam upright and let it go with enough power the ball develops an energy and will of its own. Bedser, like Maurice Tate, experienced the unholy joy of those who put themselves in trust to that raised strip of white stitching; and sometimes he, no less than the batsman, had to raise a questioning eyebrow at the result.

A metaphorical questioning anyway, for Bedser, even now that his arm has sunk with the setting sun, is not one to give anything away.

As a batsman – a Meccano figure not quite adjusted – he rarely attempted the difficult and could make the straightforward appear oddly adventurous. Yet, in Test matches especially, he had his stirring and great moments and in earlier days was not so easily shifted.

Finally, in his true role of bowler, he is, even in decline, beautifully rhythmic and sprung; not disintegrating, but like a chronometer made by one of the Swiss masters, merely running down, unable to be rewound.

P. B. H. May

THE MOST NOTICEABLE thing about Peter May's appearance was his parting, a clean, undeviating line from crown to temple in hair cut neatly short, a symbolic representation of single-mindedness and innocence.

For the whole of his comparatively short career – he retired at 32 – Peter had the look of a schoolboy. It was not only the haircut, but a certain downward demeanour, a nasal diffidence of speech. He became, at the same time, Surrey, rather than Charterhouse or Cambridge, a professional amateur among professionals.

As a schoolboy, his flair almost uniquely precocious, he encouraged protectiveness among his fellows. Simon Raven, a colleague in the 1945 Charterhouse XI, describes how he was reprimanded by the head of the school for peeing out of a train window in front of Peter May, as if the boy virtuoso's integrity might he besmirched by Raven's natural coarseness.

Raven goes to some pains to correct the impression of May as a 'po-faced booby', as he terms it, and to record his intelligence and charm.

Charm he certainly had, and quiet dignity, never apparently ruffled on the field. He had a deadpan sense of humour. In the West Indies in 1960, when he had to make a speech at a dinner amid an outbreak of gastric trouble, he remarked gravely: 'I am assured that all water in this establishment has been passed by the manager.'

The immediate impression Peter made on coming out to bat was of exhilarating freshness. He never wore a cap and it is virtually impossible to imagine him in a helmet, any more than Leonard Hutton. He had a fine presence at the wicket, his stance full of naval command. When he ran between the wickets he was a shade ungainly, his over-large pads prone to flap like a goose's feathers. As the bowler approached he tensed slightly and then anything over-pitched would ricochet off the sightscreen with a bang. His effort-less placement of the on-drive, a stroke for which he had no equal, is deservedly famous, but his straight driving was truly thunderous.

I do not remember Peter ever playing a defensive innings, whatever the circumstances. The 1954–55 Ashes series was illuminated by his magnificently noisy 104 at Sydney and 91 at Melbourne, both in the second innings, a feature of his success at the time. When the Ashes were regained in 1956 he averaged 90, holding the innings together time after time with bravura batting. The 285 that broke the heart of Sonny Ramadhin the following summer could be considered a rearguard action, but it was never other than well struck.

He was not infallible. Richie Benaud took his wicket early on more than one crucial occasion, none more so than when he bowled him round his legs at Old Trafford in 1961. In South Africa in 1956–57, he scored 1,270 runs and six centuries outside the Tests but averaged 15 in the series, so it was doubly strange.

In 1960 Peter led England to the Caribbean, his final tour. The series was won, though not due to Peter, who was suffering throughout from an internal abscess and had to come home halfway through. He was unusually tetchy and never really himself.

Peter May was a laconic, generally courteous man, with the buttoned-up ambiguity of a Pinter character. I lunched with him after he retired and he showed no regrets at having packed up so early. He disliked critical attention and his stint as chairman of selectors between 1982 and 1988 was notably unsuccessful. He had more or less settled, as recreation from the City, to driving his four daughters to riding engagements. He had no wish to play any sort of cricket just for fun. He was well out of Melbourne this week.

Lucky Johnny, Lucky Jim

THE CRICKETER J. H. Wardle is a fair, stocky man of thirty-five, with unusually square shoulders, a chin that is something of a nutcracker, a broad Yorkshire accent, and the ability to bowl left-handed, out of the back of his hand, better than anyone else in the world.

On the cricket field he passes for what is known as a card: he has a simple but highly expert sense of visual clowning, which he exploits judiciously.

He amuses the crowd both when he succeeds and when he fails. As a batsman, he hits huge sixes or, alternately, misses by huge margins. As a fielder he pretends to catch and pocket the ball when it has long since passed him. When he is hit by the ball on the behind or thigh, he rubs his elbow.

As a bowler, he is a moderate performer on the kind of wet wickets that most slow left-handers would like to take around with them. On perfect batting pitches he is, in his orthodox manner, a steady defensive bowler. When these pitches show the slightest signs of wear, often even before, and he is encouraged to bowl leg-breaks and googlies, he is unique.

So it is that in conditions despised and feared by most bowlers, the slow, bone-hard but deadish pitches of the Commonwealth, the art of Wardle extracts its fullest flavour. It follows from this that in England Wardle can be duplicated, even improved on, at least while Lock has one good leg; in Australia and South Africa his rivals have no price.

Technically, that is all there is to it. In ten years of first-class cricket Wardle has been an invaluable member of the Yorkshire side, has toured the West Indies, Australia and South Africa with MCC, and accomplished a number of impressive performances for both.

In the West Indies he saved an explosive situation, after beer bottles had been thrown on the field by over-excited spectators, by pretending to drink out of them and staggering around the boundary as if intoxicated. In South Africa he was England's best bowler, the only one capable of turning a Test Match. On the last MCC tour of Australia he was, as bowler and batsman, crucial to the balance of the Test eleven.

As expected, therefore, when the names for the coming Australian tour were revealed three weeks ago, Wardle's name was among them. Both he and Jim Laker had earlier pronounced themselves unavailable for the tour: both changed their minds.

Very soon after, the Yorkshire committee chose to communicate the fact that, in the interests of what they called 'team building', they were not renewing Wardle's contract for the following season. He was informed of this personally by a member of the committee, who inferred, under later interrogation, that his language in front of the tender-eared Yorkshire professionals and his conduct and co-operation in general had contributed not a little to this surprise decision.

Then, by writing a series of articles in the popular Press, Wardle was deemed to have infringed his Yorkshire contract, which was, as a result, immediately terminated.

What had begun as a domestic matter between Wardle and the Yorkshire committee took on far-reaching implications. It became apparent that, in the cricket world, it was not by any means only the Yorkshire committee who thought that Wardle should be brought to heel: in this great fox-hunting country of ours, the fox is supposed to enjoy the hunt, but if he should turn on his assailants, then that is considered an act conducive to a most dangerous state of anarchy. They ought to have known better than to have cast Wardle in the role of the fox.

Nevertheless, such was the publicity, the daily Press waxing fat on so juicy a bone in a season of famine, that MCC issued, for no clear reason, a statement that at the next monthly meeting of the MCC full committee, whose job it would be to approve the work of the selection committee, the position of Wardle would, no doubt, be discussed.

No doubt it will, and on Tuesday the full committee of MCC, consisting of some 22 members, meets.

The real surprise about this whole affair is that, up to a month ago, the general public at least had no notion at all that Wardle was in any sense a bad social, if not security, risk. Had he been disclosed as a paid-up Communist Party member they could not have been more bewildered.

Those in the know were not, of course, quite so taken aback. Wardle is a blunt fellow, not over-sociable, not without a cutting Yorkshire sarcasm, not without a certain healthy regard for his own capabilities, not exactly overflowing with the milk of human kindness.

On the other hand, he is more sober than most, more self-contained, more responsible and single-minded in his powers of application. No one has ever regarded him as unruly or subversive: at the same time, not everyone has found his company an unmitigated pleasure.

The pros and cons of all this, it seems, will be solemnly debated in the committee room at Lord's on Tuesday. Perhaps it will take no more than a minute or two to blow it all away: perhaps it will breed a lot of hot air and have unhappy repercussions.

In the last resort, however, the issue is relatively simple. It is one of social conformity, of an individual, in this case a professional cricketer of great renown, accepting, irrespective of his merits, the place in the social hierarchy accorded him by his employers, and not protesting.

The Yorkshire Committee, of course, are free to make their own arrangements; they can neglect, if they wish, and as they have done over the past four years, three of the leading professional cricketers in the country, and choose for their captain, if they so wish, a retired brigadier or an amateur juggler.

That is their own affair. Whether it is an enlightened attitude or even a self-interested one is another matter. But the point that escapes them is that, whether they like it or not, the power has shifted, economically if in no other way, and Lucky Johnny Wardle and Lucky Jim Laker have discovered long since that they have, not just a tongue and a pen, but something to bargain with.

Only ostriches can afford to think otherwise, and to persist in the belief that there is no need ever to come to terms. This is the age of the technician, and the best man for the job expects to be regarded, and treated, as such. Let us hope, on Tuesday, that he is.

Over to Laker

THERE WAS A TIME when the reminiscences of famous cricketers were unreadable; now, as a rule, they tend to be unspeakable. Whether it's a change for the better or not is a matter of opinion; it depends on whether you prefer noncommittal pleasantries or uninhibited plain speaking.

Jim Laker's new sequence of autobiography, *Over to Me*, certainly comes into the latter category. In essence, it offers a Laker's eye-view of the 1958–59 series in Australia, the last tour to South Africa, and the winding-up of its author's playing career.

As a result of its variously directed broadsides – which could have done with rather more substantiation – Laker has this week had his free pass to the Oval withdrawn, a token gesture as ineffective as it is trivial. In future he must pay his 2s. 6d. like the rest of us, which, after a £10,000 benefit, I imagine he can afford.

Little in the book is new, except its author's opinions and his own version of the controversies that preceded his retirement. But what is especially interesting is the cold view it provides of the relationship between a county professional and his club, a Test cricketer and his captain.

I doubt whether Laker was always the easiest of men to deal with, in the employer-employee situation, which is how, I suppose, one has to regard his position *vis-à-vis* his club: great players rarely are, and Laker, even at the height of his powers, managed, perhaps unconsciously, to suggest a detachment from the proceedings little short of mutinous. Even when bowling out 19 Australians in a Test match he revealed no overt enthusiasm: his demeanour implied that the whole thing was a fearful chore.

That was his way. Yet he was one of the great players of our time, a true artist whose variations in flight, trajectory, pace and spin were absorbing to watch, and unquestionably, through the seven years of England's Test supremacy and of Surrey's reign as champions, he was a key figure. In addition, he is a man of superior intelligence, of presence and personality and independence. Somehow, as so often before with professional cricketers, it all ended in bitterness. Why?

The answer lies, I think, in the curiously obsolescent fashion in which professionals, despite many tangible advantages, are still treated. They are not, as should be the case with a person of Laker's eminence,

regarded as part of the upper hierarchy but simply as one of the paid staff for whom, rather as with an NCO, too much knowledge is deemed to be a bad thing. This lack of demonstrated esteem and confidence develops both ways, and it leads to a personal indifference that sometimes borders on the incredible.

It is, for example, hard to credit that Laker, when he left the Oval staff in September, 1959, received no letter of appreciation from his county club, was not invited to the close season cocktail party, nor in any way made to feel that his services had been at all unusual – and, this, apparently, because he had preferred to resign rather than to be sacked. 'To them [officials of the Surrey club] the professional would seem to be very much a paid lackey who bowls when he is told to bowl, then, when the match ends, is forgotten until the next.

'They have little time for you off the field. Once a player has finished his active cricket they could hardly be less interested in them.' It stems, one is made to feel, from an insufficiently elastic and outdated attitude of mind; and whether true or not in this instance, it is often so in others.

A lot of Laker's complaints are, as he admits, seemingly trivial in origin: numerous slights by May, whose accusations of non-trying in a county match led to Laker's temporary withdrawal of his name from the availability list for Australia, favouritism by one Bedser twin of the other that resulted in Laker being dropped, Mr F. R. Brown's brusqueness and general tactlessness as a manager. Singly, they don't seem much: but in context they add up to create a picture of petty bickering and disharmony and to give emphasis to that lack of warmth and generosity in human dealings that still mark the organisation behind first-class cricket.

Unfortunately Laker damages his case by the uncharitableness of his own comments on fellow-players. He quotes Oscar Wilde's 'The truth is rarely pure and never simple' to justify a string of personal disparagements sometimes barely short of libel. With some of his strictures one can, up to a point, concur. Occasionally he makes a fool of himself. To describe Dexter, about whom he is unfailingly abusive, as 'the poor man's Trevor Bailey' is not only cheap, but critical folly. Generally, however, his comments on technique are, as one would expect, level-headed and shrewd.

Towards the end of his book Laker makes some fascinating observations on contemporary players, wickets, tactics, Press relations and most aspects of bowling, including throwing. It makes one wish that professional cricketers would get themselves better literary advisers, with more of an eye on their client's reputation and less of a one on sensation and short-term financial success. Because a cricketer of Laker's qualities has a valid case; he can bring into the open many anomalies, reveal much that should be changed. But a sustained note of professional grousing – however naturally it may come – is an unattractive one.

Now, proper respect and responsibility, for which Laker rightly asks, continues to be withheld because of the terms in which dissatisfaction has been expressed. The plea for dignity has not been enhanced by an undignified manner.

George and John

ON THURSDAY EVENING, John Langridge and George Cox, together going in first to knock off the 18 runs required to beat Somerset, played their last innings for Sussex. Since the middle 1890s there has been a Cox on the Sussex staff, since the middle 1920s a Langridge. Had John hung on another two or three years there might well by then be another Langridge on the staff, Richard, son of James, like his father a left-hander.

A professional cricketer, somewhere or other, plays the last game of his career every September, more or less unobtrusively. Langridge and Cox this month have, however, received as touching a farewell outside the county as in it. For, in their different ways, they became institutions.

Not everyone outside Sussex saw the point of John, for he appeared often to have taken to the crease as a gardener to an allotment, his devotions more distinctly appreciable by opposing bowlers than by their supporters. He was among the soundest players of the new ball, bat and pad in close alignment brushing one another, and the body always steadfastly behind the quickest bowling, but he had no graces, no abandon, and the ball at times flew impartially off all parts of the blade.

Yet since, 22 years ago, he helped Ted Bowley to raise 490 runs for the first wicket at Hove, his sudden ritualistic shift of bat and feet from the blockhole as the bowler runs up, his inclining of the body and head towards mid-on as if he were turning politely to catch a conversational remark directed at him, his little amble down the pitch and swing of the left leg after playing his shot, the affirmatory pat of the stomach and touch of a cap fading yearly almost to the colour of sand, have made of him someone who, as his statistical value decreased, acquired a fresh esteem and affection among those who watched, as well as played against him. Partly, perhaps, because he is a cricketer with a countryman's honest, bluff countenance, and calm, as patently knowing of the badger's habits as of those of outswingers and inswingers, as evidently quiet-mannered and reliable in character as he was at first slip. This present summer he has taken 69 catches, a figure only narrowly exceeded by Hammond in 1928 and Tunnicliffe in 1901.

His batting has been denigrated often, but never, by cricketers, underestimated. Only Hutton and Compton of those playing today have scored more runs than he. He has scored 1,000 runs in a season 17 times, including 2,000 runs 11 times, both records for contemporary players. His neat, pointed ears, protruding like a fox's at an angle of 45 degrees from under his cap, made him instantly recognizable at the wicket even before he swivelled that long back to face the bowler in the ancient two-eyed manner.

Statistics bear at least some relation to John Langridge's career; to George Cox's they bear none. As Langridge (Jn) begat Langridge (Jas) in contradistinction to Langridge (J), so Cox was G. Cox (Jr). For 15 years until his father's death in 1949 he was Young George, a player of dash, brilliance and perpetual promise, who seemed always, on the margin of greatness, to have some imp tilting his cap over his eyes and dazzling him. His ironic parting advice last week to the young of Sussex was: 'Don't remain a promising player as I did for 25 years.'

In a sense he did not fulfil his promise either, for he was, against all but the very best spin bowlers, technically a Test batsman, who should have played Test cricket. But in other ways he more than made up for this to the satisfaction of all but the most puritan of critics. Before the war he hit that great Yorkshire attack for 100 out of 114 in an hour (the very match after H. T. Bartlett had taken a century off the Australian bowlers in 57 minutes, in

his first look at them), in all those early seasons alternately slashing and cutting his way to imperious fifties or departing ruefully for very rapid noughts. At cover-point he moved and threw beautifully, gifts he has imparted in full measure to his successor, young Jim Parks, scarcely born when George was fielding to his father. Like John Langridge, whose golden summer of 1949 with 12 centuries came to him in his fortieth year, George Cox achieved his best season, 1950, when his noble brow had wandered far over a head shaped like those on the earliest of Roman coins. That year he scored 2,369 runs at an average of 50.

He could not always keep it up, for he was more human, and so more fallible, than most great cricketers in whose temperaments restraint and sobriety are larger elements than ever they have been in Cox's. But, on good days, usually against the strongest counties, Yorkshire as often as not, his touch and control were those of a master. No one in England cut or glanced more delicately than he; nor did anyone leave a ball outside the off-stump with more magnificent disdain. He had the grand manner as well as an anarchist's sense of farce.

This month Cox moves from the Horsham village of Warnham, where he has spent all his life, to Winchester, where he succeeds John Langridge's old partner Ted Bowley, a spectator last week at Hove, as coach of cricket and soccer.

166

Horsham born and bred, Cox has sent his son to Christ's Hospital, school of Edmund Blunden, poet and wicket-keeper, whose great pleasure it has been to correspond with George on problems of education, literature and cricket.

John this winter plans to paint and decorate his Brighton house, before, round Christmas time, reopening with his brother at their cricket school near the old King Alfred garage. Next summer, when George is wheeling down his floaters at the Winchester nets, and urging boys to the forward defensive, to 'smell her' with noses low over bat, John will, in all probability, be standing white-coated at square-leg on the county ground. If he should suddenly shoot out an arm and pluck a firm hit from the grass, no one ought to blame him. After all, it is what he and George have done all their lives, and it is how at least I who have grown up to the music of their names will always remember them with love and admiration, and the wish that they could go on doing so as long as they lived.

Schoolboy Hero: H. T. Bartlett

CARLYLE, IN HIS famous series of lectures, allowed for six categories of hero – among them the hero as divinity, as prophet, as priest, as man of letters, as King. It is an exclusive list, making no mention of statesmen, explorers, scientists, soldiers – or, for that matter, sportsmen. Carlyle, however, was much concerned with the development of spiritual power, with the manner in which authority could achieve justice. He was an idolater, certainly, but his idols were generally beyond the normal hierarchies of men. The hero, for him, had to be a great man: the idea of hero worship involved the notion of objective, abstract greatness. It was not a private human adulation of one who existed within a human scale. Carlyle was not that kind of man.

Yet the idea of a hero today, a hundred years after Carlyle lectured, has become something much more intimate. A cricket hero in this case could legitimately, of course, still be one of the legendary names of cricket: Grace, Hobbs, Hammond, Larwood, S. F. Barnes, Fry – an Olympian figure, almost without mortal failings. Any such would be a reasonable choice. Myself, I never had the affection – admiration, respect, yes – but never that warm glowing regard, for the lordly great, which my conception of hero worship regards as necessary. I prefer local heroes to national ones, on the whole: once they progress from the county to the country arena, I feel they can do without my secret dispensations or passionate advocacy.

I believe that heroes are necessary to children and that as we grow up it becomes more difficult to establish them in the increasingly responsive soil of our individual mythology. Occasionally, the adult imagination is caught and sometimes it is held: but the image rarely takes root. I do not know that we become more fastidious, more cautious; I think it is simply that we become less whole-hearted.

If I accept then that a cricket hero must belong to adolescence, I find myself choosing from among those that haunted my mind during the 1930s. It would be unthinkable that he should not have been a Sussex cricketer, though I confess I was much enamoured once of C. F. Walters (as who, having seen him bat, could not have been?). I might well have settled for Tate, the true idol of my youth, or Duleepsinhji, or J. H. Parks, especially during the year of his 3,000 runs and 100 wickets, or Alan Melville or James Langridge. My hero-worshipping really was in the plural: my heroes were, without reservation, the Sussex cricket team. I could have chosen George Cox, who has given me greater qualitative pleasure than any living batsman, not least for his

habit of driving successive pairs of Yorkshire fast bowlers through every inch of cover boundary in the county and of cutting fast or slow ones through every compass bearing between wicket-keeper and gully. I could watch him field all summer, as, with the Sussex bowling of his day, he nearly did.

Then, again, there is John Langridge, of the ritualistic gestures, more hieratical in preparatory movement than any African witch-doctor, whom I have probably observed, with bird-watcher's patience, over a greater period of time than any other player. John Langridge was not quite in the heroic mould, but, because of his value to Sussex, I forgive him anything, while in the summer of 1949 he had more than a fair share of my adulation.

Any of these could have done as symbol for the pre-war Sussex of my youth. That I have, in fact, chosen as my figurehead H. T. Bartlett represents in some ways a perverse and contrary decision, for generally we seek heroes in our own image: idealized, but also to be emulated. Bartlett was a left-hander, I a right-hander: he was batsman *tout simple*, and, for all my sudden batting cravings and hallucinatory phases of success, I was indeed a bowler. I imitated Tate as a boy, I spent two formative summers coached by A. F. Wensley. By the time Bartlett, in 1938, descended like a comet on the fairly sleepy fields of Sussex cricket, I was already absorbed at Haileybury in devising plans to bowl out Cheltenham at Lord's. What could Bartlett have especially for me? There was nothing possibly I could hope to emulate in his play. Yet, if I am to be honest, I have to admit that for two whole summers I could think of practically nothing but H. T. Bartlett. Subsequently, he provided a number of disappointments: but at that peak period, both of his career and of my fevered imagination, he was a sight to behold.

I have never cared for my heroes to be either solemn or straight-laced. I know very little about Hugh Bartlett, and then I knew absolutely nothing at all. But he always gave the impression of having a healthy detachment from the game, of having an existence outside cricket that made his excursions into it both more perilous and romantic. Perilous his first few overs at the wicket certainly were; romantic he became, because not only was he pleasing in appearance, but the very nature of his genius was transitory. He made of this ephemeral, dashing, apparent recklessness a lasting quality: to those who tend to be attracted by the elusive, he was all they could ever require. I cannot remember, even in 1938, that he at any time exuded an air of comfort.

As a cricketer, domesticity was just not in his line. He began his innings usually as one who, suffering from violent astigmatism, has not only mislaid his glasses, but has in addition a fearful headache. He made a pass or two after the ball had gone past him: he lunged fitfully and

missed: he stabbed down just in time at the straight ones: he sliced the rising offside ball over second slip; he snicked hazily past his leg stump. So, for about a quarter of an hour, it went on: or, to such an agonized onlooker as I, it seemed to go on. Then, suddenly, he would catch a half-volley or a long hop such a crack that the bowler, fearful of his own safety, lost all aggressive intention, and, with it, any idea of length.

Phase two then began. One no longer felt that the bowler was remotely interested in the stumps, but, having scattered his fielders round the boundary, relied now, in the form of bait, on a species of poisoned chocolate. Bartlett paid scant heed to these exiled boundary creatures: at alarming rates he drove between, over, and if needs be, through them. He was a firm-footed hitter, possessed of a long reach, and the trajectory of his drives was low and of a fearful power.

Something of his particular magnetism came perhaps from this violent transformation of calm into hurricane, not only in his own person, but in Sussex cricket generally. Sussex had on paper a handsome batting side in those days, but the two Parks, J. H. and H. W., were effective rather than ebullient, and in any case rather past their best; John Langridge took his time, as did his brother James, and there was only George Cox to stave off periods of total becalming.

Bartlett began that summer of 1938 quietly enough; it was at Leeds on 21 May that he played his crucial innings. Going in at No. 7, with Sussex five for 106, he set about Bowes, Verity, Smailes, Robinson and Turner to such effect that he scored 94 out of 125 in 75 minutes. He was magnificently caught by Leyland off a hit that would otherwise have gone for six. Before that he had twice hit Verity for three sixes in an over.

Of course, Bartlett's hitting powers were not exactly unknown. He hit fantastically hard at Dulwich as a schoolboy, playing for Surrey before he went to Cambridge, and he had his moments over the next three years at Fenner's. But in fact – he failed in each of his three University matches – there was not the same exhilarating, annihilating quality about his batting, and it had begun to look to many as if the best was behind, not before. In the winter of 1937–8, however, Bartlett spent many painstaking afternoons at an indoor cricket school, and the effect was immediate.

Curiously, after Leeds, Bartlett did not play again for Sussex for a whole month. It was a period of unbearable anticipation. Then at Worthing against Worcestershire he returned to make 76 and 64, and one knew that envious men of the West Riding had not spirited him away for good. He followed this with 91 not out against Essex, and Sussex began a wonderful winning run. Bartlett's next appearance was at Lord's when he scored his now legendary 175 not out for the Gentlemen. Nicholls was

hit for two vast sixes, then five fours in an over, Smith (P.) for two fours and two sixes in the next.

It was evident now that there was no fluke about it, though since they had not been made for Sussex, I could not but feel at the time that these runs had been squandered unwisely. Who could have possibly predicted they would continue? When Bartlett came down to Hove to play against Lancashire the following weekend he was a celebrity. His scores in that match were 72 and 63. Next came the Bank Holiday game against Middlesex, the first county match of the season I was myself able to see. Bartlett scored only 27 and 16, Gray bowled him in the second innings, and I have loathed Gray ever since.

But then followed one of those magic weeks whose events even now, twenty years later, I can remember in detail. Daily I took the train from my home in Ardingly to Hastings, daily the fortunes of Sussex exceeded the wildest prayers of the night before. There was in fact a certain Mephistophelian contract undertaken in those prayers. In them I vowed willingness to surrender any potential 50 or 5 wickets if Bartlett could be empowered to make a hundred and Sussex to win. I was playing two weeks of cricket that month, one of them for a club called the Vandals. I made no score of over 10, nor took more than two wickets in that first week. Sussex in the relevant weeks at Hastings beat Northamptonshire by nine wickets and Kent by an innings and 15 runs. Bartlett scored 114 in each of his two innings. I made no spiritual compact the week after, when I scored the first hundred of my life against Tonbridge on the Angel ground, and then followed this with 75 and 77 against the Bluemantles. Bartlett during those innings managed 8, 9, 0 and 0. I did not dare to bat again that summer. Without question – such heights can adolescent fanaticism reach – Bartlett's centuries gave me more pleasure than my own.

There was even greater joy in store. On 27 August the Australians came to Hove and Bartlett, batting only two hours on the second day, hit 157. He went to his hundred in under an hour – the fastest hundred of the season – and then took 21 in an over off Ward. Altogether he hit six sixes and eighteen fours. That season Bartlett finished fifth in the first-class averages; above him were Hammond, Hardstaff, Hutton and Paynter. His own average was 57.33. It could not, of course, ever be like it again. Not that it was all over, by any means. That winter Bartlett went to South Africa with MCC, and though he did not play in a Test, he averaged 51 in first-class matches. 1939, too, had its rewards. Indeed, it started rather better than the previous year for Bartlett. He opened up with scores of 49, 49, 48, 24, 33, 60, 31, 74; he made 114 (a heraldic figure for Bartlett) against Nottinghamshire, 81 against Northants, and then rather fell away. As in 1938 he played almost entirely in home matches.

He had disappointing weeks at Hove and Hastings, and then I saw him at Eastbourne later in August against Worcestershire. Sussex, facing a score of 372, were about five for 180 when Bartlett went in with Jim Parks as his partner. Bartlett raced to 89 in forty-four minutes. He was caught then by C. H. Palmer off Martin at deep extra cover, and, as at Leeds the year before, had not Palmer held the catch it would have been a six. I do not ever remember such unconstrained driving. It was not only the ball up to him that Bartlett hit: he hit as often as not on the rise, without prior reference to the length of the ball, and with little care for the correct placing of the feet. It was essentially a question of timing.

By now, this joyous performance apart, Bartlett was a more responsible – if that is the right word – kind of batsman. He hit less in the air; he built up an innings more in the approved style. He was a remarkably accomplished player, swift to hook, with a steely square cut, a solid, thoughtful air to his back play. There remained the usual left-hander's failings outside the off-stump. By the time cricket got properly going after the war. Bartlett was in his middle thirties. He captained Sussex, but with no great success, personal or otherwise. He was a memory, not a hero.

Heroes in fact die with one's own youth. They are pinned like butterflies to the setting board of early memories – the time when skies were always blue, the sun shone, and the air was filled with the sounds and scents of grass being cut. I find myself still as desperate to read the Sussex score in the stop-press as ever I was; but I no longer worship heroes, beings for whom the ordinary scales of human values are inadequate. One learns that, as one grows up, so do the gods grow down. It is in many ways a pity; for one had thought that heroes had no problems of their own. Now one knows different.

Hugh Bartlett was not the greatest of Sussex cricketers, and it might have been better if he had not played after the war. His parting from the county was not of the happiest. Yet, for two seasons, he made of every Sussex ground on which he played a place of enchantment. You do not often hear these days the buzz of anticipation that habitually preceded his emergence from the pavilion. Sometimes when Godfrey Evans goes out to bat in a Test match, or when Frank Tyson comes on to bowl, but not often otherwise. We hear a murmur at Hove on behalf of David Sheppard, and sometimes for Jim Parks, or Don Smith. But it is nothing to what we felt when Bartlett, tall, brown, bareheaded, a little Byronic around mouth and chin, but fairer, more casual, walked with toes turned a shade inwards towards the wicket.

Perhaps simply it is that one is older, less roused to excitement. I do not know. But I remember the sea glinting, the flags fluttering, the crowd settling itself, and those terrible first overs when Pope or Copson or Smailes or whoever it was, fizzed the ball over Bartlett's waving bat – the agony of it, the unbelievable survival, and finally that great ecstasy.

Colin Cowdrey

As I write this, it is 15 years to the day that Colin Cowdrey made his first, and possibly most remarkable, Test century; 102 out of 191 in the third Test, at Melbourne, in 1954. Hutton, Edrich, May and Compton had gone to Miller and Lindwall for 20, and only a batsman of superb technique and complete composure could have survived long on such a wicket against such bowling. Cowdrey was 22, playing in his first Test series. 'His century', I wrote at the time, 'had the bloom of youth on it; but the soil from which it sprang had been tended lovingly and long . . . [it was] a blend of leisurely driving and secure back play, of power and propriety.' Two runs later Cowdrey was out, playing no stroke and being bowled off his pads. The glory and the indignity, through the years, came somehow to seem typical.

Among the great English batsmen of the post-war period Hutton, Compton, Washbrook, May, Dexter, Graveney, Barrington – Cowdrey, I suppose, has looked about the best 'bred'. Yet with breeding – the inherited grace and effortlessness that combine to form the grand manner – and the assumption of authority without tokens of display that is another characteristic, there has gone mildness, indecision, a stubborn passivity. I cannot think of a great player harder to coax into awareness of his reserves, nor one who, in the mood, made the art of batsmanship seem more artless, more a mere extension of his own geniality. At his best he was a dolphin among minnows, gambolling between the green and the blue as if cares were not invented, almost patronizing. At his less good he seemed imprisoned by some interior gaoler, feet chained, arms pinioned, shuffling away a long sentence.

More than most he is a mood player, delicate in his responses to the invisible strings of memory and music. A false note and he is becalmed, devoid of will and wizardry. Lesser players create their own context, impose their wishes on unpropitious elements, defy luck and roughness of touch. John Edrich is one such. Others, like May and Dexter, had a savagery of stroke that, once achieved, meant business. Cowdrey, like Graveney, has preferred to succeed or fail on his own terms, narcissistically declining to disfigure his own reflection, never hurrying, never bringing brute strength to the caressive lullaby of his stroke-play. His refusal to hit himself into form, or in mid-innings to demolish an attack, has often been maddening; sweet words when one wanted to see the big stick, reason when one hungered for violence. He could not, I imagine, be otherwise. Sometimes it has paid off, sometimes not. As captain and batsman he has, through injury, ineffectiveness and inability to turn the screw that last fraction, missed chances galore; yet, in the final analysis, his accomplishments have been immense, his achievements legion, his consistency, chivalry and charm of character unique.

'In the final analysis?' It is, at the start of 1970, a dubious moment to pronounce such phrases. Is this longest of postwar Test careers already over, or is the most glittering prize, victory in Australia under his leadership, still ahead? They say they never come back, but Cowdrey has, more than once, and if I had to bet on it I would, on balance, just take him to do so again.

He has, over the years, changed surprisingly little, being of that outwardly heavy build and solid gait that announces itself and the maturity it represents almost from the outset. In his round, sallow features the jester and the monk share a gravity of vocation; in his behaviour at slip, his walk between overs and his running between wickets, the ferryboat and the racing yacht share aptitudes.

My first overseas tour as cricket correspondent of *The Observer* was also Cowdrey's first as a player, so that, uniquely, he has been a major part of all the Test cricket I have covered. We share, too, a background of India and Oxford, not particularly relevant except that it meant I warmed to him early on and remember his hundred for Oxford at Lord's as clearly as if it was yesterday. I cherish it with his 1954 Melbourne hundred, his superb batting in West Indies in 1959–60, and countless other purple passages in his hundred Test matches, to say nothing of his marvellous virtuosity at slip, as among the most enhancing images in my cricket experience.

He has, as few do, elaborated his technique, added new strokes (such as the latest effective but hideous scoop to long leg), refined old ones. His driving between point and mid-off, with minimal movement of the feet and gentle dismissiveness of the bat, is tidal in its rhythmic inevitability, its oceanic break. He can hook, when roused, with affronted grandeur. He cuts with the kind of glee sadistic surgeons bring to complex incisions or a wild conductor to the resuscitation of anaemic arpeggios.

He has brought to the cricket of his time high ideals, impeccable manners, an engaging presence. He has blossomed and bumbled, conjured rare tunes out of stodgy skies, suggested the richest of ports, the lightest of soufflés. He would have made my life happier if he had played for Sussex instead of Kent, but, that apart, most of the regrets in his career fade into insignificance compared to the shining rewards. He has in his comfortable way had to accommodate himself to many uncomfortable experiences; but though he has never, in a material fashion, had to struggle, I believe he has a sense of values and enough insight, if pushed deeply into himself and able to come to terms with more astringent concepts, to offset some of the deader wood at the top of the cricket tree.

Talking to Godfrey

THE INDELIBLE IMAGE of Godfrey Evans is of a stocky, squatting figure with boy-size pads and large gloves, who slightly raises himself on his toes to peer over the off bail as the bowler swings his arm. He bats without cap, so that you notice how flush his ears are to his head, and his jaunty manner makes it no surprise that, for one year of his life, he was a professional boxer, who fought his first and last fights on Herne Bay Pier as a lightweight, for a prize of two pounds.

The less familiar image is of a sturdy, well-knit man, just under medium height, wearing a black homburg, dark business suit and carrying a bulging briefcase. He dismounts from his 1936 Bentley in a side street just off Hatton Garden and bustles, with the same brisk between-wickets walk, up the steps of Marquisa Jewels, Ltd., of which firm he is managing director.

Godfrey Evans has these last few weeks acquired, through answering questions about jewellery on the 'Double Your Money' programme, an extended fame. So much so that, when we met on Wednesday at the Ritz, the barman, who has no interest in cricket, whispered, while pouring the tonic into the gin, 'best of luck tomorrow, sir.' For Thursday was the night of the £1,000 question.

Anybody who knows Godfrey at all would regard it as unthinkable that he could have stopped anywhere along the line to the four-figure answer. Instead, he announced that, should he win, he would hand over half the money to the Rev. David Sheppard, his England colleague, towards equipping a playing field for his boys at Islington. In the event, he won, so everyone was happy, except, perhaps, Associated Rediffusion, who were challenged 'to raise the ante' to £2,000 by Billy Butlin offering £1,000 to the National Playing Fields Association, win or lose.

The questions he had to answer *en route* were not so easy. What is the difference between lustre and sheen? Name the four most valuable precious stones and place them in order of hardness. How many cuts has a diamond? Which is the biggest diamond in the world and where is it? What is the irritant in a cultured pearl and how is the finished article distinguishable from the real thing? These were some of the more elementary ones. But Evans is nothing if not determined. He packed his briefcase with reference books last weekend and in between giving the lecture on wicket-keeping at the senior MCC coaching course at Lilleshall and himself taking the examination in group coaching, he did his homework.

Evans believes in mixing business with pleasure, or, rather, he makes business pleasure. Cricket represents the smallest part of his business life, though at present it takes up the greatest amount of time. Naturally, it is because of who he is that he can develop such profitable sidelines as advertising sportswear, hairdressings and milk, each of which brings in a maximum of return for a minimum of effort.

In addition he recently started, in conjunction with J. C. Laker, an insurance broking business, with offices in Duke Street, St James's. With these two activities on top of his main interests in wholesale and retail costume jewellery – mounting

Wedgwood cameos is one of his firm's functions – this rare winter at home cannot come amiss to the managing director.

'I am a selling man,' he said. looking up at the autumn sun gilding the blue cloud-painted ceiling in the Ritz restaurant. 'What I can't sell, I know is no good.'

I asked him why he thought it worthwhile, in the circumstances, to sit for a coaching certificate. 'You never know,' he mused, 'I might even take a little business trip to South Africa this winter, and then if I have the certificate I could do a spot of coaching and that would pay for the trip.'

It was on just such a trip to Australia on MCC business that he met Sir Josiah Wedgwood and suggested that Evans and Wedgwood could be of some value to each other. And so it turned out.

There are not many in the sporting world who are such shrewd exponents of the cult of personality as Evans. He is a bubbling, champagne-bottle of a man, and, as he set his homburg at the appropriate angle and jumped into a taxi to go back to Hatton Garden, the fact that he is almost certain to become, within 12 months, the man who will have played cricket for England more times than anyone in the history of the game, seemed to be of diminishing importance.

Worrell on England v Australia

ALAN ROSS: Having played against both May and Cowdrey have you any views on their respective merits as captains?

FRANK WORRELL: They have both played in the same grade of cricket for approximately the same length of time and I think they have both assimilated a similar amount of sound cricketing knowledge. At this stage of English cricket, however, I would prefer to see Cowdrey as captain as it appears that the strain of captaincy has taken its toll of Peter May. When I first met Peter May in 1950 he was a smiling and extremely friendly young man. Now one finds him an intense, retiring individual, lacking somewhat in the art of relaxation in company.

Colin Cowdrey has this attribute in his favour – I am sure that if given the job he could get the maximum effort by a nod of his head and by his genuine sense of humour when things are going badly. Cowdrey's election would be the best thing for May and England, as well as the assurance that this series will be played in keen but friendly rivalry. Benaud is a captain who responds well to any challenge, which he is more likely to get from Cowdrey than from May. Equally, if the challenge is not forthcoming, Benaud is no sentimentalist.

Ross: Do you think Cowdrey is wasted as an opening batsman despite his solid success against the West Indies last year?

Worrell: If Cowdrey has a complex about opening then he should not be asked to do the job. He is too fine a player to be exposed to the new ball if he has any apprehensions whatsoever about it. He has undoubtedly got the temperament and the technique for the task, but this position calls for men who love the job.

Ross: Would you say that the present Australians are collectively or individually more vulnerable to spin or pace?

Worrell: During our tour of Australia our spin bowlers were more successful than our fast bowlers, but that could well have been because we went into the majority of Test matches with only one genuine pace bowler, Wesley Hall – Watson was a good yard or two slower than against England in the West Indies. Our spin bowlers were also assisted by some atrocious shots by the Australian batsmen. There are now indications of a conscious effort by the Australians to rule out these shots, so the task of the England spin bowlers may be more difficult – unless, of course, it rains heavily.

Ross: What effect do you think O'Neill's injury will have on the Australians?

Worrell: Obviously the loss of a great batsman cannot be discounted altogether, but in this instance the Australians appear to have batting in hand. The two people they cannot afford injuries to at any stage are Benaud and Davidson.

Ross: How would you compare the two pairs of fast bowlers? For example, would you personally prefer to have Statham and Trueman on your side or Davidson and any other?

Worrell: If Trueman and Statham are still bowling as well as they did in the West Indies two years ago then I would prefer them to the Australian pair. Davidson by himself can be as good as Trueman and Statham put together. He is literally two bowlers in one. His natural ball is the inswinger, but without detectable change he can cut it off the seam towards the slips. But as Davidson is injury-prone, Statham and Trueman must be considered a better pair on English wickets.

Ross: In the light of five Tests against each of these sides within eighteen months, have you learnt any strategic lessons or discovered weaknesses which as a captain could be exploited?

Worrell: The only weaknesses revealed during our tour of Australia was the inclination of the Australians to hit across the ball against our spinners, but, as I have mentioned before, they seem to have rectified this.

Ross: The Australians have no off-spinner. Do you think that if Benaud is not 100 per cent fit that Simpson could do the job? And how would you compare him with Barrington or Barber?

Worrell: An off-spinner would be invaluable to the Australians here and it is most unfortunate they haven't got one. They have good round-the-wrist spinners in Kline, Benaud and Simpson, who will come into their own when the weather gets warmer and they can really *feel* the ball in their fingers in the way that English leg-spinners rarely do – by July, in the estimation of most captains, they have ceased to be a business proposition.

Simpson is a fine leg-spinner and lacks only Benaud's 'flipper' – the top spinner. Sobers never picked Simpson's googlie though he could always pick Benaud's. On the other hand, every member of the West Indies team, Ramadhin and Watson included, could pick Benaud's – except myself.

Ross: If you were a bookmaker what odds would you lay on the series?

Worrell: If I were allowed to take into consideration the weather, I'd say two to one in England's favour, given a typical English summer, and two to one in favour of the Australians in a dry summer.

Swansong

THE OVAL TEST was Frank Worrell's swansong and not even the most churlish patriot could have begrudged him the final sweetness of its melody. For three days, with the crowd packed to overflowing, West Indian as much as English, the two sides had struggled to negligible advantage. At the weekend, with the game closely following the contour of Edgbaston – England's solitary victory – the position was that West Indies, with all their wickets in hand, needed 248 runs to win. Precedent was against them, but nothing else. Trueman, suffering from a damaged heel, was able to bowl only one over on the Monday. Titmus had been foolishly left out of the original twelve, and the pitch, never other than placid, was disarmingly easy. West Indies, with scarcely a false stroke, coasted home to an eight-wicket victory. The gates had again been closed – some 97,000 people (including members) saw the match, thousands being turned away each day – and before a delirious crowd, scarcely distinguishable in character from Sabina Park, Kingston, or Queen's Park, Port of Spain – Hunte scored an inflexible, unbeaten 108, and Kanhai a lyric 77. It was all made to seem deceptively simple, despite a storming effort by Statham, and in golden sunshine, with a day and an hour in hand, West Indies reaped their just reward. Not since 1950 had they beaten England, and now it was not only the margin of their victory but the manner of it that filled the ground with chanting, grinning figures – immigrants with the red carpet unrolled at their feet. If Brixton and Camberwell that day were drained of human activity, the same evening they were centres of the wildest jump-ups and celebrations, memory stored like honey for years to come.

Frank Worrell allowed himself few words but his smile, more expressive in its lazy geniality than any film star's, was ample. For most of the summer he had displayed a sleepy air of non-committal relaxation, taking everything as it came, publicly unobtrusive to the point of indifference. He husbanded his resources as if he was 49 not 39. Thicker now all round, silkily languorous of movement, he performed as one whose mind had moved beyond the trivialities of cricket. Victory and defeat, his shrugging demeanour made plain, were much the same thing, quickly forgotten. His epic feats were behind him, nostalgia a more powerful agent than ambition. He confessed himself 'a mediocre all-rounder'. Perhaps he really did not care, for himself anyway. But his presence, on or off the field, was as pervasive as the most lingering of scents. It might have appeared to the undiscerning, judging only by the casualness of his approach, that he was merely the figurehead, a kindly father-figure dispensing soothing advice from behind the lines. Nothing could have been further from the truth. On the field, as captain, he kept gesture to a minimum, but his control, authority and astuteness were never in doubt. He had, it is true, all the weapons, but he deployed them with a single-mindedness and psychological subtlety that ensured they were never blunted.

His own performances were, again, deceptive. Much of the season he was hampered by strains and undergoing constant treatment. Yet whenever it mattered he produced the goods, with no apparent effort at all.

At Old Trafford his 74 not out seemed merely the icing on the cake, but, after nearly two days of almost pedestrian batting, it came as a revelation of a classic art and elegance. No one who saw it could forget his late-cutting on that sultry, blue afternoon. The ghostly music had begun to stir old memories and for two hours he batted, not as the legendary veteran, diffident of his own prowess, but as one whose delicacy

and aesthetic sense demanded final release. Others in his side might have to bear the main burden of taking wickets and making runs, but it was as if he wished gently but firmly to establish that, when necessary, either for display or in earnest, the magical ease and pure mastery of stroke, far from having withered, were on call, perfectly preserved. It was simply that he kept them in cold storage, offering others the limelight.

Again at Lord's, where he was bowled for nought in the first innings, he demonstrated at a crucial moment, when England, on a beautiful wicket, were getting steadily on top, all the skills and wiles of medium-paced bowling. The nip was no longer there, but the intelligence and experience were, and his two wickets that second evening crucially shifted the balance of the game. In the second innings his discreet guidance and support of Butcher in a stand of over a hundred runs saved West Indies the match.

At Edgbaston he failed, at Headingley in the first innings he ran out of partners with a surfeit of runs to play with, at the Oval he held merely a watching brief. Between overs he strolled almost gingerly into position, deprecating his right to be there at all, but when anything came near him, at short-leg or elsewhere, he pounced on it, surfacing shark-like from reflection. He put nothing down and such catches as came his way he took without effort.

Ghost Writing and Denis Compton

For the field is full of shades
as I near the shadowy coast,
And a ghostly batsman plays to
the bowling of a ghost

Francis Thompson's 'At Lord's' is about the most hackneyed, ill-quoted of all cricket poems. Every after-dinner speaker about the game, from Lord Birkett downwards, makes use of it; and Mr Denis Compton, in his provocative book, *End of an Innings*, quotes it too.

'And a famous player talks to the writing of a "ghost"' would not be an unfair description of most autobiographies to which great players lend their name; or, indeed, of the sporting columns syndicated by them. I do not personally find this practice as otiose and unethical as do some professional journalists, so long as, and it is a vital proviso, the finished work essentially represents the ideas, views and personality of their alleged author. The collaboration must be intimate. Often it is not, with the result that the book, usually ill-written, lacks flavour, is packed with non-committal clichés, and is quite unreadable.

Mr Compton gives away no secrets of composition: perhaps he wrote every word unaided though certain phrases suggest the contrary.

Perhaps he did not. It does not greatly matter, for, on the whole, one feels that this is Compton talking, this is the real thing. The prose is vivid, clear, precisely phrased: it is free of false sentiment, its arguments are sustained in adult terms, it is generally expressive of its author's warm, engaging but far from unopinionated character.

This is, mainly, the story of Mr Compton's own cricketing career, its astonishing ups and downs, its moments of poignancy and anguish. Most of it is familiar, and there is little about the man within, which is a pity, for no cricketer of our day has a more engaging personality, one moreover that is quite separable from his profession.

You get a fair idea from this book of what it feels like to be Compton batting, whether in one of those golden innings, when, as in a narcotic dream, everything is effortless and possible, or when the simplest stroke seemed too difficult to be true. You get no idea at all about what goes on in his own mind, except on cricketing topics. My own disappointment is not, like Sir Leonard Hutton's, that the book is gossipy, but that its frankness is reserved for others. There is no self-scrutiny.

What in fact is fascinating about *End of an Innings* is the author's comments on his fellow-cricketers. They are sharply to the point, revealing, considered: only about Hutton is he, I think, less than fair. I don't doubt the truth of any of his allegations about Hutton's Captain Queeg-like moments of dispirited confusion, his lack of apparent openness, sociability, and, at crucial times, authority and control, though Sir Leonard has answered these in his own terms. I think Mr Compton makes his pretty wounding criticisms without malice. But, while they spring from conviction, they are not all the story, and there is a curious absence of understanding and generosity, a failure to acknowledge the great technical gifts, the astute cricketing brain, the dry wit that are part of Sir Leonard's charm. He makes him out to be not only a psychopath but a dull dog indeed. He is far from that.

About Bradman, 'the herald of negative cricket', Mr Compton is excellent. He quotes, too, an astringent little anecdote about S. G. Barnes, when that ebullient comic was out of form. 'We had, I think, been talking about Bradman, and Barnes turned to me and said: "Mr Bradman, he gets all the publicity, let him get all the bloody runs."' There is a splendid sentence later on about the effect of extravagant appealing on the umpire: 'A great yell from six or seven Australians can be in its own way a hidden persuader.' Mr Compton, it seems, is already learn-ing from his new career in advertising.

There remains the vexed question as to whether ethically dressing-room conversations should be repeated at all. Certainly this book takes you behind the scenes in a way that no other has, and the direct speech in which Mr Compton records incidents heightens interest. It seems to me not a moral problem, however, but a matter of discretion; in the circumstances it would have been courteous for the relevant passages to have been shown to Sir Leonard. The same critical points could have been made in a less personally offensive manner without any loss of force.

Many of the best things in this book are about Lord's, about which Mr Compton is tenderly evocative. He does not forget the old days when he sold scorecards and helped to garden. He provides some skilled assessments of various Middlesex and England captains; he is handsomely loyal in his appraisements of Edrich, in his tributes to Godfrey Evans, Keith Miller, and Ray Lindwall.

The photographs are dismal, but that is one of the consequences of the iniquitous system whereby Lord's and other grounds allow agencies a photographic monopoly. As a result the standard of cricket photography in this country is the lowest anywhere.

One way and another, though, this is a unique book: as was its author a unique cricketer.

The D'Oliveira Row

THIS WEEK IN Brisbane, West Indies, having already lost two matches, take on Australia: at roughly the same time on Thursday in Dean's Yard, Westminster, the MCC Committee, having already lost two tours (to South Africa and India), take on their critics at a Special General Meeting of the club.

West Indians, outside of Test matches, rarely play true to form. They have made an indifferent start to their Australian tour and it looks as though Hall and Griffith, even before the Tests have started, have run out of gas. There was precious little in them a year ago. In consequence, Sobers is going to be crucially short of pace and seems likely to have to do most things himself.

Unless Gleeson continues to unnerve them, as he did a fortnight ago, there should be plenty of runs forthcoming. Camacho and Fredericks have settled down as an opening pair; Sobers, Kanhai, Butcher and Nurse have all made big scores. All it needs now is for Lloyd to start exerting himself.

It is not easy, though, to see West Indies bowling Australia out unless the pitches are such that Gibbs, Holford and Sobers (in his spinning role) get some chance on the last couple of days.

Interesting though this confrontation should be over the next four months, it would on all counts have taken second place to England's series in South Africa. This could have been a real thriller, the ultimate test of contemporary cricketing strength. Now it could well be that South Africa, at a peak period, will be left without any opponents. If that is so, then they have only themselves to blame.

No one now could possibly want to go over the D'Oliveira affair again, and trying to apportion blame – especially where committees are concerned – is usually a waste of time. Nevertheless, the Special General Meeting of MCC called at the request of 20 members for next Thursday has a purpose, and I hope, despite the mostly spiteful, ignorant and hostile Press (seemingly motivated by the personal loss of a winter in South Africa) that they have so far received, that their valid objections will be treated by members on their merits and given a fair hearing.

Committees nearly always hold all the cards, and whatever happens in Dean's Yard is unlikely to affect the postal vote that will have preceded it. This, however, is not the point; what is important is that a free debate on future policy should take place and that unequivocal answers should be given to whatever questions may be put.

The situation is complicated by the fact that MCC is both a private club, representing, and answerable only to, its members, and a national institution, representing, and answerable to, the whole country. There is for its members, no alternative to MCC; those who disagree with what is done by their committee cannot have recourse to another club nor would they wish to have. What they do have a right to is a say in what is done in their name.

The resolutions to be voted on have been temperately phrased (and by the committee rather less temperately answered).

They are:

1. 'That the Members of MCC regret their Committee's mishandling of affairs leading up to the selection of the team for the intended tour of South Africa in 1968–1969.'

2. 'That no further tours to or from South Africa be undertaken until evidence can be given of actual progress by South Africa towards non-racial cricket.'

3. 'That a Special Committee be set up to examine such proposals as are submitted by the SACA towards non-racial cricket; the MCC to report on progress to the Annual General Meeting of the Club: and to the Governing Body for Cricket – the MCC Council.'

In relation to No. 1, the crucial factor is that, on the bad advice of Sir Alec Douglas-Home, the committee failed to press home the inquiries they had sensibly initiated in January and to which they had received no answer. Had they done so the present situation could not have arisen in the way it did. It is really as simple as that.

In their comment on this the committee contradict themselves. 'To press for an immediate answer to the letter would have appeared to be not only hypothetical, but politically inspired.' This, of course, is nonsense. Either you don't send a letter (in itself hypothetical in implication) and hope for the best, or you expect an answer.

The question asked, after all, was simply whether the South African Cricket Association 'could confirm that no preconditions will be laid on the selection of the MCC team'.

The trouble with taking the advice of politicians is that they tend to deal in expediency, not principles, nine times out of ten with fatal results. It was so in this instance. The advice was weak and the consequences predictable.

The committee further state that the integrity of the selectors 'has been attacked by persons so violently opposed to the domestic

policies of the South African Government as to appear incapable of fair judgment.'

With due respect, this is so ludicrous as to seriously make one wonder at what repressions really seethe behind the bland exterior of a body that can so misconceive the facts before them.

In their statement the Twenty Members specifically say 'the Selectors were put in an intolerable position ... the chief blame rests not with the Selectors but with the Committee.' With this I agree, though I also think the selectors, in a purely technical sense, did a very unambiguous job altogether.

The second and third resolutions really hang together. MCC continue to go on about building bridges without seeming to understand what kind of bridges (if any) they have succeeded in constructing or where they might lead. Their critics are merely asking: What actual progress towards non-racial cricket have you made by your policies? The short answer is 'None.'

Instead the committee appear to condone and even underwrite racialism, while at the same time repeating their 'desire to foster cricket wherever it is played'. Can they honestly believe that their timid attitude to South African cricket as a whole is 'fostering cricket wherever it is played'?

In this connection, too, why do we hear so little protest from white South African cricketers themselves? The only possible conclusion is that either they support the racialist policies of their Government or that they are a pretty craven lot. Which is it?

It is in their comment, however, on Resolution 2 that the MCC Committee fully reveal, not their wickedness, but their defensive inadequacy. They suggest disparagingly that 'the terms of this Resolution give the key to the true motives of the movers of these three Resolutions'.

Well now, it is perfectly possible to agree with Resolutions 1 and 3 without going quite as far as all of 2, but anyone in his right mind must surely approve the 'true motives' of the movers of these three resolutions, which is no more nor less than a desire for some evidence 'of actual progress by South Africa towards non-racial cricket'. Is that so contemptible?

If the Committee of MCC are not in fact committed to such progress, then the sooner they are removed from office lock, stock and barrel the better. This resolution, so far from being evidence of political pressurisation, asks simply for progress on a human issue. It is an *objection* to politics in sport, not an introduction of it.

Again, if the MCC Committee cannot see this, it must only confirm the very lack of insight of which their critics complain. In these kinds of matters it is the duty of a committee to lead opinion, not just to bark gruffly from corners into which they have reluctantly retreated.

About Resolution 3 – surely an ironic one? – the committee

comment merely that the existing machinery of the Club and of the MCC Council 'will be quite adequate to deal with any such proposals as may be envisaged'. Here they are on absolutely firm ground because the likelihood of any such proposals ever materialising are precisely nil.

So there it is. The committee invite the members, either by post or in person, to vote against all three resolutions. That is their prerogative. It is also the prerogative of members to use their wits and cast their votes accordingly.

Personally, given the chance, I would have liked to add a fourth resolution to the effect that the catering at Lord's is so vile that those responsible for it ought to be deported to South Africa.

I hope on Thursday evening that the committee will feel neither the victims of a witch-hunt nor, at the close of proceedings, offensively exonerated. If I understand the motives of the Twenty Members behind the resolutions aright, then there is no call for animosity: everyone wants the best for the club.

Hove

SOME COUNTY GROUNDS owe their fame to the rural beauty of their situation, others to their metropolitan grandeur, still others to the character of their cricketers. Certain grounds have been immortalised by the matches that have taken place on them. Hove, the happy conjunction of whose letters combine 'home' and 'wave', comes into a category of its own.

First and foremost, it is a seaside ground, a mixture of the regency and the raffish, from which, almost alone in England (or anywhere else for that matter), you can actually see the sea. Not much of it, it's true, but you are always conscious of it, in a quality of light, in the feeling of the air. The sea has shaped Sussex cricket and Sussex cricketers, it has given both an alternating exhilaration and fallibility.

At Hove, sun and sea-mists, heat and cold, follow one another with bewildering rapidity, and Sussex fortunes on the field bear witness to this elemental instability. The Downs, too, are another physical factor, separating Hove from the flatness of southern England, a protective arm flung across the whole county.

As a *ground*, quite apart from its

associations, Hove cannot exactly be called beautiful. It has always been suburban, with a touch of the exotic: an odour of Empire, of curry powder and whisky, retired colonels and actresses, the ailing old, the robust young. The ground slopes to the sea, so that the villas lining it have a precarious air, their verandahs tilted like pitching steamers.

In any case, the architectural frame of Hove was always a mess, lovable in its variety, but of little consistency and no merit. In the last ten years it has changed out of all recognition and in the next ten it looks like changing even further.

Some may regret the new blocks of flats, but I think, when they're all finished, Hove will have a more intimate, marine flavour, cleaner in outline, more modern in feeling. With imaginative planting it can be a better-looking ground than it ever was.

But the physical aspect of a ground is only part of its real character, and the lifting of the spirits, the *joie de vivre*, that Hove seems uniquely to produce – at least for those in love with Sussex cricket – comes from the quality of its cricketers. As surely as vintage wines are the unmistakable embodiments of local soil, climate, skills, care, cunning and luck, so is Sussex cricket, in the atmosphere of Hove, born of unique circumstances.

What the sea is to the ground, so 'the family' has been to generations of Sussex cricketers, and to the hereditary talents in all their combinations of the great Sussex families – which mercifully show no signs of drying up – has been added just enough foreign dash to make for excitement, if not reliability. But it will be a sad day if a Sussex team ever takes the field with no player who is not the son, or brother, or cousin, or nephew of another Sussex player.

Dexter as Captain: Australia 1962–63

WHATEVER THE MERITS of the 1962–63 Tests as entertainment – and for various reasons the teams seemed finally never to get to grips – the fact remains that Dexter could have achieved in terms of results more than anyone expected before Brisbane. MCC were soundly defeated by a Combined XI at Perth and trounced by New South Wales in Sydney. The odds were that England would be lucky to draw a couple of Tests and could expect to lose three. In the event, they proved extremely difficult to beat. We live in an era of anti-novels and anti-plays and in this sense the Tests were of their period. Their particular brand of non-committal inconclusiveness might have been invented by Harold Pinter, Samuel Beckett or N. F. Simpson. The scene-setting caution with which the contestants sized one another up overlapped into, and ultimately devoured, the time that belonged to action. Nevertheless, in thirty years only one English side, Hutton's in 1954–55, left for New Zealand with a better record and victorious. England, after all, drew the series, and of the two teams they came on the very last day the closer to winning. That is not an entirely

negligible achievement. Dexter has since received almost unqualified abuse, but few captains have ever set a better personal example on the field and he joins Chapman, Jardine and Hutton as the only Test captains since the 1914–18 war to have held their own in Australia. He had his faults, certainly, but in the main these lay in his handling of his own players and they did not demonstrably affect the results of the Tests. He spent little time with his team off the field, but he was not alone in this. Jardine, Hammond, Hutton were equally remote characters, and similar complaints, one recalls, were constantly levelled at May. Bradman, during his playing days, was not usually regarded as a particularly sociable figure, nor one disposed to be free with friendly advice to his juniors. It would seem that the price of cricketing pre-eminence, added to captaincy strains and responsibilities, is a kind of withdrawn aloofness that is not entirely separable from the single-mindedness essential to the great player. Keith Millers and Denis Comptons are not thrown up every day, and neither of these was ever saddled with the burdens, social, administrative and strategic, of captaining a side, let alone on tour. Irresponsibility was part of their charm, though Miller, especially, might have been a rewarding captain.

Social responsiveness, affability, evenness of mood are not noticeably part of Dexter's personality, though he is consistent to the extent that he would as unconcernedly cut the Duke of Norfolk or the Chairman of the Selectors as he would look through a plain hostess at a cocktail party. Where he failed in his relations with his team was that he left them overmuch to their own devices, often without guidance or consideration when both would have been appreciated. Yet he is not without charm or warmth and if it lacked tact to greet the flannelled Bradman at Canberra with the remark 'Straight out of Madame Tussauds' it suggests a not displeasing irony too. He was generously accessible to the Press, and was never other than strictly to the point in his statements to them.

Much has been made of his tactical callowness *vis-à-vis* Benaud, and occasionally his field placings bore the look of a chess board that has been inadvertently knocked over by a waiter and the pieces reassembled at random. Often he seemed *distrait* during long partnerships, as if some opaque screen had come down between his private fantasies and what was actually going on. Unlike Benaud, who gives the appearance of identifying himself with every single one of his players all the time, Dexter seems to abstract himself, as if the flow of events was

no real concern of his. Yet I do not really think that Benaud, for all his persuasiveness and skill in man-management, ever got the better of him strategically. For most of the series Benaud seemed obsessed by Dexter's presence, and if his own sparse haul of wickets included Dexter's more often than anyone else's, this was of only personal significance.

In the end Dexter had too much to do, the consequence of which was that he lost his own attacking flair. In the first two Tests he raised, by his personal aggressiveness, the whole level of the English batting, and by the time he had himself gone off the boil the standard had been set. England subsequently fought all the way down the line, with Barrington in almost permanent residence, but in the initial stages, when Benaud wore an aura of invincibility, and Davidson threatened to lay waste, it was Dexter, almost contemptuously, who reduced them to human scale. He repeatedly lost his way in the suburbs of a long innings, occasionally through impatience, occasionally through exhaustion, but generally, one felt, it was because at some stage in the sixties or seventies he ceased to play instinctively and became aware of the need to go on. He was then easy prey to the spinners, prodding forward without clear idea of the googly or the leg-break. But disappointment was relative: he played magnificent strokes in nearly every innings and the sight of him pacing his crease, or bent over his bat, all restless energy, was always one to lift the spirits. He will never, perhaps, be a great player of leg-spin, though he took a fair toll of Benaud and Simpson, but few batsmen have ever driven fast bowling harder or reduced stock bowlers more ruthlessly to insignificance. He was one of the few English fielders to match the Australians in mobility and crispness, and his bowling, while only spasmodically purposeful, earned both respect and wickets.

It was one of Dexter's problems that only three of his side could be said to have come off in the accepted sense – Trueman, Titmus, and Barrington. Trueman, hair blackly flopping over a face that never lost an industrial pallor, endeared himself almost alone to Australian crowds. He never put down a catch, he threw, either left-handed or right, from the boundary to the top of the stumps, and his curving, bandy-legged run, toe-caps glinting as the broad, untidy hips swivelled, was always the signal for dead quiet. He bowled beautifully with the new ball, controlling the swing and adjusting the angles of approach, and he varied a full, swerving length with others, fractionally short on the leg stump, that reared up at the ribs. He was often genuinely fast, but even off his shorter run, at moments when he moved round the field with an old sweat's assumed resentfulness, he was never other than accurate and probing.

Taken as a pair, there was little to choose between Trueman and Statham on the one hand, Davidson and McKenzie on the other. In each case, the new ball thrust came from Trueman and Davidson, with Trueman rather the more enduring of the two. On the same side, with their contrasting methods, they would have made a glorious combination. Trueman had a slight edge in pace, Davidson exploited the more bewildering swing. Between McKenzie and Statham, one developing, one running down, there was the difference between youthful strength and honest endeavour. In his prime Statham never swung the ball perceptibly, but he had pace and the ability to make one or two an over nip back devastatingly off the seam. These days he retains his control, his almost robot accuracy, but only rarely did he get any life out of the pitch or move the ball off it. He was often no more than fast medium and he bowled on long hot afternoons rather from memory than with anticipation. McKenzie, still lacking art and frequently wild in direction, takes little out of himself, has magnificent shoulders and an open action, and always made the ball get up off a length. On anything approaching a lively wicket, like Lord's, he must be an uncomfortable proposition. Whenever Benaud needed him to bowl long spells he kept his pace to the end.

The real revelation of the series was, I suppose, Titmus. He played first in a Test match as long ago as 1955, but Laker held sway until 1959,

after which Allen, with his more pronounced spin, kept him out. Nevertheless Titmus kept bowling cheerfully away on a Lord's pitch kinder to seamers, taking his hundred wickets and making just over or under a thousand runs. He seemed a thoroughly good county cricketer.

It was not until the Second Test at Melbourne that he began to appear more than this. The Australians never played him convincingly, sweeping across the line or getting pushed crabbily back on their stumps. He varied his pace enough to deter too frequent or early moves down the wicket, and his curving trajectory, with the ball starting outside the leg stump and floating across, disconcerted everyone. He bowled few bad balls and was able to get away, for the most part, without deep fielders. In comparison with the great off-spinners his range is narrow; Booth occasionally showed up his limitations, for on Australian pitches he declined to give the ball much air, he was not able to get it to move the other way off the pitch, as Illingworth with his rounder action occasionally does, and his turn,

compared with Allen's, is negligible. But he gave himself precise tasks, and he fulfilled them admirably. His batting, especially with Trueman at the other end, progressed from the plucky to the eloquent, and apart from his one sad lapse on the last morning at Adelaide, he fielded with safety and alertness.

In figures alone, only Hammond among English batsmen has ever exceeded Barrington's performances in Australia. This is to put Barrington way out of his natural class; but runs count, and whether at five or three Barrington delivered the goods. He prefers the higher position and when Dexter sent him in first wicket down he came up with scores of 63, 132 not out, 101 and 94. No one could ask more than that. Indeed his first-class scores on the tour make remarkable reading: 24, 0, 44, 104, 219*, 19, 183*, 78, 23, 52, 35, 0*, 35, 23, 63, 132*, 33, 67, 101 and 94. These he followed up with a century in the First Test in New Zealand. He is a magnificent cutter, an effective sweeper. He plays forward with bat almost exaggerat-edly straight.

Incident at Peshawar

On reading reports from Pakistan of the ragging of an umpire by the MCC touring team.

Another Chota Peg, boys?
Let's have a go at Begh, boys,
Goddam this steamy heat, chaps,
That's what's got us beat, chaps,
The climate of Peshawar.

D'you think Begh's too hot, boys?
He put us on the spot, boys,
He'd appreciate a shower
In this stinking hot Peshawar.
Let's go and hunt for Begh, boys.
A double Burra Peg, boys.

If we're facing umpire Begh, chaps,
And they hit us on the leg, chaps,
We can go without a fuss, chaps,
For we know it's up with us, chaps.
Just walk into the shade, boys,
Don't look dismayed, boys,
Nor wait for the appeal, boys,
Just turn on your heel, boys.

If we cannot make a run, chaps,
At least let's have some fun, chaps,
If we fail to take a wicket
We can say that it's not cricket.
When you're badly out of luck, boys,
Give the umpire a duck, boys,
And even up the score
With a bucket at Peshawar.

Another Chota Peg, boys?
Let's have a go at Begh, boys,
Goddam this steamy heat, chaps,
That's what's got us beat, chaps,
The climate of Peshawar.

The West Indians at Lord's

CORDONED OFF BEHIND the nets they stand in rows, mouths slightly open as if singing, their gaze orderly and respectful, so that one might imagine a church service to be in progress. Squashed trilbies, baseball caps, trim homburgs decorate their heads; some wear bow ties, some striped wool shirts, some stiff white collars and gold-pinned city ties.

There are few white faces in this gallery, though down at the other end of the practice ground as fondly parental and critical an English audience watches the earnest endeavours of grey-flannelled boys to push correctly forward at the ripe off-breaks dropped on a length by the stiffening arms of their tutors.

These weeks Lord's is ritualistic as a ballet class: on newly mown grass that has begun again faintly to transmit its freshness, muscles are loosened, techniques and actions rehearsed and modified, footwork tested phrase by phrase, and, one by one, strokes indulged with a sensuousness not yet staled by custom. The bats are the colour of honey, oiled but unflawed: the turf is vivid green, with a baize nap on it. Practice is chidingly self-critical, but fancy has a latitude that the austerity of match play increasingly eliminates.

There are 'net' players and players who can explore their full range of possibilities only when it counts. The West Indians have a measure of both kinds, and in the early days it is not always easy to tell them apart.

At their first practice last week, under a sun warm enough to make them sweat, they batted in pairs, in approximate batting order, incoming and outgoing batsmen walking into and out of the two nets as formally in step as bridal couples, Pairaudeau and Asgarali, Ganteaume and Weekes, Worrell and Sobers. Opening batsmen are their first problem, the fast attack their basic weakness, but while the batsmen had a good work-out against Valentine, Ramadhin, Smith and Atkinson, the quicker bowlers went at it gingerly.

Gilchrist, considered to be the fastest West Indian since Martindale, is a stocky man with a bounce to his run that makes it seem he has trodden on a concealed spring, but he found length and direction, even at half-pace, steadily eluding him. The 19-year-old Wesley Hall, another fast bowler, contented himself with one delivery every ten minutes or so; Dewdney, the third opening bowler, tall, sturdy with a high action, looked the pick of them, accurate off a short economical run.

The spinners were more interesting: Ramadhin, almost portly, expressionlessly flipping off-breaks and leg-breaks with arm no higher than his ear; Valentine, preoccupied and bookish in his spectacles, until he grins suddenly as a ball hops past Asgarali like a kangaroo; O'Neil Gordon Smith, his face worried as a boxer's, turning off-breaks sharply and his feet zigzagging as if on crazy paving.

Atkinson at medium pace hit Pairaudeau's off stump, beat Weekes, alone wearing the plum-coloured West Indian cap, and generally came off quicker than seemed likely. At the other end Goddard looked on, gently appraising, talking to TV men, and occasionally delivering a medium-paced ball with arm far from his head.

It was a relaxed affair, a process of acclimatising more than tuning-up: only Worrell of the batsmen drove with much sweetness. Ganteaume, from Port of Spain, a sadder-eyed, smaller replica of him, who made 112 against England in 1947 in his only Test appearance, looked reproachfully at Valentine's hoppers, and with mournful regret at Ramadhin's absence of turn. Pairaudeau, a little reminding one of C. H. Palmer, seemed sometimes put out by the pace of the pitch. Sobers, a left-hander, who played against England in 1953–54 at the age of 17, is one of the several all-rounders who form the real strength of this West Indian team. Behind the ropes, the eyes watching him were hopefully paternal.

Who are the characters of this side? Smith, certainly, chunky and rolling of gait, whose merits are akin to Benaud's; he hits hard and high and straight, and will spin his off-breaks hugely when he gets the chance. Clyde Walcott, Everton de Courcey Weekes, Frank Worrell: no other international side boasts comparable stroke-makers.

Walcott averaged 87 against England in the last series, 82 against Australia. Weekes scored a century in each of his first five innings in New Zealand last year, and averaged 79 last time in England. Worrell, now studying optics at Manchester, averaged 89 in the 1950 Tests in England. These are giant figures among the present pygmy-sized batsmen in Test cricket. But English bowlers are also a superior race these days.

The issue, however, will boil down to whether Ramadhin and Valentine can again bemuse and leave stranded English batsmen who, in seven years, still show the same inclination to play spin bowling from the crease. The success of Tayfield, on pitches from which Laker received no response, must encourage them to think so. Meanwhile, the motor-mower whirrs, virginal bats receive their first bruises, and in basement rooms all over London guitars are being strummed to exploratory music.

Introduction to *The Cricketer's Companion*

STORIES, MATCHES, players, poems, more or less this is how I have grouped these writings about cricket. In the third section, *Men and Moments*, the emphasis is on the writer as much as on the subject. Here, Nyren, Pycroft, Andrew Lang, Neville Cardus, Edmund Blunden, and Robertson-Glasgow among others show their paces, though some of them also appear in more specific contexts elsewhere, as poets or describing great cricketers.

There have, over the years, been a number of cricket anthologies. Gerald Brodribb's *The Book of Cricket Verse* and *The English Game*, Eric Parker's *Between the Wickets*, E. W. Swanton's *Best Cricket Stories*, R. H. Lowe's *A Cricket Eleven* immediately come to mind. An initial difficulty, therefore, is to produce something fresh. Necessarily, a fair amount of this book will be familiar to the experts. That is unavoidable, though I have seen to it that there are certain items that will be unknown even to them; at the same time, the familiar can take on new life in a sympathetic context. In the last resort, however, a good anthology is a personal affair, and my pleasure in making this one has come from just that weighing and selecting that derives from reading with more than casual purpose.

I aimed at two things, the creating of a book that contained the most essential and enjoyable writing on the game, in whatever medium, and one that gave as inclusive a view as possible of the great landmarks. So that, if this book was all that a ship-wrecked mariner was able to salvage, he would get from it both a feeling of how cricket developed and a reminder of its greatest ornaments, from the forerunners through the Golden Age to the present day. It was an ambitious scheme, and all along the line there are inevitable gaps, either through lack of space or simply because certain great players failed to find their literary equivalent. It is a fact, regrettably, that writers about cricket, however knowing as commentators, or skilled at reading a match, have rarely set themselves to create a stereoscopic image of individual players, bringing forward their methods and mannerisms for the scrutiny of later generations. E. W. Swanton's extract on Compton is a good example of this. Since Nyren there have been a bare half-dozen. We live in an age of increasing reportage and anecdote, in which a literate and informed prose style, as practised, for example, by Neville Cardus and Robertson-Glasgow, has less and less place. What is missing from most contemporary writing is the power to suggest an atmosphere, to define character, or produce the kind of telling image that will linger on in the mind long after scores and statistics have staled. The discursive port-and-cigars manner went out with cloche hats. So did the essay. Nevertheless, having set myself the task of re-reading the whole literature of cricket – not without apprehension – I must admit that what started out as a chore ended with sufficient feeling of reward. There is dead and slovenly writing galore: but, if one has any fever for cricket at all, there are moments of high drama and rich character. Often these are not, for one reason or another, translatable into anthology terms, since I have determined to avoid the scrappiness that plagues most anthologies, wherein no sooner have you got into the mood of something than it is over. There is little here for the grasshopper: this book is for the reader, not the skimmer, else it would not have been worth the doing.

A note about the various sections. Cricket in fiction, which Gerald Brodribb describes in an essay, is almost exclusively rural and comic in character. It is one of the genuine mysteries that English novelists and short story writers of quality, even

when passionately interested in sport, have made virtually no use of it. What I have printed here seems to me about the best that can be done.

The chapters from Rex Warner's *Escapade* and L. P. Hartley's *The Go-Between*, both published in the last seven years, represent rare excursions into cricket by distinguished writers of prose, and they are, because of this, of unusual interest. Yet there has been no novel of county cricket, scarcely a credible character study of a first-class cricketer. Perhaps it is that real cricket offers more drama than fiction ever could. Certainly, year in, year out, things happen that novelists would scarcely dare invent. It may be, simply, that professional cricket is a specialized, exclusive world, with an idiom and a manner not easily accessible to anyone not professionally involved in it. Yet there are writers, H. E. Bates for example, or Brian Glanville, whom one can imagine as being capable of bringing off the authentic background without loss of dramatic irony and without brazen simplification. Cricket could have done with a Ring Lardner, even a Nat Gould.

However, Part I is fairly representative of the best that has been written so far.

Part II, *Great Players*, speaks for itself. Since I have imagined one kind of this book's potential readers as being the young unbored, eager to see their heroes in the round, I have gone for passages that do rather more than give plain facts.

Denzil Batchelor on Fry's Box at Lord's, for example, creates an era of vanished splendour as vividly as do the red roses that adorn the button-holes of ancient MCC members, elegant and martial, on Test Match days. Similarly, John Arlott on Tate suggests not only a fine bowler in action, but Hove in the marvellous Twenties, with Tate at one end, Gilligan at the other, and a sea-fret that spelt death and destruction to their enemies. In this, and the next section, *Men and Moments*, I have tried to focus a number of great players, from Grace and Ranji to Hutton and Miller, at the same time offering a selection of the most notable passages of cricket prose, so that some sort of development can be traced from Nyren and Pycroft, through Daft and Andrew Lang, to Cardus, Blunden, and Robertson-Glasgow. Arthur Mailey may seem a stranger in this company, though he could not but be a welcome addition to any. However, in his description of how he dismissed his hero, Victor Trumper, 'There was no triumph in me as I watched the receding figure. I felt like a boy who had killed a dove', he has achieved one of the most tender images in cricket litera-ture.

The poetry of cricket is, with few exceptions, light verse. There is nothing surprising about this, since professional poets of quality are in any case few and far between, and those who could claim to have cricket in their blood, so that a poem on cricket would be part of their experience rather than an academic exercise, even rarer. There is not much about Test matches here, except Lord Beginner's triumphant Victory Calypso, rather more about county cricket, but again not much, a few tributes to cherished or legendary cricketers, mostly nostalgic. By and large, the affec-tions have been aroused by humbler activities altogether, by country cricket grounds, village encounters, rural eccentrics. The atmosphere of these comes through persuasively and clearly, without fuss or strain, principally through the element of participation. English allegiances are notoriously local, though our pride may be justifiably national.

There remains a gap, nevertheless, the absence of 'portrait' poems that give a close-up of cricketers and transfer them in habit and stature from the field to the page. These, as I know from experience, are difficult to achieve; yet the modern idioms of both cricket and poetry demand something more stylistically attuned than the stock sentimentalities, however moving in their context, of the recognized anthology pieces. 'O my Hornby and my Barlow long ago' has lost nothing in evocative-ness over the years, but a confusion between cricket, character and moral standards has resulted in too much glutinous piety in all forms of cricket writing. First-class cricketers are no more sober and righteous than other men, and they will thank no one for saying they are. What they often have is a downright earthiness, a

197

view of one another that stops some way short of idolatory, a gift for understatement and epithet. The best of them have professional pride, a true concern for technique, integrity, robust wit and courage. Test cricket is as tough a game as they come, its beauty and fascination are essentially for the connoisseur, and no one should have it otherwise. Cricket, however, exists on a variety of levels, each with its own characteristics, and they have all, as far as possible, been represented here.

Looking Back on Old Trafford, 1961

I MUST, AT ONCE, declare my interest: I hate to see England lose, especially to Australia. In ten seasons as cricket correspondent to the *Observer*, including three overseas tours, I have yet to cover a losing series, which pleases me. I still have a chance, albeit a slim one, to keep this record intact. There are others who can observe dispassionately the changes of wind and fortune, who are not emotionally involved in the result. I am not among them.

To me, passionate allegiance is the very essence of cricket, particularly Test cricket, where knife-sharp antagonism, the ruthless pitting against each other of the higher skills, constitutes the whole of it. Without this, I would as soon watch a bridge match, a chess game or go to the ballet.

Allegiance does not, I hope, affect one's evaluation of what takes place, neither of technical matters nor of the spirit prevailing. Rather does it sharpen one's judgement and increase both awareness and vulnerability.

The Old Trafford Test match last week offered enough evidence for a profound study of the psychology of defeat. As a Test match, pure and simple, it was, in its contours and gradients, one of the most remarkable of our age. For four and three-quarter days England asserted a basic all-round superiority that since Headingley had been plain for all to see: a marked superiority in attack, a generally greater stability, as well as technical virtuosity, in batting. Yet, within the space of an hour, the Ashes, the match and probably the series were wantonly thrown away.

It is impossible to overpraise the Australians' opportunism, Benaud's tactical courage and remarkable assessing of the match in terms of outright victory or defeat, and the last-ditch stand of Davidson and McKenzie on Tuesday morning, of a gallantry to rank with the Eureka Stockade and the siege of Glenrowan (Ned Kelly's undoing).

The best Australian characteristics, independence, generosity of endeavour, refusal to surrender, thrust and aggression, were displayed to the full like a spread peacock's tail. Benaud, with three Test runs in four innings, and not a wicket in the match for over a hundred, showed himself possessed of that sort of daring and faith in his own powers that is the mark of the great leader.

He has, in this series not least of all, had his reverses but, without doubt, he is one of the few Test captains with both visionary genius and a febrile, almost seismographic sensitivity to dramatic potentiality.

Lawry's craggy, rugged defiance; Davidson's sudden summoning of the old sweet masteries, a half-crocked, tired Neptunian figure, hair flecked with foam but magically regenerated as if by some Faustian potion; McKenzie, brash and unabashed when resistance seemed all but pointless; O'Neill, living for the moment as immediately as any paid-off cane cutter; Benaud, mercurial, buoyant, tigerishly lazy of movement. They are truly Australian, with something of the renegades' camaraderie about them, the outlaws' independence. Harvey, lightfooted, smiling, trim as the VJ's that skim Sydney harbour, I cannot regard as particularly Australian. He stands outside origins, just as did Hutton, a Yorkshireman for whom the Ridings and dales were merely chance frontiers, not redoubts.

But what now can one say of England? That had Cowdrey been fit, not simply would the runs have been eaten up as a Bentley swallows miles, but that it is inconceivable that three of the four crucial dropped catches would not have been taken. Certainly one can say that and make an end of it. But England had other chances galore.

They failed to move with the tide, on Saturday morning. The slip fielders, first, then the bowlers, at vital points, lost their sense of urgency (something the Australians, no matter how unpromising the context, never did) and finally, with victory sniffable, there was a loss of nerve among the middle and later batsmen of a kind one can even now scarcely credit. (In just such a way, though, did England, in Johannesburg in 1957, throw away a Test. Chasing 231, with time in hand, they collapsed from 147 for 2 to 214 all out as if similarly bent, in the quickest possible time, on self-destruction.)

Can one reasonably say, with any truth, that May was out-captained? At Headingley throughout, and most of the time at Old Trafford, his hold was tight, his setting of tempo brisk. Had any of the various catches at slip or gully been caught the match would have been wrapped up by lunch-time. The initiative was certainly lost on the last morning or rather wrenched away, but Dexter, magnificently and as if by divine right, stole it back.

What one must question here is whether any captain could have curbed the wanton excesses of the batting when only a run a minute was needed. I don't know, but I would be interested in Benaud's dispassionate view.

At least, we had a good, if slowish wicket. We saw memorable batting by May, Lawry, O'Neill, Davidson and Dexter; bowling of high quality by Statham, Davidson, Allen and Benaud. And if the sky was only as momentarily blue as at Siena, one must remind oneself that it was Manchester and that the match was played to a finish. It would be greedy to expect more.

Flawless Summer

THE END-OF-SEASON Blues that in September descend on the counties with Bessie Smith melancholy are this week not evident in Scarborough. Traditionally, this is where Yorkshiremen, in their week's cricket by the sea, shed their inhibitions after the stern gravity of the Championship, but this year the inhibitions were thrown to the winds a week early at Hove and the proceedings at Scarborough are taking place on the high exultant note of Harry James's trumpet.

So, at last, Surrey's seven-year stranglehold has been loosened. To be honest, they still remain, at full strength, quite plainly the best side in the Championship. Next year, without Laker, they may not be. But the absence of May for most of the season and of Barrington for ten matches has this time proved more

than even they could afford. But only just. A month ago they were free-wheeling to victory and had Sussex, in one of the most fascinating matches of the summer, held off Yorkshire on Tuesday with more determination, Surrey's final meeting with Northamptonshire would have been crucial. They could still have got home, as, indeed, could Warwickshire also.

As it is, anybody who watched the final day of the Sussex v. Yorkshire game with any kind of attention will know that Yorkshire, if not actually presented with victory, were nevertheless given an opportunity where none need have existed. Sussex were not bowled out by Yorkshire; in a quixotic excess of gallantry they simply threw away their wickets.

Some of them may even have had

visions of a Yorkshire defeat. Yet it could only have been pure hallucination to suppose that while they, themselves, scored 300 against Trueman, Illingworth and Close without losing a wicket, except gratuitously, they, in turn, might take ten Yorkshire wickets for under 200. No, what it boiled down to – and few complained – was that Sussex, by their own volition, produced the conditions for a dramatic finish, and at no time did their captain, unnerved though he may have been by the astonishing violence of Stott's and Padgett's onslaught, make any legitimate attempt to control it.

This may sound churlish, but it is merely another way of saying that neither in this match nor in any other have Yorkshire looked of true champion class. They lack both presence and dash in the field, and their batting is still in the formative stage. Burnet may, in the eyes of the Yorkshire committee, have dispelled or rather acted as a buffer to the mutineers, but he has not yet produced an inspired team.

What is interesting about their present triumph – premature only because the top five or six sides are all much of a muchness – is that essentially it was a co-operative efort. Five batsmen scored over 1,000 runs, five bowlers took over 50 wickets, and one player after another, at moments of crisis, took the crucial part.

This flawless summer, during which the county championship so flourished, has been tragically squandered on the Indians. These were never as bad as they themselves made out, but, insipidly led, the undoubted gifts of several of them came to disappointingly little. Yet from an English point of view, three players – Barrington, Pullar, M. J. K. Smith – made what one hopes will turn out to be a lasting impression, and three others – Illingworth, Greenhough and Swetman – have now the chance of making the positions of Laker, Lock and Evans their own – though as far as the last is concerned, it is hard to see how Parks, if he continues to develop as he has over the past three months, can be kept out much longer. This winter in the Caribbean one will see more exactly what these six are worth.

This has, all the same, been a sad summer in some ways, for it has brought to an end the Test, and in certain cases first-class, careers of the last survivors among those who, throughout the post-war decade, were automatic choices for England. Our commanding players since the war were first, as batsmen, Hutton, Washbrook, Compton and Edrich, as opening bowler, Bedser, as wicket-keeper, Evans, as all-rounder Bailey, as spinners, Laker, Wardle and Lock. Now the last of these, Evans, Laker, Bailey and Lock, have been jettisoned.

We shall not again see Evans, who spans the whole period from 1946 to 1959, keep in a Test. Eighty-eight times he represented England, more than any other player in the history of the game, and he has, as much as anyone, been part of the cricket lore of our time. Standing up to Bedser, taking the late inswing or outswing with a superb, inspiriting smack, or diving horizontally to save off Tyson or Statham, his performances created and sustained professional standards that will survive his lifetime. One indifferent Test this year at Lord's ended his career. The disappointment will not be only his, for Evans, morning-afterish and dissemblingly slap-happy, fighting fit or hung over, remained a great wicket-keeper, even in his sleep.

Nor shall we see Laker, with that seemingly fatiguing and bored little trundle of a run, again demonstrate that spin bowling, with its endless variations and disguises, its constant need for patience, is essentially an intellectual pursuit. Old Trafford, 1956, will be written on Laker's heart like a vintage, and there are none better. Lock, on the other hand, remained an aggressive Oval man through and through, though at backward short–leg in any climate he dazzled and astonished.

Finally, Trevor Bailey, who played the first of his 56 Tests for England exactly ten years ago. His relentless forward prod has made of his name a byword for doggedness. He has irritated bowlers of every pace, colour and political persuasion to fabulous frenzies of frustration. He has been an ever-present help in trouble to cartoonists. But he has never, throughout these ten years, been anything less than a magnificent and undaunted all-round cricketer, who, more than most, kept English dignity afloat at its worst moments.

His partnership with Watson against Australia at Lord's in 1953 – on which our string of three victorious Test series against them was founded – is deservedly historic. Yet, times without number as well, whether as opening batsman or at number six, he blunted rampaging enemy fast bowlers and staved off apparent defeat. And as many times, when the conditions were right, he changed the course of a Test with the controlled swing of his medium-pace bowling. Nor will one forget in a hurry certain of his catches at slip and elsewhere.

Evans, Bailey, Laker, and to a lesser degree Lock – these were an essential part of our Test cricket over more than a decade, and they have each of them contributed images of a clarity that, whoever may succeed them, is unlikely to fade.

Four Miniatures

David Gower

A confusion between the apparently effortless and the casual has done David Gower no good. He will never look a grim, dogged batsman no matter how hard he tries. So that when he gets out after having languidly stroked his way to thirty or forty he appears to have had a lapse of concentration.

Yet his approach to batting, his instinct to take the bowling on from the very start, leads to a demoralisation of the bowler quite out of proportion to the runs being made. For such is the sweetness of Gower's timing, the fluency and elegance of his strokes, that the bowler is made to appear to be doing all the work while Gower simply waves him away. Woolley was the archetypal left-hander of this sort, taller and harder hitting than Gower, but they are recognisably members of the same persuasive club.

In Test terms Gower has only been around for five years but while Randall and Gatting and various others have had to earn their place match by match, he has never looked back. He hit his first ball in a Test match for four, scored fifty in his first Test innings and a Test century in the same season.

Gower's manner of batting, his slightly vague and angelic appearance, contribute to the overall impression of a fair weather cricketer. In county matches, nowadays, it may be that his attention wanders or the demands made of him seem insufficient. But this has not been the case when he has been playing for England. Time after time he has not only redeemed an appalling start, but held the innings together for long hours against the fastest bowling.

Still, it ought not to be as a defensive cricketer that Gower is remembered. He is the most graceful batsman of his generation, who never makes an unpleasing or awkward movement at the wicket. When he leans out on the offside the ball races off his bat, though contact appears to have been minimal. His judgement of length is usually impeccable, to an extent that there is an air of inevitability about his strokeplay. He and the bowler seem accomplices in an illusory magic.

Ian Botham

No one since Ted Dexter has hit the ball as hard as Botham or so electrified a Test crowd. No English all-rounder since the war has approached him in success or – at moments – in failure. He reached the top quicker than anyone, descended abruptly, and now mercifully is back near where he belongs.

Botham remains rustic in manner despite a classically correct technique. He retains the raffish grin of a poacher even when bent on the most solemn of enterprises. He can look overweight and out of condition one minute and then make it seem an optical illusion the next by taking a staggering, split-second catch in the slips. He can lollop up to the wicket bowling medium-pace long hops and then a few overs later wreck an innings with lift and swing.

The bowling, perhaps, was always something of a bonus, never quite perfected in the way of the real professionals. But the wickets came in large quantities, there was a bounciness and enthusiasm that made up for a certain waywardness and looseness in delivery.

The batting was another matter. No one who chances his arm and takes up the challenge as Botham does is not going to fail from time to time, but so surely grounded is his batting on a proper attention to basic principles that his failures stem from extravagance not from inadequacy.

He is a magnificent hitter, blessed with great strength, a fine eye and an absence of inhibitions. His two hundreds against Australia in 1981 will deservedly go down in the legends of the game, and there have been others scarcely less brilliant.

There is no wastage when Botham is batting, no marking time. What is drivable is driven, what is pitched short is pulled or cut. There are few deliveries, once Botham is set, which do not fall into one or other category.

It is the greatest of blessings that Botham took to cricket; it might have seemed too long drawn-out and calculated a game for one of his temperament, one too demanding of time and patience. Shooting, fishing, flying, footballing, he has a go at most things but miraculously he brought to bear on cricket enough attention to cultivate the essential skills. All the rest, the soaring sixes and the plundered boundaries, are the result of his own exuberance, his delight in the contest.

Derek Randall

Great cricketers come in all shapes and sizes but Derek Randall, in what with him passes for repose, must be among the most unlikely of all. Who would expect this restless figure loping about the place to be the finest fielder of his generation, as a cover point possibly only excelled by Colin Bland in the whole post-war period? Or this neurotic fidget at the wicket, going through as complex a ritual as any fetishistic tribal African, to be a batsman of dazzling virtuosity, capable of taking any attack apart? Randall moves with the disjointedness of a rag-doll, the sawdust running out of it and arms and legs going every which way. But when finally the strings are pulled and the decisive moment arrives, everything miraculously comes together. In the field the head is out and low, like a pointer dog's, and the body is tensed and poised. At the wicket the body suddenly settles, the head stills. He freezes like somebody waiting for an old-fashioned photographer to get under his hood. Meanwhile a butterfly could alight on him with perfect confidence.

In the eight years since he first played for England, Randall has been in and out of the Test side more than most, not always with much justification. He has never been a particularly heavy or consistent scorer for his county, though in one memorable match in 1979 he made 209 and 146 against Middlesex. But he rises to the occasion and when sufficiently challenged he can always make the sparks fly. For England he has had to bat as low as number seven, a position which did not stop him making 164 against New Zealand at Wellington in January 1984.

First and last, though, Randall will be remembered as an entertainer. There are not so many of them about. He is worth travelling a long way to watch for his fielding alone. Like most players who rely largely on eye and who are laws unto themselves, Randall can look disorganised and unco-ordinated, his feet far from the pitch of the ball. But when his eye is in he can leave the field standing with audacious cuts

and drives made with the minimum margin for error.

A courteous, vulnerable, entirely human cricketer, Randall makes of idiosyncrasy an art. He is the strolling player, the troubadour of the modern game.

Geoffrey Boycott

Geoffrey Boycott appeared in 1962 as an awkward, balding youth, with steel-rimmed specs, the antithesis of what one might expect a potentially great cricketer to look like. In the twenty years since, the baldness has been thatched over, the specs replaced by contact lenses, the gauche manner planed to something approaching the debonair. Such a transformation from the roughly local to the smoothly metropolitan is entirely in keeping with the immensely prosperous, widely travelled and experienced cricketer that Boycott has become. It is an indication, too, of his dedication to improvement, his determination to make the most of what nature has given him. If nature only half did the job, Geoffrey would do the rest.

Unathletic in appearance as Boycott might have appeared at first glance in those early days, his technique was never in doubt. His stance was relaxed but upright, he picked the bat up as convincingly as he brought it down, his striking of the ball was clean and decisive. Boycott at the wicket aged 22 was almost as authoritative as at 42. Anyone with half an eye could see that here was someone with a technique in the same classical mould as that of his great Yorkshire and England predecessor, Sir Leonard Hutton.

Hutton had his ups and downs, but they were nothing to Boycott's. Hutton, when he had a mind to, could charm the birds off the trees, introspective though he was by nature. Boycott has the introspection, but with it a kind of blinkered cussedness that appears to make only his own interests visible. As a result, though at several different stages of his career he seemed indisputably the best batsman in the world, he lost out on the England captaincy, was ousted from the captaincy of Yorkshire and has been consistently at the centre of dispute.

Boycott taking guard for England was always a comforting sight. The times when he was rattled could be counted on the fingers of one hand. On all sorts of wickets in nearly 20 years of Test cricket he displayed a concentration and technical mastery that were unrivalled. He is a beautiful striker of the ball through the covers, especially off the back foot, and a fine on-driver. On his balmy

days he imposes himself on the bowling in a fashion that leaves the bowler no hope at all.

In Australia and in the West Indies in the early 1970s Boycott did England proud. For Yorkshire he amassed vast quantities of runs, averaging over 100 in both 1971 and 1979.

Yet from 1974 to 1977 he declined to be considered for England, so out of humour was he with the selectors. On his return he was as successful as ever, scoring his hundredth hundred and fourteenth Test century in the same innings at Headingley in 1977. He again showed his great qualities in Australia in 1979–80 but before long he was in trouble again.

There is something inescapably sad about this great, lonely technician, who can bat so boringly and with such little regard to the needs of others, whether they be his colleagues or paying spectators. He has been responsible for the greatest divisiveness and bitterness in the history of Yorkshire cricket. Yet there were those heady months over two decades when no batsman performed on the world's stage with the ruthless superiority of Geoffrey Boycott.

Brian Lara

THE BATSMAN AS accountant, the accountant as batsman. He could be wearing a three-piece suit, beautifully tailored for his neat figure. He looks as used to presiding over board-rooms as over a team of cricketers.

He is almost the smallest in the West Indies team, only the diminutive wicket-keeper, who seems to have strayed in from a boys' game, more insubstantial. But Lara, with the sweet moody name, redolent of snows and ice, of fur hats, has presence. He may only reach just above the waistband of Ambrose and Walsh, of Bishop and MacLean, but he is confident in his occupation of space, of his whereabouts.

He keeps very still and at the wicket he is stillness personified. Alert as a gundog, scenting something, giving nothing away. Leaning on his bat between overs he may be dreaming, perhaps doing mental arithmetic.

The bowler approaches and now everything works together in harmony, the bat an extension of the arms, the legs and feet as in the first steps of a dance, abruptly halted.

In defence he is classically correct, body and head aligned, something of the martial arts in his position, pose held just long enough to be admired.

Runs appear to flow from him rather than he make them. He is anticipatory, a sixth sense making him ready, even before the bowler lets go. He strokes not hurts, times, caresses, even in moments of aggression melodious.

You might think his shape, his roundness, works against elegance, but his style is of another sort, one deriving from mastery. He can perform without reference to text, note-perfect. A small Buddha, perhaps, some musk or incense emanating from his waistcoat. But when in mid-afternoon he decides to leave the field for a moment you feel it is not nature calling but his broker.

Curtly Ambrose, 1998

Kensington Oval. Over Pickwick Pavilion a tall palm like a gangly schoolgirl, a row of flags fluttering over the poppy-red corrugated roof of the Banks Beer Stand. There is a conch shell blown, like the moo of a sea cow, a brass band starting up.

Around the boundary white-shirted men on stilts prepare for lunch-time cabaret and Ambrose coming up to bowl looks at first as if he is one of them. Lara, small, compact, his pronounced buttocks like a bifurcated peach, adjusts his fellow slip fielders.

Ambrose yesterday was the only West Indian batsman to attack the bowling, launching his right leg half-way down the pitch and swinging his toy bat. Sometimes, proud of his technique and restraint, he presents a classically correct forward stroke, lingering in position, though no mirror in which to admire himself. But batting is a hobby; now for the real business. He begins his run, high-stepping like a show pony, arms and legs struggling for priority.

Mouth like a slice of cut papaya, teeth like a keyboard, he glares down the pitch as if sighting Van Diemen's land from the bridge of a frigate. His gaze goes far beyond the batsman, a treasure to be located on a tropic isle, if only he can find it.

He is parsimonious, Ambrose, his grin suggestive of indulgence or cruelty, but from his great height he delivers with a final twirl ball after ball on an exacting length, a loss adjuster not a clown.

Between overs at long leg he seems out to grass, you expect to see him good-naturedly cropping.

He signs an autograph or two, bracelet on his right wrist glinting as he reaches over the chicken wire. A ball comes his way and in patriarchal, stately fashion he condescends to stoop and pick it up, some kind of hydraulic system secretly in operation.

Inactive for a while he patrols the boundary in his wide sun hat, a plantation overseer keeping an eye on the workers. Two-thirds leg, up to the shoulders is a straight line, the buttocks negligible.

Time for another bowl, not so prancing and aggressive this time, the heat taking something out of him, so a couple of bouncers come up tamely, pussycats not tigers.

He gets a wicket off a long hop and that is it for the day. The sun is dropping behind the palm trees, the light turning melancholy.

There will not be many more such days.

Stanley Matthews

THE BLACKPOOL DEFENCE work the ball clear, or maybe it was Stoke or England, and a longish pass finds the outside-right waiting on the halfway line. He has been standing apparently idle for some time, a nicely built but slight figure about medium height, rather saturnine in appearance, in fact rather like George Raft, dapper, only with his shirt hanging loose over his shorts.

Without fuss he brings the ball immediately under control and starts his run down the wing. He makes some yards, and now one of two things happened: an opponent comes in to tackle or else, and this is more common, the whole defence, mesmerised and probably acting under instruction, retreat *en masse*. As they do so, the winger takes the ball closer and closer, showing it to them and giving the impression that he is chasing them to return something they had dropped.

Speed in this particular demonstration, except for the first few yards, is an incidental, an inessential. A wing-half or a back, by now emboldened by the coarsely expressed advice of the supporters massed behind the goal-line, comes out to join issue. The winger makes to move his foot to cut in, sways the other way, and he is off.

Five yards from the goal-line he will drop his centre exactly in line with the far post. If by any chance the tackles are made earlier on, the ball will be held still, just as the *torero* is motionless till the last second of the bull's charge, and then, with as economical a movement, flicked after the tackler has begun his lunge forward and so unable to recover. Then, with the other forwards running up into position, that superbly confident run down the touchline is begun.

Such is the routine, familiar by now if no less effective, that has created the Stanley Matthews legend. But, as with all great artists, his methods have been criticised constantly.

His tactics, it is said, and it is undeniable, enable the defence against him to recover, for he is the exponent of the three-cushion shot as against the straight pot. But these tactics are not unwitting. 'By taking the ball down to the goal-line,' Matthews wrote in his autobiography, *Feet First*, 'I cannot make an offside pass; think how many wing breakaways are cut short by that and of the dangers from a free-kick.' Then about dribbling: 'I dribble to destroy the confidence of my opponents.'

Yet there is one thing this unassuming, domestic man, the possessor of more international caps even than Billy Meredith, still hankers after: a Cup-winner's medal. Perhaps, he notes in *Feet*

First, it will elude him like it did Bob Crompton and Steve Bloomer, and like the Derby seems to elude Gordon Richards. Perhaps it will. But when all else is considered, it will appear of little account.

Soccer Star, 1952

ASSOCIATION FOOTBALL in England is an industry for professionals as well as a recreation for amateurs, and, at its best, an art for both. It is to the English what the bullfight is to the Spaniards, a ritual, a drama, and only then an entertainment. Cricket, with its slower, gentler rhythms, is bred by the English countryside, but football is the product of the towns. In it are invested the passions, hopes, and frustrations of those who live hard lives in big cities.

The proper background for the football stadium is narrow grey streets, a skyline of chimney-stacks smoking like half-submerged ships, factories, cranes, docks, pitheads, warehouses, shipyards, mills. Big football blooms at its most beautiful where the soil is stoniest, the air dirtiest, the people most congested.

In many English cities, in Scotland and, to a lesser degree, in Wales, football is the *leitmotiv* of men's off-duty senses, a subtle music blended with the noises of street,

office or factory, throughout the week. Its interest is fanned by gambling, but it in no sense depends on it. It is as deeply rooted in British life as are the theatre, poetry, public houses; as reflective of it as are music-halls and the English climate. The final round of 'The Cup', this year played off as late as May, is the climax; the player's summer is short; he will be training long before he goes into action again in late August.

What, then, is the role of the professional footballer, the artisan in this industry, the artist of this culture, both its star and its victim?

Take the case of Tom, eventually a local hero and an international Name. He is a son of working people in an industrial town. His career begins in the street, where they play a kind of football uninhibited by rules or touchlines, a swaying, yelling storm-centre that never pauses for breath until a goal is scored between the piled-up jackets. It is a game without art, without even a proper ball, but from its turbulence Tom picks up stamina and pluck, and the quickness of reflex a player can scarcely do without when the ball is constantly rebounding from walls and lamp-posts.

At school, where the game has formality and a referee, Tom practises the swerves, feints and nonchalance of his favourite players in the local First Division club. The style of almost every boy in the school team is equally derivative, but Tom attracts attention because with him there is a much less obvious gap between self-conscious artistry and real accomplishment. Already he has the controlled neatness of move-ment, the confidently, even impudently, restrained expense of energy, and a way of thinking about what happens next, that set him above the blind impulsiveness of the others.

Football has become Tom's way of expressing himself, and when he leaves school, his place in one of the clubs of the local minor league is at least as important to him as his job. The local paper starts printing his name in the headlines ('Tom Nets Three For Rovers'), and before long the Talent Scouts arrive.

Everyone knows they are there, though the convention is that they travel incognito, as unobtrusively as men from the CID. But in the one small stand the club possesses, they cannot hide among the familiar Committee members and, in any event, they set themselves apart by their obvious lack of partisan emotion. They are, after all, business-men, trained buyers looking for a healthy youngster who in a few years may be worth big money to their club.

In spite of any anxiety he may feel, Tom is like the Talent Scouts in that he can detach himself from the wayward feelings of the crowd and become absorbed into the technical pattern of the game. He acquits himself well and the two gentlemen from the United come into the dressing-room and invite him to sign professional forms.

This is the crucial moment. If Tom's promise of football genius is real, there can be only one decision for him, even though it means giving up a settled industrial life for a glam-orous career which is known to last, on the average, seven years. He finds himself at once in surroundings quite different from those of his amateur club with its spare-time secretary, its Committee of shop-keepers and works foremen, and a bottle of liniment for training resources. He has joined a big enter-tainment industry, a club which, instead of holding a whist drive to buy a new ball, may make a profit of £10,000 or £15,000 on the season out of match receipts in the region of £100,000. It should be said that, where there are shareholders, they make very little out of it; their motive is primarily 'the good of the club'. But in this great organization, Tom is still an employee, subject to a Manager who, however unsullied his passion for the game may be, must deploy his resources without sentiment, without too carefree an interest in the merely sporting chance. His job is to keep his club at the top end of the League and in the running for the FA Cup, or (graver problem) to prevent its relegation into a lower League, a misfortune which may mean a drop of one-third in the season's receipts.

For a time Tom plays in the reserve team, among last season's giants whose glory is fading and before crowds far too small for the stands they occupy. But the winter comes when Tom is ready to be blooded, when he runs out in the first team's Indian file and stands dancing on his studs, wringing his hands slightly as all footballers do at this moment, and being elaborately unaware of the multitude roaring for battle. Up in the Press box under the dark roof of the main stand are the critics who govern his fame and who hereafter will write every week to tell their millions of readers about Tom's tactics or the current state of his kneecap.

Tom establishes himself with the first team and is with it for season after season. Not for him the dying fall of those who are sold down the table, for £20,000 to the Second Division, or for £7,000 to the Third. For him football is a genuine creative expression and playing it he is probably happier than he could be if he were doing anything else. Soon he gets his first cap for England and his future seems assured.

After four or five years, Tom begins to feel his value and to look ahead. The United have had good service from him, and they feel that he is restless. They agree to end his contract, put him up for sale, and at a transfer fee of £30,000 (of which he gets, at best, only a trifling percentage) Tom joins a London club. He has married recently; his wife has inspected several houses near his new club's ground, and he has met the directors of the sports outfitters who have guaranteed his future. Though the sale suggests a serf, his chains may be golden.

He advertises a breakfast cereal; he invests his £750 benefit money from the United; his international fees, and the bonuses over and above his £14 a week wage, help to bring him a much larger income than that.

Tom is now 33. A shrewd businessman, he has got his finger in several promising business 'enterprises'. His career as a player is fading now, but there are offers of managerial posts; he is listed as a member of the sports staff of a Sunday newspaper, and he has only to choose the moment of retirement.

He is not badly off. He has a detached house in a London suburb, a car; his wife dresses well, his children are sent to good secondary schools. Yet he is well off only in comparison with his colleagues. He is one of the great stars of his profession, worth literally thousands of pounds in 'gate' money, and he has certainly made ten times his annual salary for his club. Compared with the rewards of a successful jockey, a film actor, an ice-hockey star, a music-hall comedian, a boxer or speedway rider, his income is absurdly small. The others frequently marry out of their class, move in higher social circles, have a certain playboy publicity. They command their own future, they employ agents.

The professional footballer never achieves this freedom. This mentality of a strictly employed person remains with him because he can never negotiate from strength. Football is a narrow world with its own rules; the player must accept the terms laid down or get out of the game. He cannot move to another club if he is unhappy, except on sufferance. He cannot sell his own skill, but it can be sold by his club. He remains a small individual inside a name that may be a household one.

Tom has done as well as it is possible for a footballer to do, and if, at the end, he still feels frustrated, he may perhaps console himself with the sad spectacle of Dick's greater frustration and of poor Harry's collapse into unprofitable disrepute.

White Hart Lane in 1950

LOOKING OUT OVER the Spurs ground from the Press Box, through windscreens like those of a car, you get an aerial view. The players move in fluid, highly wrought patterns beneath you: dribbling with the ball as if on a string, swerving, the body altering course as if in sudden contact with a windpocket, or running into reverse positions to anticipate a through pass. Through the open windscreen the noise of the crowd, the particular Tottenham roar, comes up in gusts like doors opening and shutting at a party. But drama is strictly controlled. At moments, the air relaxed, the atmosphere easy, the players go through their complicated manoeuvres with the confidence of mastery. The ball runs nicely for them, an ally in the formative process of the work of art. A quick throw-in, an overhead kick, the ball trapped easily by an inside forward and then out to the wing who, beating his man, cuts in and lobs across the goal. The opposite winger coming in at top speed flicks the ball with his head into the corner of the net. It is the rare, finished product of months of training, rehearsal and planning. The *beau idéal*: the far shore. At other times, everything misfires: skill is suspended, the fluid movements grow jerky and peter

213

out; the equations no longer balance. The crowd becomes restive, ribald, wanting the extremes of feeling. Only aesthetic perfection or ridiculous ineptness soothe their nerves or drug their craving for sensation.

At half-time the teams go in, diving into recessed tunnels in the grandstands. Bands fall in on the crimped green turf, dispensing martial airs to stamping spectators eager only for the half-time scoreboard to put up the scores in other matches, and the teams to come out again. Mist begins to intensify over a skyline of smokestacks and chimneys, gasworks and churches. It thickens over parks and parade grounds, a grey wool clinging to blackened, leafless trees like mould on ghosts. The streets rise to the north, intersecting roads filled like fountain pens with mist thinning in patches over outlying blocks of flats. Darkness comes choking in, district by district, as the second half begins and tails away tamely, or grows desperate and dogged, ridden by partisan spectators to a storming finish.

An hour-and-a-half a week. Yet somehow, the Saturday match is one of the end products of a hot-house culture: the perfect forced orchid, the final cutting produced at the expense of every devotion that could be lavished on it. It is the catharsis of emotion throughout a wide social strata, a pastime built to an industrial pattern. It is the masses' great flirtation with beauty which gives them a new life, a new death, every seven days. In between is the post-mortem

and the planning, the retrospection and the promise. But in the dead months of the year football breeds the imagery of nostalgia.

Tottenham is N.17. Going north from the West End on a Saturday, you cut through successive architectural belts, through pauses and compressions in social tensions.

The last half-mile to White Hart Lane picks up the pedestrians, a moving, thickening swarm of people who seem to adhere to the sloweddown traffic like insects battening on a carcass. There is a Jive Palais, a Roxy Cinema, and local government offices with turrets and pale green cupolas set back in disappointed trees. Everything converges, expectant, purposive, hurrying. You see the long winding queues outside the Stadium itself, the men selling blue and white favours and official programmes, the pub on the corner, the fish-and-chip shop and the ornate, formidable urinal that marks the last bus stop.

Huge grey walls surround the ground, a barrier to revolution. They might have enclosed a prison or a mental home; instead they house an expanse of green turf, pampered as a rare bloom, and worn by this struggling suburb like a button-hole at the end of a workaday week.

The Spurs are something of a myth. It is a myth that transcends performance, or class or individual players. They have won the Cup twice, in 1901 and 1921. A page in the Tottenham Hotspur Football Club handbook for 1949–50 gives some of the Red Letter events in the

Spurs' history. It is an astonishing graph of expansion. The first available record of the club is a document headed 'Origin of Tottenham Hotspur', under which is an exhortatory verse from a poem by Sir Walter Scott:

Then the strip, lads, and to it
*   though sharp be the weather.*
And if, by mischance, you should
*   happen to fall.*
There are worse things in life than
*   a tumble in heather,*
And life is itself but a game at
*   football.*

'In August 1885,' the document reads, 'a meeting was called by postcard, sent out by J. G. Randall for the purpose of forming a football club. This meeting was held at the rooms of the Y.M.C.A., High Road, and the Hotspur Football Club started ... The ground was Tottenham Marshes, Park Lane end.' In 1884–85 the club's receipts were £5 0s. 1d., and expenditure £4 11s. 1d., a close budget. In 1888 the club moved from Tottenham Marshes to Northumberland Avenue and eleven years later to White Hart Lane. In 1909 the Spurs became members of the recently reconstituted Football League First Division. By 1935 they had been relegated to the Second Division, promoted and relegated again. Each year since the war the F.A. Cup and promotion have seemed to be within their grasp. Each year, some time after Christmas, the brilliant early promise has faded. Last season,

however, hailed from beginning to end as 'the team of the year', they got too far ahead ever to be caught, and now they are back at the top where they naturally belong. For the Spurs are the aristocrats of present-day football. They are the aesthetes for whom football is an end in itself, for whom, with sometimes fatal results, artistry has always meant more than the brute score. It is a striking thing, part of the myth, part of the Spurs' continuation of the classic tradition of English football, that every Saturday over 50,000 pay at the gates – as a rule more than at any other club. This was so even when, as last year, the Spurs were in the Second Division.

What has produced this streamlined, highly expert machine? There are two main reasons: firstly, at a time when football club directors, like nervous stockbrokers, have bought and sold players for fantastically high sums, out of all proportion to their merits, the Spurs have developed their local talent. In an age when football has switched, disastrously, to the Hollywood Star system, the Spurs continue to run like a provincial repertory. Sometimes their refusal to buy star players has caused discontent amongst the supporters. Last season saw the vindication of the Spurs policy. Eight of their eleven regular League team have been chosen to play for England or Wales in one or other kind of International. The second determining factor has been the exclusive football view of the new manager, Arthur Rowe, an ex-captain of the Spurs. Many clubs take their players on part-time, allowing them to work at different jobs during the rest of the week. But though nearly all the Spurs players learn trades to practise when they finish with football, as long as they are with Tottenham Hotspur they are full-time footballers. It is a perfectionist attitude, but the Spurs on the whole justify it. The executives live, breathe, and think football. A highly organised system of scouts work throughout the country, watching and sifting players from all grades of football. Reports are sent in and collated. Players are drafted to junior clubs affiliated to the Spurs for training in nursery teams. Other scouts watch the tactics of future opponents: every move is studied, and counter-moves are prepared to exploit observed weaknesses.

There is nothing haphazard about modern football. It is as specialised and precisely developed as the Ballet, to which it has more than spectacular affinities. Yet it has always been a 'popular' sport in the generic sense. Nearly every other English game has at one time or another been the object of a cult. Football, perhaps the most strictly theatrical of all in its appeal, has remained the preserve of what was once called 'the working class'. A first-class football match is a planned and rehearsed *performance*. Cricket, more detached in its emotional engagement, is a stylish ritual; racket games are personal encounters; rugby and hockey are pastimes, often highly skilled and beautiful in their intricacy. First-class football alone is a performance in the final sense of the word. At the moment it lacks two things: anything approaching comfort for its spectators, and a literature. These are boom days and the money pours in, regardless of the amenities. Most supporters of football come from a class who expect little in the way of personal attention. If the quality of the play is all right, then they are satisfied. Excitement, the gambling instinct, become substitutes for a natural right to enjoy something in comfort. It is this more than anything that keeps football a 'working-man's' game. It is a pity; it narrows its frontiers, lowers its standards and deters many from an authentic and stimulating aesthetic pleasure. Literature? Football needs a Cardus, a Robertson-Glasgow, a Nyren; possibly a Graham Greene. In an age of utilitarianism, it still lacks class in presentation. Something to bridge the gulf between the prison-like walls of White Hart Lane and the mossy talents of its encrusted mediums, the split-second precision of the Spurs in action and the hardware atmosphere of Tottenham High Street. The green orchid and the black cockerel of the White Hart Lane stadium are emblems in an age of streamlining. But it is a long way back from Tottenham, and the No-Man's Land of summer, with its evenings of crude wickets chalked on back-street walls, doesn't last long. Football is a nine-month season.

Jack Groom and Tennis

THE GAME OF TENNIS, with its many courtly and historic associations, played modestly by Henry VIII and Charles II of England, and rather better by Henri II of France, is returning to favour. It may no longer be a Royal pastime, though Jack Groom, professional at Lord's for thirty years, demonstrated it recently to the Queen and the Duke of Edinburgh, nor a particularly aristocratic one, though the present amateur champion, carrying on a family tradition, is Lord Aberdare.

But the private courts attached to the great country houses, long converted by disinterested owners into furniture stores, chicken runs, even skating rinks, are here and there being restored and handed over to new clubs. The court at Hatfield House, for example, where Groom was brought up, reopened two years ago.

Those who play in it are not likely to put up stakes of £2,000, as did Latham, the world champion, when he defended his title against Pettitt at Brighton in the 1890s; nor wear knee-breeches as did the third Earl of Lytton; nor kill their opponents out of pique as did the famous Lombard painter Michelangelo da Caravaggio at Rome in 1603: nor acquire the notability of Benvenuto Cellini, the Florentine all-rounder, who was devoted to the game. But it is no less encouraging that the sweet music of this antique and complex art, still subtle and gracious where most racket games have become fast and brutal, will echo now in ears other than those of a few lonely peers and professionals.

Over lunch last week, in a small restaurant near Lord's, I questioned Jack Groom, who, at 67, still plays and coaches regularly, has a head and nose that would not discredit a Roman emperor, and who was British Open Champion exactly twenty-five years ago, about tennis in his time.

'I was lucky enough to be born at Hatfield. Before the 1914 war the militia used to play on Lord Salisbury's court and Lambert, the professional there, wanted a ball-boy and I went along. One day he threw a racket on to the court and told me to pick it up. I did so, and he just said: "You'll do", because I had by instinct picked it up with the proper grip. When he died in the war, I took over. I used to play with the present Lord Salisbury's grandfather when he was Prime Minister, and Lord Grey, the Foreign Secretary, and then I coached the grandson and we got him an Oxford Blue. We made all our own balls, you know, sewing together bits of rag, pieces of billiard cloth and soldiers' tunics.

'Then I went to Princes' for a bit, back to Hatfield again, finally to Lord's in 1925, and I stayed there for thirty years.'

Most great players come to tennis via racquets or squash, but Jack Groom is an exception. 'I never had time,' he said. 'I was keen on cricket, but once I got to Lord's I was in the court from nine in the morning till seven at night. It was mostly princes and gentry then, people with time on their hands. Later doctors used to come from Harley Street, and people on their way to the office.'

I mentioned Pierre Etchebaster, the Basque former pelota player, who was world champion from 1928 to 1950, and who is the subject of a new poem by the distinguished American poet Marianne Moore. 'Oh! Etchy was a great player all right, but we had to teach him the game. And I think Covey, who was champion before him for ten years, was the better of the two. Covey was at Crabbet, you know, the Hon. Neville Lytton's house. Mr Lytton was a fine player, amateur champion in his day, and Lady Wentworth, his wife, she was a good player too. Of course, it's rather strenuous for most women,

but she was a strong 'un, a proper horsey type.'

Groom swallowed some chicken, sipped his wine, and looked lyrical. 'Compared with tennis, squash and lawn tennis are not an art at all. Tennis is like chess, you can play till any age and you have to think every move. "Head always beats legs," I say. Another thing we say in tennis; "You stoop to conquer", the commode position is the proper one, the racket head-up and not too close to the body.'

I asked about the increase in popularity. 'Well, it's not an expensive game like racquets, and it is skill that counts, not stamina. As long as you can walk you can play. Before the Revolution there were hundreds of courts in Paris. It will never be like that again. But there are fourteen or fifteen courts in use in England now, more and more are playing at the universities, and Mr Whitney, the American Ambassador, has a court in Long Island.'

For all its democratization, one was back in that lost Scott Fitzgerald world of the romantic rich, of the Drexel Biddles and Jay Goulds, the Baerleins and Aberdares, the du Viviers and van Alens. Perhaps, whatever social class future generations of tennis players may belong to, it is only right that they should look back to their noble and individual predecessors.

How to Play

THERE IS ALWAYS something both comforting and vaguely comic about books with titles like 'How to Win at Chess', or 'How to Play Cricket' or hockey, or whatever you like. It conjures up visions of some fiendish and bepectacled intellectual, text-book in hand, word-perfect, advancing confidently on to the field and surveying with calm supercili-ousness the crude oafs around him.

He can, of course, carry it off by sheer cunning, on the Games-manship pattern; but more likely he will become a *divertissement* in the Charlie Chaplin manner. He will attempt, shall we say, a leg glance, most cultured of strokes, yet the ball, no reader of text-books, will hit the edge of his bat and pop ungrace-fully up towards the slips. Of course, it will be the text-book's fault.

Yet this divergence between the attempted and the actual is one of the most comforting things to the spectator; one of the most comic, too, for did not the great French philosopher Bergson, in his study of laughter, put forward the idea that what is funny about a fat man falling on a banana skin is his fond belief that, at the moment we see him sprawled on the ground, he is still walking pompously along.

In professionals, however, we do not care for too much deviation from the classic. We wish perfor-mances at Lord's or White Hart Lane or Thurston's or Twickenham to conform as nearly as possible to what the text-book has led us to hope for. When we are young they really seem to; and we rightly carry these memories of perfection with protected awe through life.

But, alas, the more we see of the best players at work (for work is what it is these days), the more do we grow aware of their fallibilities. It is nothing unusual to see a slip-catch dropped in a Test match, of the kind that would earn a small boy at his preparatory school a sharp cuff, or to see a corner-kick put behind the goal in a football international, a crime usually rewarded by expulsion amongst well-bred adolescents. Yet we learn to put up with these frail-ties, even enjoying them, for if we no longer look with awe, we give to our sporting heroes a more tolerant human interest.

This may seem a long way to get round to Mr Joe Hulme's 'How to Play Soccer' (Eyre and Spottiswoode, 9s. 6d.); but the great virtue of his book, a rare one, is that he combines instruction with readability. When he explains a common fault, he remembers how X, playing for Chelsea or England, made just such a mistake. That is good for morale. So, too, is the way in which, going through every position in the field, he contrives to make each in turn seem the most important.

No student, of whatever grade, will in fact find 'How to Play Soccer' without comfort, encouragement, or stern technical value. It may not enable the literary critic, the balletomane, or the ship's doctor, simply by digesting its lessons, to expect an immediate contract with Tottenham Hotspur; but it will at any rate greatly increase their pleasure, both aesthetically and tactically, if they should happen to watch them play.

Folkestone, or Hockey and the Inner Life

THE RIGHT END of the stick, as opposed to the wrong end at that lesser resort, Margate. The programme, at first debilitating – the Fifth Triennial Conference of the International Federation of Women's Hockey Federations – grew wings when a casual flick of the pages revealed, under the title of Immediate Past President, the name: M. Dietrich. An image nevertheless that warred with the idea of St Trinian's schoolgirls from sixteen hockey-playing nations. The cigarette-holder and the arched knee in the cool silk stocking, or the gym-tunic revealing a slash of scraggy thigh, scout-knife thrust in black drawers, specs perched on a pimpled pier of a nose? Would the Leas, those wooded cliffs so enticing to murderers and suicides, be full of wolfish talent scouts, or addicts of John Betjeman's Pam—

See the strength of her arm, as firm
    and hairy as Hendren's;
See the size of her thighs, the pout of
    her lips as, cross,
And full of a pent-up strength, she
    swipes at the rhododendrons,
    Lucky the rhododendrons,
    And flings her arrogant love-lock
Back with a petulant toss. . . ?

Neither. This was a serious world, despite M. Dietrich's presence. Consider again the Programme: Rules Sub-Committee and Umpires Meeting; Eight Matches; Country Dancing and Folk Songs by Member-Countries, Majestic Hotel; Two-Hour Conference Session. Blonde entertainers and lethal schoolgirls had no place here. Murderers mostly boarded the first train back to Bournemouth, Pamaddicts to Newbury or Woking.

The Leas, with their barricade of smart hotels, showed no congestion. The same well-wrapped exiles took the lift down to the harbour and fish-market, or the path leading to the Secluded Walks, or ambled diligently to the Indoor Rock Pool, the Marine Gardens and past the peeling Bathers' Cabins.

Everywhere on their walks, from sun-lounge to coffee-room, from bandstand to yacht club, the Conference is posted; and programmes are available, with full details of the afternoon's entertainment.

There is no play yet, no performers to be seen, for they are in sisterly committee. The programme, however, is revealing, is entertainment enough meanwhile, for hobbies are listed – the hobbies and ambitions of one hundred and seventy-six women. Miss Pollard, lively and legendary figure of the twenties and thirties – did she not, in 1927, score 8, 5 and 6 goals in successive Internationals for England? – has conveniently analysed their occupations in her hockey magazine, and it is tantamount to a poem:

Air Hostess, Almoner, Accountant,
Barrister, Bookkeeper,
Comptometer Operator, Company
  Director, Clerk,
Display Artist, Doctor,
Farmer, Furrier,
Housewife, Hotelier,
Journalist,
Landgirl, Lawyer, Lecturer,
  Librarian,
Machinist, Medical Technician,
Painter, Pastry-cook, Precious
  Stone Sorter, Professor,
Receptionist,
Sculptor, Schoolgirl, Shop Assistant,
  Solicitor,
Teacher, Ticket Writer, Translator,
Umbrella Maker,
Watch Regulator, Weaver,
  Welfare Officer.

Turn the pages: hobbies and ambitions (the English excepted) are as various. Miss Heilbuth, goalkeeper of Denmark, is interested in farming, forestry, and ballet; Miss Burgersdijk, of Holland, in the flute; Dr Watson, of Scotland, very properly in reading; Miss Woods, of South Africa, in tropical fish collecting; Miss Loulou Doret-Stump, Swiss inside-forward, in fashion design; Miss Louise Swelt, USA defender, in model 'planes and beadwork. Understandably, the lift attendant, a man of persuasive moustaches, has read and re-read this Kinsey of handbooks on his ceaseless journeys from Harbour to Bandstand. For what could be more exciting than to know, before play begins, that Mrs Pepper Merkh, the Philadelphia forward in the delphinium-blue tunic, is a detective, the Belgian Nany Renkin a sculptress of repute, the Austrian Fräulein Prkic a dreamer about educational reform?

After lunch, when grizzled dogs,

returned from coffee, daydream by snoring masters, and the sky thickens over a chain-mail sea, the ladies emerge from the purdah of conference, put ambitions and hobbies to sterner tests.

And the biographies take on deeper significance: for they show, what had hitherto not been suspected, that single-mindedness, even here, is an asset. Americans, confessedly ambitious to be writers, their neat heads full of Hemingway, Dos Passos, perhaps even (though one hopes not) Truman Capote, go down hopelessly to merciless South Africans, ambitious to be better sports girls. Swiss housewives, ardent philosophers as well as skiers, retrieve the ball fourteen times from their net, the English, those ruthless games mistresses, barely out of breath. Belgians, with a taste for

whisky as a reviver, not orange-juice, though urged by enthusiasts biting strong cigarettes and crying *Allez la petite Belgique*, are no match for Australians, intent upon hockey. The eye rests fondly on graceful Indians, newly freed of saris, on muscular Austrians, on a Danish team with two lots of mothers-and-daughters . . . even on the blood sprinkling the pavilion steps (red ink thrown by a disappointed cartoonist?) but the Empire, whose biographies proved so undistracting (seven out of eleven English are Physical Education Mistresses), are everywhere triumphant. One cannot, it seems, have it both ways; neither the French, however, nor the Belgians, deftly re-shaping their lips, inhaling ecstatically from secreted packets of cigarettes as they removed their shinguards, seemed to mind much.

Peter Waterman, Welterweight

IT WAS NOT the kind of room, nor the kind of conversation, in which Harry the Horse or Nicely-Nicely Johnson would have felt much at home. The room was not full of smoke, nor littered with used glasses, and the only racing paper was one which I had brought myself.

The wallpaper over the fireplace was of a bold ivy pattern. There were paintings of Spain round the walls, scenes which might have been

chosen for their picturesque quality by Sir Winston Churchill and whose awkwardness of technique was compensated for by vigorous brush-work.

The only clue that this first-floor flat, in a suburban villa off Leigham Court Road, Streatham, belonged to a boxer came from the various paintings of old-time pugilists over the staircase and one or two portraits of Waterman himself. Unlike the coloured photographs in sports magazines, which show him as having the skin of a Red Indian, these are of an exaggerated paleness. He is, in fact, very pale, and he himself puts his colour, when he is not actually sunburned, as being 'billiard saloon green'.

On Tuesday, at Harringay, in a contest that takes second billing to that between Pastrano and Richardson, Peter Waterman, holder of the British welterweight title, fights Ben Buker, the Spanish champion. It is not a title fight, but it is one that Waterman, as he is well aware, cannot afford to lose. For his name, with a handful of others, is about to go into the hat, or into what passes for a hat in American boxing circles, for the right to fight for the welterweight championship of the world, vacated when Carmen Basilio, who recently defeated the holder, Sugar Ray Robinson, moved into the middleweight division.

Waterman is sanguine enough not to imagine he will be allowed an early crack at that title. In May, he fought a draw in Rome with the European title-holder, Marconi, with whom he is due for a return fight. There is talk of a meeting with the Empire title-holder, the Australian George Barnes; and if these eliminating contests are satisfactorily concluded, there will doubtless be a little group of American nominees, one of whom he will have to beat to establish a final right to fight for the championship itself.

It used to be said, perhaps still is, that economic necessity, and single-minded passion were the best spurs to ambition in sport as well as in the arts. The Olympic Games, athletics generally, professional lawn tennis, and even Test cricket, have recently proved this view to be false. Certainly, the ability to think in international terms, not to be satisfied with purely national rating, is an essential. Yet ugly thoughts of the breadline no longer force a boxer back to his feet, nor, any more than was the case with Tunney or Carpentier, is the ring the only burning area of the great boxer's consciousness.

Has Waterman that final ruthlessness, the elasticity of imagination that must be greater than all his opponents', to take him to a world title? This, more than any technical issue, is the crucial question, and it is not an easy one to answer. For Waterman, who is not yet 23, though he has held his British title for eighteen months, is a realist. He takes things very much as they come, his eye only on the next rung and not so far up that he is in danger of toppling off altogether through having to crane his neck.

For example, the new house he is thinking of buying is not in a smart residential area 'up West', but five minutes' walk away, in a better road with a garden and with a view of trees that gives the illusion of being in the country.

Boxing, ever since the age of 11, has been his life. He won 121 fights out of 130 as an amateur, boxing for Britain in Helsinki in 1952. Since turning professional he has fought nearly fifty times, losing only to Kid Gavilan in the second of their two encounters. He defeated Wally Thom, to become welterweight champion, and he successfully defended against Frank Johnson.

He tends to regard American boxers as overrated because their boxing writers put on such a 'flowery' show on their behalf. 'Flowery', it would seem, denotes the inessential trimmings, the panache for which he has little use because it is not 'the real thing'.

I kept thinking as we talked – about Swedish furniture, about women's hats, about Capri (where he went for a week's holiday after fighting Marconi) – that perhaps there was not in Waterman the dominant passion for fighting that is generally regarded as the passport of a world champion. Then again I thought of Tunney and Carpentier.

I asked him if he ever felt nervous before a fight. 'No,' he said, 'not since I was an amateur, not really.' Was he much aware of the crowd? 'Only when I box badly,' he said. 'What does happen', he went on, 'is that I wake up on the morning sometimes and suddenly I know I am going to win. It's a wonderful feeling.'

Joe Davis at Home, 1957

JOE DAVIS DECLINED my telephone invitation to lunch. 'When I'm on circuit, with two sessions a day, I prefer to potter around in the morning. I hope you understand. Come round to my house instead.' I understood, and went round.

Mr Davis, of course, is a snooker player, not a judge. His sessions are at the table, not in court, and though his circuit may not be so dissimilar to that of a recording magistrate, it involves somewhat separate qualities.

Now in his middle fifties, he is a dapper figure with glossy hair and the hooded tortoise eyes of a man who spends a lot of time staring. He lives alongside the Royal Cambodian Embassy in Phillimore Gardens, his hall is covered in ivy-leaf wallpaper, and his billiard room is entered through the doors that once opened on to the green baize table at Thurston's, Leicester Square, the former temple of billiards, to which, for over thirty years, he was high priest. Mr Davis bought up the doors marked 'Pull' at the closing sale three years ago, so that presumably he will keep on going through them for the rest of his life.

One might think that Joe Davis, who gave up championship play ten years ago through the sheer monotony of having won the world snooker title twenty years in succession, could now afford to relax, or at least dispense with the larger part of his customary five hours' daily practice. But whether he can afford to or not, he doesn't. Even while we talked, sitting on the stools round his private bar, he put in a shot from time to time, demonstrating for me the nursery cannon stroke that Willie Smith could never play and which virtually put billiards out of business as a spectacle. After he had caressed the ball into several dozen cannons that never disturbed their intimate relationship, we both grew tired of a feat which not half a dozen professionals in the world could have done.

'The trouble with billiards', said Mr Davis, who still prefers it as a game to snooker, 'was that we got too good at it. At our level a player sometimes made only one visit to the table during a session. The rest of the time he sat out watching his opponent.' Joe Davis speaks with authority, for it was against him that Walter Lindrum made his record break of over 4,000, taking three two-hour sessions over it. When it was over Joe went to the table, feeling, he confesses, the size of a pin, and proceeded to make 1,200, which says much for his temperament.

The superseding of billiards, a thoroughbred game, requiring, in addition to superior qualities of stamina and character, an exact assessment of possibilities, a soothing touch, a complete control, by snooker is a concession to public taste. No snooker player can remain at the table for more than about ten minutes at a time, usually it is for much less, and for the same reason as people tend to prefer seeing wickets fall to watching one man bat all day, they prefer the choppier rhythms of snooker to the solo grace of billiards.

It is partly, of course, a question of personality: once it was regarded as a privilege to watch Bradman or Hutton bat all day, just as it was to be present when a Lindrum or a Davis made a four-figure break. 'Showmanship comes into it,' Davis admitted. 'This young boy, Rex Williams, whom I've been playing this week, now he's going to be the best of the coming lot; he started at the right age, but he makes a labour of each stroke.

'But there was never big money in billiards,' Davis went on, 'though in my last championship match at Kelvin Hall, Glasgow, when I beat Horace Lindrum, we took £11,000 in the fortnight. Against that, you must remember that the staging of it cost £2,000 alone.' I asked how many professionals today could expect to earn a living at snooker. 'That's one of the troubles, only about six, which means that there is no intermediary period of keeping going while you learn. It takes fifteen years practising full-time to make a top-class player, and it's ten years before anyone will pay to see him. Even now ten years after my official retirement the takings at Burroughes Hall this week are three times as great when I play as when I don't.

'You know, one of the sad things is, one can play a complex shot, putting on stun or screw or side, and people observe the result, but they don't begin to understand what has gone into it. Before the war *The Times* carried three-quarters of a column every day on billiards, discussing individual strokes, tactics and so on, so that there was an informed public.'

I suggested that lack of informed criticism was common to many arts and sports, though perhaps to a lesser degree, and asked Davis how he began his career as a billiard player. 'My father was a publican in Derbyshire. I began playing regularly when I was 11. That's the time to start. It's like music or ballet, you have to grow up with it.'

One of the fascinations of the great is their single-mindedness, their acceptance of slavery as the price of perfection, and their necessary belief that it is worth it. 'Of course, I lay off a bit in the summer now, that's partly why I retired. It's no use having a home if you're never in it. And I like gardening. I've got a bungalow on the river and there's 200 bulbs waiting for me to plant when I can get the time. But I'm playing at Ipswich next week and I don't know whether I can risk messing my hands up. You've got to be a killer at this game; if you start taking it easy or feeling sorry for your opponent, the balls can begin to run against you and you're done for.'

A man from Derry and Toms called for Mr Davis to inspect some stuff. It was time to go, and time almost for the great man to make his way to Soho, where, an hour later under the smoking lamps, to a gallery as absorbed as if watching a surgical operation, he would once more soothe the coloured balls into familiar surrender on the green baize.

Even after five hours' practice a day it seemed a more beautiful way of earning a living than going to the office.

The Amateur Game, 1953

IT'S NOT OFTEN THAT amateur football, for most of the season played in pleasant obscurity, attracts any public attention. However, two things have created a slight stir of interest, even among those who find amateur soccer about as exciting as amateur ballet. One was the experiment of holding the University match at Wembley, where a goalless draw was played recently; the other the Amateur Cup semi-finals on Saturday, as a result of which Harwich will meet the winners of the Pegasus and Southall replay in the Final. The University match, whose 5,000 spectators looked strangely lonely in the great grey stone amphitheatre that holds 100,000, was not, in fact, a success. The quality of the play was intelligent enough, but no one seemed to know where the goals were, and many of the elementary arts had just not been mastered. Perhaps, more than anything, the funereal emptiness of the stadium contributed to the anaesthetic gloom.

Either way, it was a pity, for University soccer and amateur football in general are greatly on the mend. But if this recovery, after a period when soccer, once the preserve of the Beau Brummels of sport, sank into total social disrepute, is to be maintained, great attention must be paid in the next few years to details. The problem of housing the University match is, of course, this: which, for the players, is better – to play at Wembley unnoticed, or before a passionate crowd, near enough to smell their breath, at Iffley Road or Dulwich?

Curiously enough, the Amateur Cup Final has suddenly caught the imagination, and Pegasus, a team composed of Oxford and Cambridge players, excited the admiration of one and all when they won the Cup two years ago. Here, people said, were the present-day Corinthians. They began to rout about in their memories for the great names, the Hon. A. F. Kinnaird (who used to take the field in long flannel trousers, blue-and-white cricket cap and wearing a destructive red beard), De Paravicini, and A. T. B. Dunn, all of Eton and England, C. W. Alcock of Harrow, Vidal of Westminster (both internationals), and many others. When the Amateur Final is played next month there will be a full house of 100,000.

University football will certainly increase in stature during the next decade, but in the meantime some niceties of sporting aesthetics, techniques and social values are worth discussing.

For there is no doubt that, put beside its professional counterpart, amateur soccer still looks a sadly weak bloom. The amateur cricketer, Rugby player, squash player, tennis player, rider, can hold his own with anyone, whether as an undergraduate or businessman who plays in his spare time. It is not unusual for undergraduates to play in a Test Match or to represent their country at Twickenham, yet Oxford and Cambridge soccer players are pygmies compared with the general run of 1st, 2nd or 3rd Division professionals. They are, in relation to the stars that grace international soccer, as stumbling chorus-girls to ballerinas, or as the vicar playing snooker in the youth club to Joe Davis. Why is this? It should not be fitness, for University Rugby players can get as fit as they ever will be; it should not, though undergraduates are notoriously obtuse in many matters, be a lack of intelligence. The best professional soccer produces a spectacle of controlled passion, trained skill and beauty only matched by ballet dancing or bull-fighting, and accessible to anyone who is moved by painting, grace in action, or subtlety of strategy.

The only conclusion possible is that while squash, tennis, Rugby and cricket can be taken in an ordinary man's stride, provided the natural gifts and determination are there, the professional soccer player must be a dedicated, special sort of man. Because of this extension of skill into a profession, with its ceaseless demands, football became an industry, with the responsibility of competing as an entertainment with every other form of popular art. When this began early in this century, the great amateurs, who had helped the Wanderers, Oxford University and Old Etonians, among others, to win the FA Cup, dropped out of the game. Professional soccer is now an industry that is also the highest level at which the masses can appreciate art.

University soccer and amateur soccer are just not the best of their kind, and it is because of this alone that they tend to arouse little interest. It has become impossible for an amateur team to give professionals a game, with the result that the contempt of the spectator for the inferior has been confused with social snobbishness. Winchester, Charterhouse, Shrewsbury and Westminster still produce their occasional player of talent, but there is only one from the Public Schools, H. A. Pawson of Winchester, who could, and has, commanded a place in a First Division side.

Those interested in comparative anthropology or aesthetics might well visit Wembley on 11 April, Twickenham next Saturday (when England play Scotland), and Wembley again for the Cup Final on 2 May. They will, even without looking at the field of play, find much to speculate about.

Knights of the Baize Table

I LOOKED IN A WEEK or so ago at the final of the World Match-Play Snooker Championship, played at the Leicester Square Hall. The finalists were, as usual, Fred Davis and Walter Donaldson, who have both now reached the final for six years running. Snooker finals consist of two six-frame sessions (lasting about 2fi hours each), played every day for a week. It was an afternoon session which I attended and the score before play was, Fred Davis (the holder) 16 frames, Walter Donaldson 20 frames There were still two days to go.

I arrived shortly before 3 o'clock expecting to find some signs of occasion. But the Leicester Square Hall looked desolate; about fifty people occupied about a third of the seats. The Hall is tastefully decorated with pale green walls and pastoral murals. Rows of comfortable maroon armchairs rise in tiers.

Light music was being relayed through a loudspeaker and most of the audience, all men, seemed to have the furtive look of those who know they ought to be doing something else. At 3 o'clock the house lights were put off and the only illumination left was over the glowing green baize. An attendant drew the black curtains to make it still darker and an official introduced the players. As he did so, both appeared, like the figures in Swiss weather houses, on either side of the screen that masked the entrance. Both bowed slightly. Fred Davis was round, dark, smiling and bespectacled, and Walter Donaldson tall, gaunt, baldish and naturally melancholy in feature. Both wore dark blue waistcoats and trousers, exquisitely pressed, white shirts and black-and-white spotted ties.

The start was slow, for each player seemed more concerned in these opening exchanges not to leave the reds too pretty for his opponent. It was quite a while before there was any scoring. The audience shifted about mutely, coughing between shots. Then Donaldson thumped a red down from the whole length of the table and went on to make 30. Fred Davis scored only in ones during several visits to the table.

Donaldson went to 47 with a group of splendid shots that rattled the balls down precisely but with no sense of any force being used. Now Davis got in, looked for the first time with some satisfaction at the table and made a couple of breaks of about 15 each. Neither player had yet made what could be called a mistake, though there was nothing spectacular about any of their shots. When the ball hung on the lip of a pocket there would be a hoarse exclamation from the darkness, a noise of religious protest rather as though the candles in church had refused to light.

Davis eventually won the first frame 61–47, but then Donaldson again went to 40 in three or four visits to the table before Davis had scored. They had warmed up a bit now, they even smiled to one another and the balls were going down with greater frequency. Davis made a break of 36 and then Donaldson polished the frame off with a 20.

Fred Davis seemed not to be interested in any disposition that left him without a good chance of scoring at least twenty, so that while Donaldson progressed steadily Davis stood smiling in the shadows like an acolyte, cue in hand, and then overtook his opponent in a single break. In the third frame Davis, with his score 11 and Donaldson at 2, cleared the table with a break of 102.

There was, for the only time, a sharp round of applause.

For long periods there was no sound at all except for the skeletal kiss of the balls, the ritual cry, in the tones of a muezzin, of the marker. Davis especially was playing beautifully. Sometimes he would look along his cue with the serious air of a dentist about to make a difficult extraction; more often he appraised the table with the lofty rapid glance of the company commander who knows his weapons are equal to his task.

When either player was not sinking his pots with unruffled ease, he was leaving the table as bare as he could. Davis took the next frame to give him a lead of 3–1, but then, apparently satisfied, let Donaldson take the next two.

The perfection and the stuffiness had by then almost drugged one, and emerging into the open air again was like climbing out of a submarine. Fred Davis, I thought, as I went away, looked always to have just that little bit in hand. And sure enough, two days later, he retained his title by 37 frames to 34.

A Great Day at Wembley

FORTY THOUSAND uniformed schoolgirls, seated in groups like blocks of coloured tulips, cheered England's women hockey players to a great 4–1 victory over Holland at Wembley Stadium.

An astonishing volume of noise encouraged each succeeding English attack. The ears of Lofthouse would have burnt with envy had he heard the crescendos of pure joy, rising into a blue sky, that accompanied the dashes through the middle by the dark and graceful Miss Susan Hyde, scorer of three goals. Her shots rattled the woodwork like gunfire in a Hollywood western.

This was not, nevertheless, an outstanding English team: in stick-work, accuracy of passing, and general intelligence it was well below the level one would have expected. Since the war England have lost only two out of a great many international matches; for a team considered to be as good as any in the world there are now weaknesses that were not apparent a year or two ago at the Folkestone Festival.

Early on it was the Dutch who looked better. The tulips handed over by the Dutch captain, the only married player among the visitors, had scarcely been laid to rest when a series of Dutch attacks had England's goalkeeper, a rotund padded figure in a white peaked cap such as male Americans sometimes sport in such places as the Rue de Rivoli and the Borghese Gardens, crouching anxiously.

Dominating the opening phases was Miss Terlingen, Holland's centre-half, as powerful as a Rubens but more mobile, breaking up attacks and sending away her speedy left wing, Trix Nillesen, nicknamed Jet. Compared with the Dutch in their orange blouses and blue skirts, England, playing in cardinal red skirts and white blouses, seemed very sluggish. Just on half-time, however, a long sequence of penalty and short corners brought a goal, Hyde shooting in from the edge of the circle.

In the second half England were a changed team: faster, more direct, now timing their passes. Hyde soon put England two up with a rising shot that would have decapitated Holland's goalkeeper had she been in the way, and Rylands, an energetic centre-half, was not long in making it three. Nor were any of England's goal scorers greeted by the effeminate effusiveness ladled over one another by professional soccer players.

Holland's centre-forward, Van Nierop, reduced the lead with a nice shot a moment later, and then came a textbook goal for England: the ball flashed from forward to forward and Hyde, racing clear on the final pass, swept the ball into the net.

Scarves and hats went flying, the rancours of the classroom dissolved for ever. For these were, almost without exception, schoolmistresses playing for schoolgirls, and not even a renegade from St Trinian's, puffing a Player's Weight and sipping cherry brandy from a concealed flask, would have dared to question the honest enthusiasm and delight of it all.